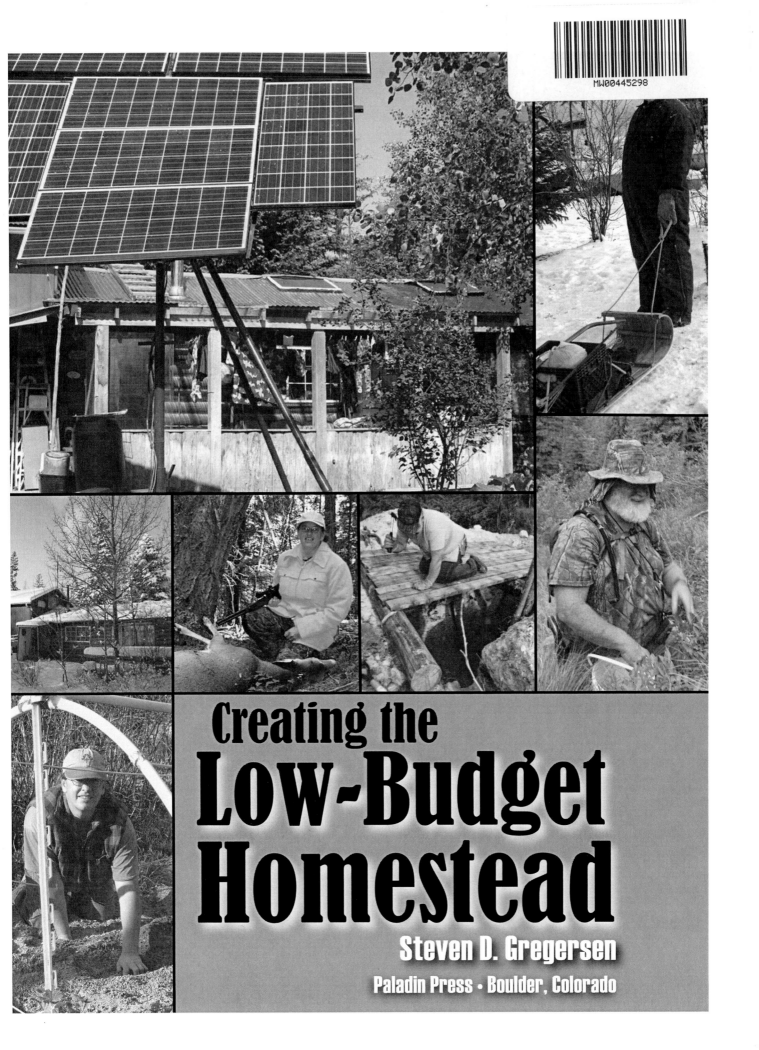

Creating the
Low-Budget
Homestead

Steven D. Gregersen

Paladin Press · Boulder, Colorado

Creating the Low-Budget Homestead
by Steven D. Gregersen

Copyright © 2012 by Steven D. Gregersen

ISBN 13: 978-1-61004-762-3
Printed in the United States of America

Published by Paladin Press, a division of
Paladin Enterprises, Inc.,
P.O. Box 1307
Boulder, Colorado 80306 USA
+1.303.443.7250

Direct inquiries and/or orders to the above address.

Visit our website at www.paladin-press.com.

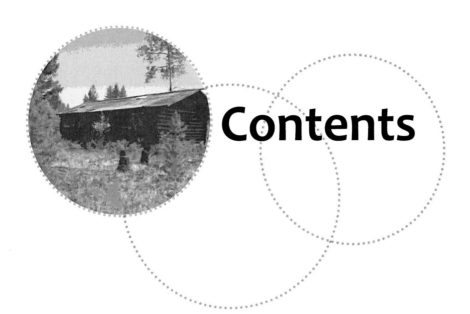

Contents

Warning

The information in this book is based on the experiences, knowledge, research, and beliefs of the author and cannot be duplicated exactly by readers. The author, publisher, and distributors of this book disclaim any liability from any damage or injury that a reader or user of information contained in this book may incur from the use or misuse of said information. This book is *for academic study only*.

Acknowledgments

I'd like to give special thanks to my wife, Susan, who encouraged me to keep on writing all through the hard times when the words just wouldn't come. She's the one who took on extra tasks on our homestead to give me time to write. Much of our success is due to her knowledge and tenacity. There are very few women with the wisdom she possesses or who would live the life that we live . . . and do so without regrets. She's always ready for an adventure. I am truly fortunate to have her by my side.

I'd also like to mention our good friends John and Denise McCann, who are sources of encouragement and inspiration. It was their interest in our lifestyle that kept me writing in my blog, which opened my eyes that there were people who really wanted to know how we live the life that we live.

Thanks to Jon and Donna at Paladin Press for all the work they did to bring this writing to you. I never understood how much work was involved in publishing a book. Thank you, Jon, in particular for your editing skills. This is a much better book because of you. It's been a pleasure working with you.

And finally, thanks to all those who read my blog and offered encouragement. Some of you I met at Dirttime. Others I have yet to see. Hopefully we can remedy that in the near future.

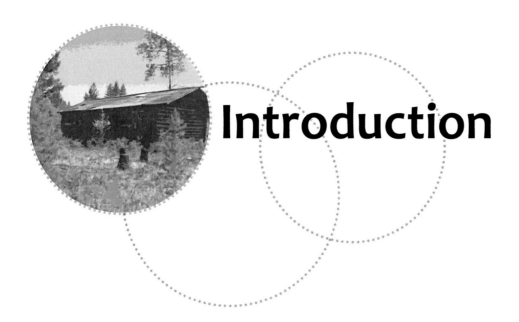

Introduction

Why another book about modern homesteading? There are already dozens, if not hundreds, of similar books on the market, so why one more? What makes this book different from the others you'll find about pursuing the homestead life? Why should you read this one?

I'll tell you why. We'd like to see more success stories.

When we bought our 20 acres in the northern Rocky Mountains, it had two buildings on it. One was a two-room frame structure on a post foundation put together with plywood and poles. It was insulated and had interior walls of unpainted drywall. Pack rats had moved in and built nests in the wall insulation. A leaking roof allowed rain and snow to destroy the Sheetrock ceilings. There were piles of insulation and crumbled sections of drywall on the floor. When we cleaned it out, we found an intact wall where former residents had left their names and the dates they lived there. But they were long gone.

The log cabin we renovated for our own use

A partially completed cabin in our area, evidence of a failed attempt at living the homestead life.

Another abandoned building in the very early stages of construction.

was in the same state of disrepair and neglect. It, too, was another testimony to shattered dreams and tenants that had left long ago.

The evidence was everywhere on every parcel of land around us. Collapsed structures, old foundations, and partially completed buildings long since abandoned to the elements. Their owners were gone, now pursuing a more "practical" way of life.

It was disheartening, to say the least.

There was a nagging fear in my mind that our story would end as theirs did. From the looks of the buildings, they were people like us. People pursuing their dreams of a self-sufficient life but without enough money to do it "right." We, too, had big plans, but nothing to back them up except determination and a vision of our future.

We've been here over eight years and now feel confident that, with some good advice and a mountain of resolve, it is possible to successfully pursue a self-sufficient lifestyle even if you don't have a safe full of money to back you up.

So, what will you find in the pages of this book? You will find practical steps and instructions to take you from dreaming about a self-sufficient lifestyle to living one.

We will tell you how to define and set goals and how to locate land (we purchased our 20 acres with owner financing, no money down, and no interest on a five-year contract). We'll show you a different way of looking at life that's going to be absolutely essential if you're going to be a successful low-budget homesteader. We'll give you some advice on self-sufficient, sustainable gardening and on how to keep vehicle costs low. There are chapters on inexpensive, off-grid entertainment, how to schedule time for the greatest productivity, and how to avoid burnout. We'll also give some tips for low-cost housing and things to think about when designing an efficient off-grid home. We'll address some questions like what skills you'll need and how to acquire them, how to set up a simple off-grid power system, and the advantages and disadvantages of pets and livestock. These are just samples of the practical ideas you'll find inside the covers of this book. And in every instance, we'll look at them from the low-budget angle.

So, if you've ever thought about pursuing a self-sufficient lifestyle but feared you didn't have the money to do it, just keep reading. We'll show you how!

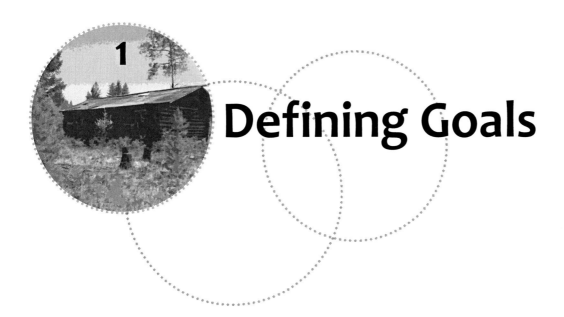

1 Defining Goals

Since you're reading this book, I'm going to assume that you're at least a little bit dissatisfied with life as you know it. I can identify with that, because we felt the same way when we made our move. We had some goals in mind. We wanted to be free of the cash-based economy and the accompanying enslavement to a steady job, where we were only slightly better off than indentured servants of the 1600s. We wanted to declare our independence from the grocery store and food that had been planted in dead soil, nurtured with petroleum-based fertilizers, bathed in herbicides and insecticides, and then picked green, injected with artificial coloring, and shipped halfway around the world to be sold weeks or months later in the "fresh food" department at our local grocery store! We especially wanted to give a one-fingered salute to the gas pump and utility companies. (We'd already done that with network TV!)

In short, like a teenager on his eighteenth birthday, we wanted to declare our independence. A person who's reliant on others for the necessities of life will always be subject to and dependent upon the people and companies who feed, house, and protect him. It doesn't matter whether it's the grocery store, the utility company, an employer, or the government.

Compounding our frustration was the simple fact that all of these entities are extremely complex in operation, and the breakdown of even a small part could deprive us (and the entire United States) of necessities for daily existence. Gasoline embargoes in the Middle East have left Americans waiting in long lines for rationed (and expensive!) fuel. The irresponsible actions of the government and banking system plunged us into an economic downturn that may take decades to recover from. A large part of our agriculture relies on a steady influx of illegal immigrants for planting, cultivation, and harvest. The government's response to even moderate-scale emergencies is woefully inadequate. I shudder to think of how long it would take to react to any wide-scale disaster, terrorist attack, or civil unrest. The entire system we depend upon for our very existence seems as fragile as a house of cards just waiting to collapse with the first stiff breeze. In short, we don't have much confidence that the "machinery" of our world is reliable enough to trust with our lives and livelihood.

Not only were we seeking independence, we wanted security as well.

We summed it up this way: "We want to be able to live our life in relative comfort and security without depending on outside resources."

So what's so important about goal setting? Or better yet, what is a goal and how do you choose it (or them)?

A goal can (according to the thesaurus) also be described as an objective, aim, ambition, end, destination, purpose, or target. It's something you aim for or seek to attain. A goal gives you a direction to go, a reason to prepare or work, and a way to measure progress.

Can you picture a football game in which there

Our goal is self-sufficiency. We do not want to depend upon others for the basic necessities of life.

We spent the first couple of weeks camping out while we began cleaning up and restoring the cabin. Breakfast is being cooked over an open fire.

were no goals? Imagine the opening kickoff as the players line up in opposing formations. The ball is kicked and the other team catches it and begins to run. But which way and how far? Without goals, they have no direction and no way to measure success. What's to stop them from turning around and running in the other direction . . . away from the other team! Goals keep you on track in the direction you want to go. Not only that, they tell you when you've reached your destination.

Once you've determined your ultimate goal, you'll need to break it into bite-size segments. It's nice to say you want to be self-sufficient, but what does that mean? We'll go into more detail in later chapters, but it surely means you'll need to supply your own food (although maybe not as much variety as in the grocery store), clothing (again, maybe not

what L. L. Bean offers, but it ought to keep you warm and protected), shelter (it may not have central heat, but it should keep you warm, dry, and safe from the elements), medical care, security, and anything else you need to sustain life. All of these are waypoints or subgoals to be attained on the ladder to your eventual goal of self-sufficiency.

Break these into bite-sized pieces as well. There are sections in the food chapter on gardening, hunting, fishing, foraging, gleaning, preserving, and preparing. Each one of these can be broken into smaller pieces. Food preservation, for example, includes canning, dehydrating, root cellar storage, pickling, smoking, spring houses, and other methods.

Medical care can begin with taking a class on CPR and first aid at your local chapter of the American Red Cross. You may want to go further and become

In the early days we saved our batteries for running the laptop computer and used kerosene lanterns for light.

The first winter we did not have a woodshed, so our firewood was stored under a tarp.

One of the first tasks was to set up the outhouse. Our progress was stopped only momentarily by this large boulder.

One of the highest priorities was construction of a root cellar to keep our canned goods from freezing. We had very little money, so we used old lumber and poles to make the roof. We covered this with plastic, then piled on the dirt. It's still in use nine years later.

an EMT or first responder. There are even ways to get someone else to pay for the class! In chapter 3 (the money chapter), I'll show you ways to learn, for free, almost every skill you'll ever need for self-sufficiency without spending anything except maybe transportation costs (which might be shared if you carpool).

Don't let fear stop you! There's an old saying that you can eat an elephant if you do it one bite at a time, and that's what we're doing here. You can become skilled at everything you need to know to be self-sufficient if you break it down into manageable pieces and take every opportunity available to learn and do.

Goals provide a way to evaluate progress (or the lack thereof). Football fields have lines at

10-yard intervals as a visible reminder of how far the players have come and how far they've yet to go. Every year we look back and see ways we've learned more than we knew the year before. Your homestead life should include ways to measure your development.

In summary, goals keep you on track, direct your efforts, and help you measure your progress. But how do you determine what your ultimate goal is, and how do you keep it attainable?

THE FIRST THING TO REMEMBER IS THAT YOUR GOALS ARE *YOUR* GOALS

We've never told anyone they should live life like we do. Everyone has different desires and different ways to attain them. We see nothing wrong with living an 1800s lifestyle if that's what we must do to survive. But we also like many of the things available in the twenty-first century. The result is a "blended" life of old and new. We have telephone and Internet service, but no cable or satellite television. We have a propane cookstove but do most of our cooking on a wood-burning stove. We used kerosene lights the first couple of years, and it was more than two years before we acquired our first solar panel. The first four years we had no refrigerator (and could still do without it quite easily if need be). We have an outhouse and composting toilet instead of a flush toilet and septic system.

We know other people living the homestead life who do things much differently than us, and that's fine. Some are working toward total self-sufficiency, while others just like gardening and hunting and living in the country. Some continue working regular jobs and hire work done, while we tend to do everything ourselves on a shoestring budget. Others are growing their own food and producing their own electricity while living in the city with no plans to move anywhere else. That's great, as long as that's what they want out of life. This is your dream and your aspirations and should be designed for your life and no one else's.

SECOND, BE REALISTIC

So many people have told us that "if things get bad," they'll just throw some seeds in the ground and grow their own food. Any experienced gardener will laugh hysterically when hearing comments like

Our first winter in our Montana homestead.

The east side of the cabin today.

that. Even the fastest growing plants still take weeks to mature, and that's in fertile soil under ideal growing conditions. Try doing it on virgin ground. Just as naïve is the person who's going to grab a rifle and live off the land. It wasn't that long ago when whitetail deer were almost extinct in much of the United States due to unrestricted market hunting. Imagine what it will be like if every adult male with a gun hits the woods at the same time! Populated areas will be devoid of game within weeks.

If you've never planted a garden, hunted or fished, cut and split firewood, treated an illness, or earned an income on your own, start learning how to do these things now. (And don't quit your day job yet!) Remember the quip about eating an elephant? You aren't going to do that in one day!

That being said, homesteading isn't rocket science. With diligence you can learn the basics in a relatively short amount of time, even if you've never grown anything more exotic than mold on stale bread or hunted anything more elusive than the closest McDonald's franchise.

THIRD, PRIORITIZE

When the paperwork was finished and we took possession of our land, we had three months before winter ended outdoor work. In those three months, we needed to make the cabin livable, which included some major cleaning and restoration, a new roof and floor, chinking the logs, cutting a hole for and installing a new door and repairing the old door, cutting holes for and installing 10 windows and the roof insulation, building a root cellar, digging a new pit for the outhouse, and cutting, splitting, and storing 10 cords of firewood. I was also working three days a week on 12-hour shifts at a job 55 miles away. Me, my wife, and the four youngest children still living at home with us put in a lot of hours, but by the end of October we were snuggled inside our warm, dry cabin with a root cellar full of food and enough firewood to keep us toasty warm all winter long.

FOURTH, BE FLEXIBLE

Things don't always work as they should. Have some backup plans. While we don't lose any sleep over things like an electromagnetic pulse (EMP) attack or solar flares plunging the world into the next Stone Age, we do have backup plans even when traveling. We are experienced cross-country bicyclists, so we take our bicycles with us and put our clothes and supplies in our bike panniers. If there's a widespread disruption due to a cataclysmic event, or something else makes motorized transportation impossible, we'll use our mountain bikes to get home. The way we pack, we can be out of the car and on our way again in minutes with enough dehydrated food and survival supplies to get home safely even if the journey is a thousand miles.

On the home front, we have power tools like saws, drills, rototillers, grain grinders, welders, and other devices that make life a little easier, but we also have handsaws, hand drills and bits, shovels and hoes, hand-powered grain mills, blacksmithing tools, axes, and everything else needed to continue life as we know it without electricity or gasoline.

Sometimes unexpected opportunities arise, so you need to take advantage of them. Our first solar panel was acquired through barter. An acquaintance needed some vehicle repairs and yard work done and had a solar panel to trade. We hoped to acquire solar panels in the future, but it wasn't on our schedule for that year. On the other hand, deals like this didn't come often, so I dropped what I was doing and took on the job.

Other times a project gets stopped for unforeseen reasons. In that case, do the next thing on your list. Be willing to shift gears when needed or even take a different road. Just keep moving forward and eventually you'll reach your destination.

2 Setting Priorities

I read an article this morning that debated whether or not the "modern woman" can "have it all," possessing a highly paid, professional career, enjoying a fulfilling marriage, and being the perfect mother to her children. One of those commenting below the story pointed out that everyone featured on the program had at least one failed marriage, and many didn't have children. Those who did have children had nannies to care for them. The only thing they had in common was that they had all risen to the top in their chosen careers.

Trying to have it all is one of the main reasons I've seen people fail at their attempts to live the low-budget homestead lifestyle. Everything has a price, and the wise person knows this.

Satisfaction and success cannot be measured by the accumulation of possessions, wealth, or fame but must instead be sought through things like family, security, contentment, and a sense of fulfillment. Living like we do requires a completely different philosophy of life.

COMFORT VS. CONVENIENCE

I had a friend tell me once that he couldn't live like we do. I was really puzzled by that, so I asked him what was so hard about the way we lived? He looked me right in the eye and said, "That's exactly what I'm talking about." I didn't have a clue what he was talking about! On another occasion, I talked to someone else who said something about how many things we gave up to live the way we do. I was puz-

zled by that one too! Then I put those two comments together. What I believe both people were referring to was the issue of comfort vs. convenience.

The dictionary defines comfort as "a condition of ease or well-being; a feeling of being relaxed, cozy, contented."

It defines convenience as "something that increases comfort or makes work less difficult." Synonyms include expediency, ease, and handiness.

Which got me pondering the question: Do laborsaving devices make life more comfortable?

Example one: You are a wife in 1955. In the kitchen you have a refrigerator, gas or electric range, and an electric mixer. The utility room contains a wringer washer, you hang your clothes on a clothesline, you iron your husband's shirts and jeans and your dresses, and you have a Hoover vacuum cleaner. In the living room you have one telephone, one black-and-white television with an antenna (no cable), and 13 channels to choose from. In the morning you fix a hearty breakfast and send your husband off to work and two of your four children off to school with sack lunches. You still have two preschool kids at home to care for. After school, your children are greeted at the door by the smell of home-baked cookies. They grab a couple on their way to the backyard to play. Your husband gets home an hour later, and you all sit down to a home-cooked meal and relax in the evening watching *I Love Lucy, The Jackie Gleason Show,* and *You Bet Your Life* on TV, or maybe you read a book or magazine while the kids play in their room. In your bedroom you have a bed, closet, dresser with mirror, and a radio. You have one car that your husband drives to work, and you all share one bathroom. The dog sleeps outside in his own house (which the husband shares with the dog on occasions).

There is no automatic dishwasher, microwave, permanent press clothes, computer, or video games, and you have no "outside" job.

Example two: You are a wife in 2012. In your kitchen you have a refrigerator, range, dishwasher, microwave oven, toaster oven, automatic bread maker, automatic coffee maker, blender, food processor, a telephone, and an electric can opener. In the utility room you have a freezer, automatic washer and dryer, vacuum cleaner, and a dusty iron and ironing board. You have two kids, one in school, one in daycare (no lunches to fix, but don't forget to send lunch money). In the living room you have two telephones, surround-sound stereo, a computer, Internet connections, DVD player, Xbox, Wii, PlayStation version 99 (or whatever is the newest and latest), high-definition large-screen television, and satellite or cable service with 99+ channels, not including pay-per-view channels. You also subscribe to Netflix. In your bedroom you have another phone, computer, television, stereo, and digital alarm clock, in addition to a sleeping apparatus (i.e., a bed), walk-in his and her closets, dresser with a mirror, and your own bathroom with double sinks. You have two vehicles—wife gets the minivan; husband gets the SUV. Everyone over the age of 10 has their own cell phone.

Mornings begin with a quick cup of coffee (you'll get breakfast on the road), kids get a bowl of cereal or breakfast at school (don't forget to send money), mom drops the youngest at daycare on her way to work, dad takes the oldest to school on his way to work. Both parents work all day (you have to in order to pay for all of those "conveniences") and eat lunch out. You have a rotating schedule telling you which kids are at what activities and who picks them up after work. You'll need to stop at the store for your evening meal and pop it in the microwave when you get home, or just order takeout. Then you eat supper, stack the dishes in the dishwasher (or trash), swap clothes from washer to dryer, fold clothes out of the dryer, watch TV and/or get on the computer or help the kids with their homework. Later, dad is in his home office with his laptop finishing up his "home-work" from his job, while mom is in the bedroom. Kids watch their own TVs or play on their computers or play video games in their own rooms.

Which couple lived the life of greatest comfort? Why? Which had the most convenient life? Why? Does convenience increase comfort? Why or why not?

One of the most important questions is "how much does convenience cost?" If both parents were not working full time, would all those conveniences be needed? Suppose one parent stayed home. How many of those expenses could be eliminated? How much would *not* be needed to pay for such things as childcare, eating out, multiple vehicles, cell phones, and wardrobes? Now suppose you downsized on housing, which means you pay less in insurance, taxes, and mortgage. How much will that save? We'll look deeper into the money issue later, but you should also think about the mental aspects of modern life. When was the last time you actually felt relaxed in the evening?

If you ever want to get off this treadmill, you're going to have to reprogram the way you think and

Water is our biggest inconvenience. In the summer we use collected rainwater for washing and watering the garden. In the winter we melt snow. In the late fall and early spring we collect water in buckets as the snow melts from the roof. Often it freezes during the night, so we melt super-sized ice cubes like this one.

CREATING THE LOW-BUDGET HOMESTEAD

In keeping with our goal of never becoming dependent upon electricity, we wash clothes using washtubs, a "Rapid Washer," and a hand-powered wringer. It's easier than most people imagine.

act. One of the first things to do is evaluate the difference between needs and wants.

NEEDS VS. WANTS

"Need" is a word we use with great ambiguity. As I write this chapter, I'm looking at Lake Mead through the open back door of our 14-foot U-Haul truck that's been converted to a motor home. My wife is outside soaking up the sun on a lounge chair. We're over a thousand miles from our home in Montana, where the snow lies deep and the thermometer still registers in the single digits at night. We aren't going home until two things happen: we have to experience at least one day of 90-degree temperatures here, and the snow has to be gone

from the yard at home. We really needed this extended vacation! Or did we?

I remember a question posted on a computer forum asking which was most important in a survival situation: fire, water, shelter, or food. The only correct answer is, "it depends on the situation." If you fall through the ice on a lake, the most important thing might be fire to prevent hypothermia. If you've spent a day in the desert without water, the most important thing is going to be water. If there's a storm heading your way, the most important thing might be shelter. If your plane has gone down in the wilds of Alaska where you have shelter, fire, and water, the most important thing might be procuring food. What you need most depends on a lot of factors. Your needs as a homesteader must be evaluated the same way.

On our homestead, we have certain needs that must be met. They are food, water, shelter, and paying our property taxes. These are essential, meaning that if you take away any, our life here is over (in some ways more permanently than others). We have a couple of common household expenses that are wants but are very important to us. These are the phone and Internet service and insurance for the vehicle we're driving. In tight financial times, these will go if necessary in order to keep the property taxes paid. If it comes to that, we can take bicycles or snowmobiles to town to use the Internet, we have ham radios for emergency communications, and we'll park the vehicles. Everything else is negotiable.

We've established what's most important to us and have planned our lives accordingly. We've found that by eliminating those things that were of less value, we have more time and money to pursue those things we really want. Hence, even though we make very little money, we still have enough to take our camper out for a few months every year for an extended vacation.

One of the most important skills needed for creating a low-budget homestead or retreat is the ability to differentiate between needs and wants. The more of your resources you use to obtain wants, the less you'll have available for your needs. Meet your needs first; then prioritize your resources to get the wants you truly desire.

In order to determine if an item is a need or want, we ask the following questions:

Firewood splitting is just one area we do the "old" way. Splitting by hand is cheaper, and the exercise keeps you in better health.

A. Will life cease if we are deprived of it? If so, it's a need.
B. Will our quality of life be severely impacted in a negative way if we don't have it? If the answer is yes, depending upon the degree of negative impact, it may be a need or it may be a very important want. It's important to note that B is subjective and will depend on your goals and attitude toward life in general.
C. Assuming that something is an obvious want, we ask, "Is this something I'll really use, or will I regret buying it and sell it later at a loss?" We also ask ourselves if we'd be happier not buying it and using the money saved for something we'd enjoy more (like traveling).

On those rare occasions when we're feeling deprived, we remind ourselves that for the vast majority of man's existence, there was no television, Internet, telephone, motorized vehicles, running water, indoor plumbing, washers and dryers, air conditioning, microwave ovens, refrigerators, or Reese's Peanut Butter Cups. Yet people who came before us still enjoyed life.

Suicide was less prevalent in the past than it is today, so it's safe to say that more "things" do not make life more enjoyable. In fact, studies are proving that more things can actually lead to a lowering of life satisfaction. The best way to avoid clutter in life is to not get it cluttered in the first place. The best way to do that is to decide what's really important and avoid those things that aren't. Get your priorities right.

Think critically about your choices in housing, vehicles, tools, toys, and equipment. Do you need a large house or do you just want a large house? Do you need a new truck or just want one? Do you need more guns or just want more guns? Do you need a backhoe or just want one?

On the other hand, don't take this to extremes. I know people who have 10 years of food supplies stored up along with thousands of gallons of diesel fuel and gasoline and hundreds of thousands of rounds of ammunition supporting an arsenal that

We kept our electric grain mill, waffle iron, and microwave oven. We have nonelectric alternatives for the grain mill and waffle iron. The microwave does not like being run on the inverter, so it's used mostly as a high-tech breadbox unless we're running the generator.

would make a third world dictator gleeful. If you have lots of money or you've acquired these things slowly over time and the responsibility of possessing them brings no added stress, there's nothing wrong with this type of abundance. But if you've denied yourself and your family everything else to go to this extreme, you need to reexamine your priorities.

There's nothing wrong with wants and luxuries as long as you have your basic needs covered. Determine what's most important and then make that a priority. Above all, be very careful about going into debt even for necessities. There are low-budget alternatives to nearly everything. (I'll cover this in more detail later.)

I want to repeat again: one of the most important skills needed for creating a low-budget homestead or retreat is the ability to differentiate between needs and wants. The more of your

resources you use to obtain wants, the less you'll have available for your needs. Think critically about the choices you make.

TIME VS. PRODUCTIVITY: A NEW PERSPECTIVE

In a recent conversation, a man asked me, "Why are we busier now than when we had jobs?" I told him it was because we were now doing everything we used to pay other people to do!

There are times I've thought about getting a "real" job long enough to earn enough to hire someone with a dozer to come clear and level a few acres of our property for a larger garden and hay meadow. He could get more done in two days than I could in a month of hard labor.

If I got a job, I could make about $15 an hour. By the time taxes and Social Security are deducted, I'm making about $12 per hour. Plus there's the driving time, which in our area would be about 90 minutes each way. Now figure in gasoline to drive to work, which at current rates will be around $120 per week minimum. I'm making about $480 per week take-home pay and spending $120 per week of that for fuel, which leaves me $360 for my effort. But remember, not only am I working 40 hours a week, I'm spending another 15 hours in travel time, plus losing another five hours per week due to the hour allotted for lunch. My job is eating up 70 hours of my time each week, and after taxes and fuel I'm "making" roughly $5.14 per hour of effort expended. (Remember, the government is taking $3 per hour right off the top before I see any of it.)

Now out of that I'll have extra maintenance on my vehicle, plus the eventual replacement cost since it's going to wear out much faster and we'll have to pay insurance on an extra vehicle since my wife will need a licensed and insured vehicle while I'm at work. Since I'm in town every day, we'll spend more for things we wouldn't normally have purchased.

So let's pretend I'll end up with an extra $150 per week to hire a dozer and operator to clear five acres of land. He's going to charge me $100 per hour, and it will take him about 15 hours to clear and level that five acres. His fee is going to be $1,500. Now do the math. I have $150 per week to apply toward his work, so it's going to take me 10 weeks to save enough to pay him. In that 10 weeks, I'll have devoted 700 hours of my time to pay him for 15 hours of work. It would take me about 350 hours to clear and level that five acres by hand. Also, if I do it myself, I won't be paying $1,200 to the government in taxes and another $1,200 to the gas station, and I won't be insuring, maintaining, and replacing another vehicle.

The key here is that I'm not going to do it all at one time. In fact, it might take me a couple of *years* while devoting a few hours per day to the project, but that's okay. There's no rush, and I'd rather take the extra time working at home than spend it in the city breathing polluted air, putting up with the constant noise, enduring the harried atmosphere, and supporting the government, insurance companies, and oil industry. I've done enough of that in my life already. I've paid the price of convenience, and it cost too much.

Now, I could buy a tractor and backhoe and farm implements and get the work done in less time, but then I have other problems. If I didn't pay cash (believe me, if I had that kind of cash I wouldn't be writing this book!), I'd have to use credit. Then I'll owe a bunch of money, and I'll have to use the equipment to make money. So, now I'm working 40 hours or more per week to pay for my equipment, plus liability insurance and other business-related costs. Now I'm a contractor rather than a homesteader, and I'm in the same trap I moved here to escape from.

Always remember that homesteading *is* your job. You've traded the nine-to-five rat race for your present life. So what if it takes three times as long to get things done!

We go through periods when we wonder if it's worth it to grow our own food and directly provide for most everything else we have. For example, we were having peas for supper. By the time we've worked the ground, added compost (making compost is another task by itself), planted the seeds, weeded and watered the crop all summer, picked and shelled the peas, and canned or dried them, we've got a lot of labor in that jar of peas. Now, for those working a job, how many hours do you work to be able to pay 75 cents for a can of peas at the grocery store? At $10 per hour, it would have taken about five minutes of work to earn that money.

Is our way convenient? No! But the finished product tastes better and is healthier than any commercial alternative you can get at a store. Is it an efficient use of time? No! But we are not dependent on factory farms thousands of miles away or

We grind our meat using a hand-powered grinder that we've had for 20 years.

migrant labor for the harvest or distant canneries or the petroleum industry for fuel and fertilizer or long-haul truckers or wholesalers and distributors or delivery trucks and grocery stores for our food.

Remember, this is your job. You used to spend 40 hours a week at a job, plus your commuting time and the time you were allotted for lunch to provide a paycheck to buy your food, pay your mortgage and insurance, and buy natural gas, electricity, or whatever to heat and cool your home. Now you've traded that time to directly provide those necessities. If it takes me 50 hours a week to provide those things, I'm still "working" 20 hours less per week than I was before, and we end up with two or three months of vacation time every year to spend wherever we want to be.

The irony of the situation is that I used to work my regular job, then come home and work in my garden, pick huckleberries, and go hunting, fishing and trapping for fun. Now I get up every morning and do the things I've always truly enjoyed doing.

The electric toaster didn't make the move with us. We make toast by sandwiching the bread in a sheet of aluminum foil on top of the woodstove. If you use foil on one side only, the bread dries out and curls. It can also be made in a frying pan or on a cookie sheet in the oven.

FANCY VS. FUNCTIONAL

My grandfather was a frugal farmer. He never owned an electric air compressor. When he had a low tire, he pumped it up with a hand pump. I asked him why he didn't buy an air compressor since they'd be faster and easier. He said he had lots of time and the exercise was good for him. When a tire needed repairing, he removed it from the rim using two broken leaf springs for tire spoons. I asked him why he didn't just go buy tire spoons from the auto parts store, and he said he didn't see any sense spending money for store-bought tools when his worked just as well and didn't cost him anything. The wagon we hauled hay on was made from the frame of an old worn-out truck. He removed the drive train, cab, and bed and made a new bed out of used lumber. It was nothing fancy, but it actually worked better than the wagons sold just for the purpose.

It wasn't that he didn't have money. He just didn't see the need for "fancy" when "free" (or cheap) worked just as well.

In another instance, I saw a man forge a knife with a campfire, a plastic trash bag, a piece of leftover rebar, and two rocks. He has all the blacksmithing tools he needs at his shop, but he did this to demonstrate a point: functional doesn't have to be fancy.

Cultivate creativity. For example, my wife once got a nail in her tire out in the backcountry. She had a tire pump and "space saver" spare, which was completely inadequate for the road she was on. She pulled out the nail, gave it a liberal coating of superglue, and stuffed it back in the hole. Leak fixed, problem solved!

We live in an era where specialization is the norm. Go to a website catering to cross-country bicyclers and you'll find endless discussion on the "right" bike and the "right" clothes. Skiers, both downhill and cross-country, are another example of people who focus on specialized clothing and equipment.

There's nothing wrong with having a specialized bicycle or anything else unless not having it would keep you from riding. Don't become a slave to the "right" equipment or methods of accomplishing a task. In today's society, "right" is a product of advertiser's hype and has more to do with cosmetics than functionality. Remember, people crossed the United States with handcarts, covered wagons, canoes, and horses. They got the job done.

Learn to make do with the things you already have and save yourself money and time.

KEEP IT SIMPLE!

We say that primitive people needed almost nothing to survive, but that isn't true. They needed the same things we do: food, clothing, water, shelter, security, and friends, family, and community. The difference is that their needs were supplied locally and their circle of dependence was small. When they needed tools, they made them from locally available materials rather than order them from factories half a world away. When they needed food, they harvested it from their fields or foraged locally. When they needed security, it was supplied by the men in their tribe or village. When we say their needs were "simple," what we mean is that their needs were supplied through simple—i.e., uncomplicated, low-tech—methods.

The modern way of life is extremely interdependent. An oil embargo in the Middle East leaves long lines at the gas pumps in the United States. A volcano in Iceland stops air traffic across broad areas of Europe, leaving people stranded in airport lounges while looking for alternate modes of transportation. Oil price increases lead to higher fuel costs, which lead to increased expenses for farmers in fuel and fertilizer, leading to higher prices at the grocery store.

One of the major benefits of the self-sufficient homestead is that you distance yourself from this interdependency. If the stock market crashes, it will take months for us to notice the effects. When oil prices increase sharply, we cut back on driving or leave the vehicles parked until things stabilize.

The key here is to keep things simple and local. That doesn't mean reverting immediately to a Stone Age existence (although we're working on the skills to do that if the need is there). What you want to do is keep whatever modern amenities you desire without becoming dependent upon them. I have an electric table saw and radial arm saw along with an air compressor, drills, sanders, and various other electrical tools. The stationary saws and air compressor must be powered by a generator, but everything else can be powered by our solar power system. Our electrical needs are supplied locally and completely independent from the power grid. In addition, we have hand-powered counterparts to every item mentioned so if for some reason we cannot generate our own electricity, we can still build things. If you check your history, you'll find it wasn't that long ago when everything was built with hand tools. It just took longer.

I often receive calls from people wanting to set up their own solar power system so they can get off the grid. After a short conversation, they're usually disappointed and shelve their dream, returning to the tyranny of the power company. Why? Because they want to live life off-grid in the same style and excess as they lived life on the grid. Unless you have piles of money to invest, that's just not going to happen. You're going to have to simplify your life and get down to what's really important to you.

• • • • •

In summary, you're going to have to make some choices. You can live free with less, or you can sell your soul to your "conveniences." Option one offers freedom, but it's going to come at a cost. Things take longer and life may not be as convenient. Option two offers you every comfort and convenience, but you're little better than a dependent child needing others to provide your every need. And like a dependent child, you'll live your life at the whim of your benefactors. In this case, your benefactors are your employer (or clientele), the power company, the grocery stores, the oil industry, the automobile industry, the entertainment industry, and even the workers who harvest your food. Which option will you take?

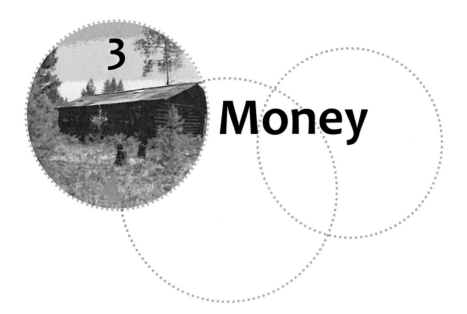

Money

Money, at least for now, is part of being self-sufficient. If I had to guess at the number one reason people abandon their dreams of self-sufficiency, I'd say it was money. Within a few miles of our cabin, I can show you the remains of homes, outbuildings, and foundations where people came to escape the rat race, only to succumb to the heart-wrenching reality that money is still a necessity in self-sufficient living.

We've seen people come here with piles of money and pay cash for their land and home, then run up enormous debts and lose it all. We've seen others come from out of state who had jobs paying $50 an hour, only to learn that the same job here (if they can find one!) pays a third that amount. Even those who tough it out sometimes face years of deprivation and stress before fiscal progress is seen.

Don't be naïve about money. You're still going to need it, but if you follow some of the guidelines in this chapter, you may find you'll need a lot less than you thought and may find ways to make it while still pursuing your dream of self-sufficiency.

The first step of our financial odyssey began long before we moved to our cabin in the woods. We were at a point where we probably weren't going to make more than our current income, so if we wanted to improve our lot in the financial world, we'd have to find ways to save more of what we made.

WAYS TO SAVE MONEY

Having enough money is a problem many people face every day, and we're no different in that regard. But we've found ways to stretch the small amount of money we do have a long way! Here are some of the things we and others have done.

Decide What You Want

What level of preparedness or self-sufficiency do you want to attain? Are you just planning to use your retreat until conditions stabilize? Are you aiming for complete self-sufficiency? Are you equipping a place as an insurance policy so that if it is TEOTWAWKI (The End Of The World As We Know It), you'll have someplace to go with family and friends and live your life in relative security? Whatever your goal is, you need to make a list of the skills, tools, knowledge, and equipment you'll need to reach your desired level of preparedness. Now go through the list and set priorities. As you save money, get the most important items first. A list like this will keep you on track, and you'll be able to see the progress you're making, which will motivate you to continue your efforts over the long haul.

Pennies Add Up to Dollars, Dollars Add Up to Big Bucks

Years ago I kept track of every penny I spent for one full month. That was illuminating, to say the least. The biggest shock came when I added up my expenditures on snacks. I averaged a mere $2 a day for snacks and soft drinks from the machines at work. That didn't sound like much until I made the yearly connection. That $2 per day times five days per week for 50 weeks came to $500 a year spent to rot my teeth and expand my waist. So, I made a few changes. At break time, I had coffee (free where I worked) and brought snacks from home. The trade-off was better health and a pile of money saved over the years.

How much do you spend on things like snacks, soft drinks, and cappuccinos? If you can save just one dollar a day every day of the year, you'll have $365 dollars to spend on other things. Even cutting out $10 a month will net you $120 in a year's time. The key here is to set that money aside for the things you really want.

Start Saving Dollars and the Money Adds Up Even Faster

A coworker used to eat his noon meal at a restaurant with his friends. The average cost was $7 a day. That's $35 per week, or $1,750 per year. If he packed a lunch, it would bring the cost down to $2 a day for a savings of $1,250 per year. What could you buy with $1,250? Add on the $500 a year saved on snacks and you have $1,750 total savings.

If you substitute coffee from home, cutting out the $7.50 per day spent on cappuccino, your annual savings will come to $1,875. Add that to $1,750 already saved and you'll have $3,625 in your special purchase fund. What could you do with $3,625? Divided over a 12-month period, that's $302 per month. With a careful purchase, that would make a monthly payment on property for your retreat.

Save By Downsizing

Can you eliminate a vehicle? You'll spend less on licensing, taxes, insurance, repairs, tires, maintenance, and gasoline.

What about housing? Could you get by with something smaller or cheaper? If you rented an apartment within walking distance of where you work and eliminated a vehicle as well, you might be able to save enough to buy a piece of land in the country somewhere for a retreat.

If you're at the age where you can buy that retirement home, think carefully about what you get. Do you really need four bedrooms and five bathrooms? Large houses are costly to heat and cool, difficult to keep clean, and expensive to maintain, and the taxes and insurance are atrocious.

One of the best ways to save money is to make things yourself. I wanted a heavy wool coat but couldn't afford a new one or find a used one like I wanted. We purchased two wool coats from a thrift store for $7.50 each. I combined them to make a coat exactly like I wanted. Not including my labor and thread, I saved over $100 compared to the price of a new coat.

Reevaluate Your Insurance

The typical American pays insurance on his or her life, health, home, and vehicles. It's important to have adequate insurance, but remember that the more insurance a salesman can talk you into, the fatter his commission—and the thinner your wallet—becomes. Savings can amount to hundreds of dollars per year. Meet your legal requirements on property and vehicles; carefully analyze what you do and do not need after that.

Medical care and insurance is a difficult obstacle to overcome. If you're a veteran, you may qualify for health care benefits from the U.S. Department of Veterans Affairs. There are also county-, state-, and city-sponsored clinics that handle most routine medical needs. Those I'm aware of bill you according to your income. In the event of a long-term or serious illness, and if you qualify, Medicaid or Medicare may be options.

Utilizing government-subsidized health care may be offensive to some, but as long as the systems are not being abused, I have no problem with those using them.

There are alternative, home-based treatments for many of the ailments people purchase drugs to cure. I know of one family battling a chronic condition who, after spending thousands of dollars on doctors, began pursuing home remedies. They made some dietary and lifestyle changes and got better

You'll save money on automotive repairs by fixing parts whenever possible. The dimmer switch on my pickup quit working, so I disassembled it, sanded off the corrosion, and put it back together. It's worked like new ever since. If the repair hadn't worked I'd have had to buy a new one anyway, so I figured I had nothing to lose by trying.

results than following the $3,000 a month regimen of prescription drugs their specialist prescribed.

The most important way to cut medical costs is to live a healthy lifestyle. Eating healthier food is a cinch if you're growing it yourself! If you smoke, stop. If you consume alcoholic beverages, do so in moderation. The homestead life itself takes lots of physical labor, which helps a person avoid many of the complications brought about by a sedentary lifestyle.

Be Energy Efficient

Trading in a gas-guzzler for a more energy-efficient vehicle may save money on fuel, but be careful here. Add up the difference in miles per gallon savings vs. the cost of the newer vehicle and you might find it's cheaper to drive the old clunker until it's worn out. However, when the time comes to trade it in, get something that's fuel efficient.

The same holds true of appliances. If your water heater, refrigerator, or freezer have a few years under their belt, they are probably power wasters. As they wear out, replace them with energy-efficient models. Little things like wrapping insulation around hot water tanks and putting the freezer in a colder room make a difference as well. Turning down thermostats in winter and up in the summer and using a lower setting on your hot water tank will also save money.

Connect the television, microwave, computers, and Xbox to power strips and turn them off when they're not in use. Many of these items have clocks and "instant on" circuitry that use power even when the appliance is turned off.

Replace incandescent lights with low-watt fluorescents or LEDs. Use reading lamps instead of overhead lighting. Turn lights off if you aren't using them. Use motion-sensitive lighting outside rather than leaving the light on all night.

Personal savings may be anywhere from a few dollars to over $100 per month. However small or large, it all adds up over time.

Be Cautious of Phone and Internet Extras

The more extras the phone company sells you, the more money they make. Sure, call waiting is only a couple of bucks a month, but do you really need it? What about caller ID, voice mail, or unlimited long distance? We save about $30 a month by using a calling card for long distance at three cents per minute. That's $360 per year available for other things.

What about family plans and the other extras that cell phone companies offer to save you money? They operate on the same principle to make money that we're using to save money: they know that an extra 10, 20 or more dollars added to your account equals big commissions over time in their pockets. They sell these things by "saving" you money. That's pretty smart. You spend more to save more, and they get bigger checks by saving you money! You leave feeling good about the bargain you got, they order a steak dinner to celebrate their commission for selling you the "super saver's package deal!"

Now this is great if you really wanted or needed the things they sold you. But if you wouldn't have bought cell phones for the entire family without the package deal, did you really save money or did you just sign a contract to buy toys for your kids?

Internet providers have different plans as well, and the same rules apply. Get the plan that's best for you, not the plan that makes the salesman the best commission.

Are There Some Habits You Could Do Without?

Cigarettes, alcohol, drugs, gambling, and pornography are not listed here as moral or health issues. A pack of cigarettes in my area costs $5.75. One pack a day will cost you $40.25 a week, $161 a month, and $2,093 a year. That's more than a month of income for some people, and that's only for the cigarettes. The decline of your health and productivity add even more! A case of beer is $7 around here. Two per week is $14; the annual costs approaches $728.

I knew a couple who, before they quit, spent more on cigarettes every month than they did on their house payment. They could have bought another home with the money they spent on cigarettes. Again, I'm not judging anyone for these activities, but if you enjoy these things in excess, you'll pay for them in excess.

Use Free Resources

The public library is your friend. People pay others to clean debris from rain gutters, to paint their house, to pour cement for simple jobs like sidewalks and patios, to shampoo or lay a carpet, or any number of tasks they could do themselves if they'd just go to the library and check out a book on the subject. Do it yourself and pocket the money you saved.

YouTube is a treasure house of information. In addition to the entertainment videos, there are literally thousands of posted videos teaching you how to do almost anything. Just a short search brought up videos on field dressing a deer, baking bread, threshing wheat at home, and learning how to build a stone wall. What would you like to learn?

Skills can be acquired through donating time to nonprofit organizations. Want to learn how to ride and care for horses, or the ins and outs of backpacking, canoeing, skiing, rappelling, archery, shooting, or lifeguarding? Volunteer as a scout leader or summer camp counselor. Most organizations will teach you how to do these things and more so that you can teach others. When I was a youth camp director, we were always looking for lifeguards and medical staff and would gladly pay to train people in these areas if they'd donate a week or more of their time. Sign up for your local search and rescue group or serve as a volunteer fireman and you'll receive intensive training in many survival-related skills for free.

Clubs and organizations are filled with people who love to teach others how to do the things they do. You can learn shooting, hunting, reloading, fishing, mountain biking, swimming, gardening, quilting, knitting, weaving, and more this way. We got our ham radio licenses by taking free classes

Buy the best you can afford. It'll save you money in the long run. This Troy-Bilt tiller was purchased over a quarter century ago and is still running great. It was built to last, and last, and last!

given by the local ham club. The only things we paid for were the book and the test fee.

When I wanted to learn how to rebuild automatic transmissions, I contacted the local vocational school. They told me that they didn't offer the class normally but would if there was enough interest. I needed 10 people to get a class going, so I spent some time on the phone calling repair shops and had 18 people signed up within two days. The state paid for everything except textbooks.

Many colleges and universities offer adult education classes for a nominal fee. If there's a subject you're interested in, suggest it to them. Many times they'll line up instructors to teach the class if you can get enough people to sign up for it.

Years ago I took a $35 correspondence course on photography and made money on the side doing weddings and graduation pictures. You can get the same knowledge from a library book for free. I already had the equipment, so I used it to pay for itself and made some profit as well.

Utilize government resources. Did you know that you can get free information from sources like the Federal Emergency Management Agency (FEMA), Department of Agriculture, U.S. Geological Survey, Forest Service (state and federal), county extension offices, and most colleges and universities? FEMA has a wealth of information on survival-related subjects. The county extension office has information on gardening, livestock, off-grid power, and dozens of other preparedness topics. Go to their websites and see what they have to offer.

Get Out of Debt and Stay Debt Free!

We could not live the way we do if we had any debt. Sit down with your monthly statements and add up the amount of interest you pay every month on your credit cards, home and vehicle loans, school loans, or any other loans you have. What could you buy with that amount?

Beware of those "no payments or no interest for six months" and similar deals. Always assume that they're making up the difference somewhere. Often they've added extra charges or higher interest rates to make up for the lack of payments.

Be careful of consolidation loans and second mortgages. If you cannot control your spending, consolidation loans will just get you that much deeper in debt. I've seen too many people get a consolidation loan to pay off credit cards, then immediately buy more things on credit. They ended up making payments and interest on the consolidation loan *and* the new credit card debt.

Our son is changing a tire on our $49.99 Harbor Freight Tools tire machine. He saved over $200 by buying his tires online and mounting them himself. We save over $100 per year using this machine and doing our tire swaps and repairs ourselves. It comes with instructions.

Instead of buying on credit, use layaway at the store. Or save up the money and pay cash.

Stop Impulse Spending

One of my biggest problems was buying on impulse. I'd see a good deal. I had the money in my pocket and I'd spend it. (Or worse, I'd use the credit card!) The problem was that I didn't have what I really wanted and needed, and usually the item I bought ended up being sold at a yard sale—at a loss! Know what you want and how much you'll spend before you go into a store. If it isn't on your list, don't buy it!

Buy When Others Are Selling, Sell When Others Are Buying

I purchased a complete reloading setup for $100. It included a press, several sets of dies, a powder scale, two complete sets of dipper-type powder measures, a hand priming tool, case lube and pads, a loading block, over 8,000 primers, several pounds of powder, hundreds of cast bullets in .357 and .44 calibers, and a box full of other loading accessories. A friend at work was moving and needed the money in a hurry. He made the offer; I took him up on it. I later sold some of the dies that I didn't need and made back my investment and a little extra. It wouldn't have happened if I hadn't had the cash on hand.

On the flip side, buying when everyone is buying gets expensive. I saw people happily pay five times as much for ammo in 2009 after the presidential election as I did in 2008. And they were glad to get it at any cost. Why? Supply and demand. Anytime there's a shortage, prices go up.

If you must buy when prices are high, get only what you need. The prices will probably stabilize and may even go down if you can just wait out the current crisis.

Look for the Best Deal

We seldom pay retail prices on anything. Most of our food supplies were bought in case lot sales at half the retail price. Watch for seasonal sales and after-season clearances to get good prices. Use the Internet to find new and used merchandise for a fraction of the retail price. Figure up what you would have paid normally and pocket the savings.

You'll have to decide if it's worth the membership costs to shop at places like Coscto and Sam's

Club. In our experience, we can often beat some of their prices with careful shopping. However, our local Costco (65 miles away!) has some things we cannot get in the same quality anywhere else without paying much higher prices. What we've done is split the membership fees with one of our kids and leave the account in their name. Since we have to travel there to shop anyway, we just do it on days when they can come along, or they pick up what we need and bring it up when they visit.

Be Frugal

Spend only on what is needed. We live by the maxim, "use it up, wear it out, make it do, do without." This is easier if you've prioritized and know the difference between needs and wants.

Stay Home

Fewer trips out mean savings on food, fuel, impulse spending, and vehicle maintenance. Consolidate your trips and make each one accomplish multiple purposes. If you're going to be out all day, pack a picnic lunch and eat at the park instead of a restaurant. Take some ice from the fridge and a cooler of soft drinks. Bring snacks from home. Pocket the savings.

Reduce Your Times of Eating Out

I'm not saying you should never eat out, but cooking at home from scratch saves money and you'll probably eat healthier too. The crockpot and barbeque grill are your friends.

When you do eat out, spend less. We take advantage of dollar menus and coupons when we go out. A $5 Little Caesar's pizza, soft drinks from our cooler, and a city park provide a pleasant meal for a price that doesn't break the bank. Pocket the savings.

Don't Let the "Joneses" Control Your Life

Many of our friends have newer vehicles, bigger boats, larger houses, and unlimited electricity. They also depend on others to provide food, fuel, electricity, and heat. With the current economic meltdown, many of them are on unemployment, with no prospect of a decent job in the foreseeable future, and are struggling to keep their homes out of foreclosure and food on the table.

Instead of marching to the beat of a different drummer, *be* the drummer! Develop an independent spirit and lifestyle. Break free! Why go into debt to buy things that will drag you down, just to impress people you may not even like?

Rent Items You'll Only Need Once or Twice

Specialty ladders, paint sprayers, carpet cleaners, backhoes, motor homes, trucks, and trailers are among dozens of big ticket items that can be rented at a fraction of what it would cost you to own them.

Tough It Out

Don't sell anything you'll have to replace or buy back later. I've known people who sold or pawned guns, cameras, musical instruments, tools, jewelry, and other valuables when they were caught short at the end of the month. Usually they got much less than the item was worth and ended up with no money and no gun (or whatever they sold). Once you've bought something, keep it. If it's expendable, you shouldn't have bought it in the first place.

Set Aside the Money You Save

When you forego a cappuccino, take the money you would have spent out of your pocket and put it aside. Keep an envelope at home and deposit the money there, or open a separate bank account for these funds. Do the same with everything else on this list. Set that money aside and use it only for the things designated in your master plan. Then, when that super deal comes along, you'll be able to cash in on it.

This plan will only work if you are truly motivated. Start now.

WAYS TO MAKE MONEY

Saving money is great, but without a source of income, no matter how frugal you are, you'll eventually run out of cash. When that happens times will get really tough!

My wife and I have made money lots of different ways since our move. (Notice I didn't say lots of money in different ways!) She has tuned pianos, given music lessons, sold homemade children's clothing and hot pads, written magazine articles, cut boughs for Christmas wreaths, cut and sold firewood, done proofreading and editing, and cleaned houses in addition to employment at "real" jobs.

I've had magazine articles published, designed and constructed off-grid power systems, and done

This is my wife on her way into town for the farmer's market. She's taking everything on her bicycle and trailer to save gasoline and get some exercise. The trailer was originally a child carrier, but she modified it to haul cargo. It's about 40 miles round trip.

Everything you see (table, chair, umbrella, and merchandise) was transported on the bicycle and trailer (except for the boy at the table!). We sold raspberry plants, dried huckleberries, and a few other things we'd grown or foraged from the woods.

mechanical repairs of vehicles, machinery and small engines. I've earned money doing carpentry, logging, welding, photography, trapping, and cutting and selling firewood. I've also worked "real" jobs as a mechanic, truck driver, janitor, security guard, preacher, and children's camp director.

The Internet has opened up possibilities for those living in remote areas, if it's available. I know a man who "works" in California yet lives in a lakeshore cottage in Montana. He commutes once a month by plane to the jobsite, but everything else is done at home in front of his computer screen.

We've made money selling items on Internet marketing sites like eBay. We peruse yard sales and thrift stores for bargains we can resell and make a profit on. I recently purchased two recurve bows, some arrows, and a case and accessories for $40 at a yard sale. Two weeks later, I sold one of the bows for $175 on eBay and kept the rest of the items for my own use. However, if you're going to do this, be sure you know the value and marketability of what you're buying, and don't use cash you cannot afford to lose.

One of our sons makes extra money housesitting for people on vacation. He has earned a good reputation that has spread, so people now call him directly.

We know others who work as wilderness survival instructors, hunting guides, taxi and shuttle drivers, wild-land firefighters, snowplow operators, auctioneers, greenhouse owners, rain gutter installers, foresters, and heavy equipment owners/operators. Others are Dumpster divers who restore other people's "junk" and resell it at yard sales, and who salvage aluminum, copper, and other materials for its scrap value. Some do seasonal work picking and selling mushrooms in the spring and huckleberries in the summer; selling produce at farmer's markets in the spring, summer, and fall; and selling Christmas trees in the winter.

Often there are part-time and temporary jobs available in government service or with private firms and individuals. Our state's job service site has special sections for temporary jobs. One example is during the potato harvest. The farmers hire people to sort, sack, and ship potatoes at harvest time. If you're a good worker, let people know you're available for small jobs in the area. A lot of people need help for a few hours on a particular project and will call you if you're a good worker and available.

My wife tunes pianos for some extra cash. While she has a strong music background, you don't even need to know how to play a piano in order to tune one. There are correspondence courses that can teach you everything you need to know, and the tools are relatively inexpensive. With the advent of electronic tuners, even someone who is tone-deaf can tune a piano to perfection.

We know some folks who do chainsaw carving and others who build kayaks and canoes out of wood strips. Another couple makes money selling firewood. I've often wondered if an accountant could make money on a part-time basis doing tax returns. It would be an ideal homestead job in this area, because tax time comes at a slack season for us. It's still too cold and snowy to plant the garden or do much else outside, so why not bring in a little income in the warmth of your cabin?

If you're contemplating a homestead lifestyle, it helps to be versatile. The best homestead and retreat locations tend to be rural, and jobs can be difficult if not impossible to find in these places. The more salable skills you can bring with you, the better off you'll be.

There are numerous opportunities to make money even at remote locations. The problem is that it usually isn't steady income, and it usually isn't a lot of income . . . which brings us to the next part.

Our son makes money installing rain gutters. It takes a little cash outlay to get started, but he's built up a thriving business that's going strong even during the current recession. His tips for those entering the business: do quality work, and answer the phone. The number one complaint he hears about his peers is that they don't return calls.

WAYS TO NEED LESS MONEY

We've never talked the county into taking potatoes or other garden produce in place of cash when our property taxes were due, nor has the doctor ever been enthused about the idea of trading chickens for a visit to his office, but many times you'll be able to barter goods or skills for some of the things you need. We've traded eggs for milk and mechanical repairs for a solar panel. We've received traps and other homestead tools and equipment for helping others move. We've traded garden produce for tires and tires for pigs.

Barter is alive and well in the countryside. Some things to remember are to be fair and considerate when striking deals. Don't approach anyone with the attitude that your stuff is gold and theirs is garbage. Don't pass off junk as valuable. We've all heard horse-trading stories where someone got a really poor deal, but the thing to remember here is that these trades will most likely be done with neighbors and friends, and a bad reputation in the countryside will spread faster than an influenza outbreak in the public schools.

One of the best things you can do is buy less stuff! Review the section on needs vs. wants in the last chapter and the section on saving money in this one. Remember: it's easier to live without many of the things money can buy than to make the money to buy and maintain them. Engrave this on your front door, the fireplace mantle, the refrigerator door, the mirror, your computer, your wife's (or husband's!) forehead—everything you see. Most Americans are buried in clutter. There are even studies telling us that less clutter makes for less stress and advising people to get rid of all the nonessentials if they want happiness in life. (Well, maybe they don't go quite that far!)

When you spend money, spend it wisely. I remember seeing an advertisement in a tool salesman's truck that said, "we'd rather explain our price than apologize for the quality." There's a lot of wisdom in that statement. Now, I know that some things are horribly overpriced, but generally, you get what you pay for.

Yard sales and thrift stores are your friend. I've purchased name-brand clothing, tools, and appliances at yard sales at a fraction of their price when new. However, be sure you know what you're buying and how much it's worth. I've also seen items priced higher than local stores sold them for brand new. Be especially cautious about things you'll have to repair. I've seen ham radios at what seemed to be a good price, but the battery pack needed to be replaced. By the time you bought new batteries, you had more invested than an equivalent radio

The local sawmill encourages people to salvage slabs from their leftovers. These are the round parts of the logs that are left after the tree is milled into boards. We pick these up for use as firewood and for unique building projects around the property.

We used some of the free sawmill slabs to make the railing around our front porch.

purchased new (battery packs and chargers included). Be cautious buying rechargeable tools for the same reason.

Take care of what you've got. Perform scheduled maintenance on schedule! Fix minor problems before they become major issues. We had a neighbor tell us that Briggs & Stratton generators lasted a lot longer if you changed the oil twice as often than the manufacturer recommended. He was right. Clean your tools and store them in their proper places when you're finished using them. When you're short on cash, it really hurts to have to replace something you lost or broke because of carelessness or abuse. When you use tools or equipment, pretend it can never be replaced and treat it accordingly. Someday it may be true!

Take care of yourself. Many if not most of the illnesses people seek treatment for could have been prevented through proper diet and exercise, not smoking or drinking excessively, less stressful living, or being safety conscious.

One of the benefits of the homestead lifestyle is that you'll probably be more active and eat healthier than you used to. Not only can you avoid many of the chemicals and preservatives found in food sold in stores, your food will be fresher, tastier, and healthier. Plus the homestead lifestyle is an active lifestyle. Gardening, woodcutting, construction projects, foraging, and the dozens of other tasks you engage in will keep you bending, stretching, sweating, and working as a natural part of life. You can cancel that membership in the health club and save both money and time while still enjoying good health and flexibility.

There are some cautions also. You'll be working with tools and in situations that can destroy your health and life in a heartbeat if you aren't careful. Some of the things we've had happen include a broken wrist in a horse accident (my wife), broken ribs in motorcycle accidents (both of us on different occasions), ribs rebroken in a slip on the ice (me—hurts a lot more the second time!), and 13 stitches from an accident with a hatchet (me, and that was *after* I sternly lectured the kids on axe safety!). My wife had a row of stacked firewood fall on her once that could have been very serious, and a neighbor

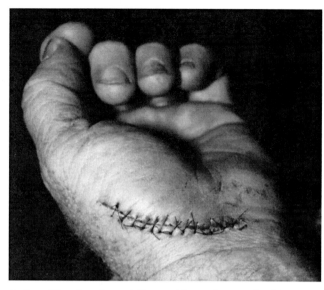

A slip with a hatchet while notching a log resulted in a trip to the doctor's office on Saturday morning. Always try to keep a stash of cash on hand for emergencies. We try to keep a hundred dollars or so available. We are fortunate that our doctors will come to the office for minor weekend emergencies. Otherwise it would have been 65 miles to the nearest emergency room and a much greater expense.

broke his wrist on our trampoline. And that's just the short list! Granted, not all are related specifically to homestead life, but it's far safer to play video games at the computer than to engage in the outdoor activities commonly found on the homestead. The moral here? Be careful; it'll save you a pile of money.

Now, here's the disclaimer. Don't become so frugal that life is no longer a joy. We sometimes take long vacations to a warmer climate in winter. We occasionally go out to eat or take in a movie. We go fishing, kayaking, backpacking, snowmobiling, skiing, and bicycling for fun. When we do these things, we still remember to keep the cost low. When we head south, we take a tent or our U-Haul truck converted into a motor home. We bring food from home and prepare it ourselves, camp where it's free, and generally do things on the cheap. Gasoline is about the only extra expense beyond what it costs to stay home. We take home-dried food when backpacking, bicycling, and on other activities. Having fun doesn't have to cost a fortune.

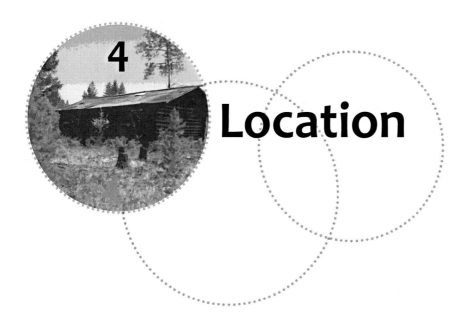

4 Location

The mantra of real estate agents is "location, location, location!" Now, while location is a part of the picture, it isn't your only, or even most important, concern. Let's face it, people have adapted to every climate and land mass known to man. For most of the earth's history, they did so without electricity, super insulated housing, or central heat and air conditioning. Additionally, you aren't a land speculator with the intention of gleaning huge profits a few years down the road. What you need is something in your price range that you can use to provide for your needs. With that in mind, there are some things you need to think through.

DECIDE WHAT YOU WANT

Finding *affordable* land can be a challenge. The first thing to recognize is that cheap land is cheap for a reason—or a lot of reasons! Usually it's remote; jobs may be difficult to find or nonexistent; it will probably be lacking in amenities such as water, sewer, and electricity; roads and/or access may be seasonal or by four-wheel drive only; or it may be in such undesirable locations as deserts, mountains, or swamps. In short, it's going to be a challenge to live there.

However, there are still bargains to be had and, in the current housing market meltdown, there may be more in the future. What you need to do before you even begin considering land is to decide what you consider to be essential and what is negotiable.

Again, be realistic. Don't get dreamy eyed believing "everything will work out in the end." If you can't find a job or make money from home, you're going to be faced with some harsh options. You may have to temporarily work out of state, as some do in our area, or you may have to dip into retirement savings. If you're going to hate the climate or the people living there, find someplace else. If on-site water is nonnegotiable, don't buy property without it. If you have a minimum acreage requirement, stick with it. If you have a maximum price, don't go beyond it. If you plan on utilizing solar power, don't buy land on a north-facing mountainside. Don't start your new life on a shaky foundation.

That being said, at least take a look at alternatives. Many people think that a homestead or retreat must be remote, inaccessible, and at least 10 acres or more. In some cases that might be the best option, but there's a lot to be said for living in a small town even in bad times. You'll have neighbors to work with and the security of numbers if you work it right. There are numerous examples of people growing almost all of their food on small lots in cities. You'll be able to trade and barter goods and services with your neighbors. You can pool resources and draw from the talents and skills of those around you.

Going it alone has a whole set of problems to be wary of. Security can be a real issue when you're alone or your numbers are small. Standing watch takes valuable time and energy at the expense of other tasks. Many jobs are easier with help or even

Cheap land is often remote, with very poor, often seasonal roads. Think carefully about finding (and getting to!) work, repairing and replacing vehicles more often, the amount of time it will take to get emergency medical or law enforcement assistance, transporting your kids to and from school, and the time and expense involved to get groceries and attend church, school, and community functions. Do your homework before putting any money down.

impossible without it! When illness or accidents strike, you'll need someone around to nurse the sick or perform essential duties. Remember, in tribal cultures, banishment from the tribe was often a death sentence. People can be your friends and allies instead of enemies to avoid or defeat. I can think of a lot of small towns that would be a great place to live if things got bad. Even in rural areas, it's best to have reliable neighbors at your side.

If you're thinking of homesteading, remember that you don't need a lot of land to take care of your needs. This is especially so in areas where the climate is mild and growing seasons are favorable. I once had a home on three acres in a small farming community in Kansas. The neighbors were great. Our growing season was long. I had a hand-drilled well with a shallow well pump to water the garden. I had permission to hunt, trap, fish, and camp on thousands of acres of private land owned by local farmers. I worked out of my garage repairing trucks, cars, and farm equipment. It was a great place to live—except for my allergies. I just got tired of being sick all the time and finally headed for a more allergy friendly environment.

Where we live in northwestern Montana is not the ideal place for a wilderness homestead or retreat. Our growing season is short. Winter (and the need for heat) is long. Food for people and livestock must be grown and stored for the long winters. Game is relatively sparse and difficult to hunt compared with many places, and it takes a lot of land to pasture a cow or horse. Predators such as weasels, skunks, hawks, eagles, coyotes, wolves, mountain lions, bobcats, and black and grizzly bears put small animals and livestock (and sometimes people) at risk. These difficulties can be overcome, but it takes more work to provide for yourself than it would in places more friendly toward survival.

FINDING PROPERTY

If you're looking for cheap land, don't expect Realtors to fight for your business. In our experience, they'll first try to talk you into something more expensive. If they can't do that, they'll give you directions to locations that might meet your desires and then expect you to find it on your own. I can't blame them to a degree. They work on commission, and the profits from cheap land won't go far toward purchasing gasoline at today's prices. And, like I said earlier, cheap land is usually remote and access can be difficult. One piece of advice, though: get a good map of the area and have them trace the route on the map before you leave their office. It will also help if they have GPS coordinates (assuming you have a GPS).

We found our 20-acre parcel when we looked at an adjacent five-acre piece of property listed by a Realtor. His directions were so poor it took three trips to locate the property. While there, we noticed that the land across the road looked like it had been abandoned for years, so we decided to locate the owner and make him an offer. We visited the plat room at the county courthouse to determine owner-ship, then obtained an address from the tax assessor's records (it's all public information). After that, we wrote the owner a letter asking him if he was interested in selling. A week later he responded saying to make an offer. We did a little research on land values, added about 10 percent, and shot back a proposal to buy the land on a five-year, no-interest, no-down-payment contract. He made a counteroffer, which we accepted, and the deal was done.

The lesson here is that you have nothing to lose in trying some unconventional methods. The landowner wasn't desperate to sell or he'd have had the land on the market, but he wasn't against selling it either. There are others out there who'd be open to the same type of deal we made, but you're going to have to find them.

In addition to real estate websites, eBay and Craigslist are good places to search for land on the Internet. Once you're on the sites, you'll have to enter data relevant to your search, such as desired location, type of property (residential, rural, commercial, etc.), with or without dwellings, and price range. There will be lots of options to choose from, so narrow them down to the most desirable and check those first. Once you have results, read the listings carefully. Sometimes the posted or bid price covers only the down payment.

If you have an area in mind, drive around a bit and look for land you might be interested in. If you see something that catches your eye, find out who owns it (ask someone living nearby or visit the county plat room). Next, contact the owner and ask them if they're interested in selling. If they say no, then ask if they're aware of any land in the area that might be for sale. Remember, you have nothing to lose by inquiring.

If you're not familiar with a plat room, check the county courthouse in the same county the land is in and ask the clerk at the information desk how to find the plat room. Once there, you'll be directed to a room where the county keeps large scale maps of the county with each parcel listed by number. Find the numbers corresponding to the parcel you're interested in. From there, go to the records of ownership (probably in the same room) to learn the name of the current owner. Take the numbers identifying the parcel of land along with the name of the current owner to the tax assessor's office, and they'll give you the contact information for the owner. From that, you can obtain an address or a phone number and write them a letter or call them to make an offer.

We've always found the county employees very helpful, although if you go in with a long list of properties, they'll probably just give you a lesson on finding things yourself so they can take care of their regular duties. The information is also available online. Call the county or a local Realtor and they should be able to give you the web address for your state. It can be kind of fun once you know what you're doing. You can find out who owns any piece of land, along with records of ownership dating back a hundred years or more.

There is also free land available. It may take some searching to find, but many cities and counties offer free home lots or commercial land to qualified individuals. These are usually residential or business lots in small towns that have been losing population. Some will be bedroom communities where most of the people commute to work someplace else. There will be restrictions and expectations to fulfill, so check them out carefully. In most cases, they're trying to build up their population and tax base, so you'll probably be required to build a home and live there. Many of these places are within commuting distance of larger towns, where work may be available. If the land is free and you build a modest home, you could be living mortgage free or at least be able to pay the loan off quickly. This may be a good option for some people. As noted above, small towns can be very good places to live.

Contacting banks for properties that have been foreclosed on might be an option, although if you can find a real estate agent specializing in such sales, you can save a lot of time. Contacting the county sheriff's department for land being sold for delinquent taxes is another option. In both of these examples, you'll need to know the rights of the seller as well as your own. In many sales such as these, the former property owner has a time period in which they can redeem the property (i.e., buy it back), so you may not receive a clear title on the land for one or more years until the redemption period expires. Be cautious about this option, though. Neighbors could be quite hostile if you bought land that belonged to a friend or relative.

If you're looking for land close to where you live, check the local newspapers and bulletin boards for properties. Many small towns have public bulletin boards at stores and community centers. Local people often post notices there selling everything from services and vehicles to pets and land.

If your job situation is in flux, you might want to move to an area you're interested in, get a job, and rent a place to live for awhile. It will give you a chance to get to know people and the climate. Ask those you meet if they know of any land for sale in your price range. Check out schools, libraries, churches, police departments, and shopping opportunities. Go to the library or newspaper office and read both current and back issues of the local paper. Spend some time in the coffee shops or restaurants and listen in on conversations. Be especially aware of local political leanings and the attitudes of people toward newcomers. (More on that in chapter 17.) Check the phone books to see if half the last names are the same. (Don't laugh! I've seen small towns where two or three families dominated almost everything!) Check out the churches as well, and for the same reason. It will give you a feel for the community before you make a commitment to purchase land.

You might also want to consider running ads in the local newspapers in areas you find desirable. Just run a small ad in the real estate section stating what you're looking for and specify that only those who can meet that criteria contact you. Do the same with Craigslist for the region.

Some survival/preparedness websites have real estate listings. The last time I checked the Rawles site at http://survivalblog.com, he had real estate listings with land in various parts of the country. Don't forget magazines aimed at self-sufficiency or preparedness. Most of them have websites with ads accessible to the public. Check hunting and fishing magazines as well. They'll have hunting or fishing

properties or "camps" listed, and many of those would also make good homestead or retreat locations. Other options include magazines catering to outdoor pursuits, like *Backpacker* or *Backcountry*. Go to your nearest magazine retailer or library and look through all these publications. If you find one that has sections advertising land that's suitable for homesteading, write down its name. Now find it online. That way you may be able to look over back issues for old real estate ads. I'd be willing to bet that many of those properties are still on the market.

Be cautious about ads listing "XX acres with low down payment." I can't speak for all of them, but some of those I've looked at were very remote, windswept acres with poor access. None had water available, and it would take a person at least an hour just to reach the nearest improved road from most of them. They might make a decent retreat location if you can get water and grow food on them, but be careful here. Be sure it's a place you'd like to spend the rest of your life if it comes to that. Disregard promises from the Realtor about road improvements he'll make (he might declare bankruptcy after selling a few parcels and leave you and the bank holding the bag) or glowing prognostications about some future "homeowners association" that's going to make improvements when more people buy land. Generally, what you see is what you get.

Be absolutely sure that the land you're being shown is the land you're purchasing. I had one Realtor show me a parcel I was considering on the map he was holding, but the map had contour lines stacked upon each other and the land we were on was flat as a pancake. I was sure the lot on the map was the one next to the lot we were standing on, but he insisted I was wrong. The lots hadn't even been surveyed yet! I asked him if I would get my money back if he was wrong, and he replied they didn't make refunds but they would apply the down payment to a different parcel if it came to that. I said no thanks, call me back when you get it surveyed. I never heard from him again. I drove by that area several years later and there wasn't a habitation of any kind on the entire 640-acre section of land.

In another instance, here in our area, an out-of-state purchaser came to look at land. After he went back home, he closed the deal on one of the parcels by mail with the Realtor. However, when he moved

Be creative. We originally looked at the land for sale behind this sign. While there we noticed the vacant property on the other side of the road. We located and contacted the owner and purchased it on a five-year contract with no money down and no interest. Sometimes the best deals are not the obvious ones.

a year or so later, he learned that the parcel he was sold was not the one he wanted. Whether he messed up or the Realtor did is for the courts to decide. In the end he accepted the lot he actually purchased, even though it wasn't the one he wanted. It would have been too much hassle and expense to straighten things out, and he would have been homeless while the case went through the court system. It was a hard lesson. Be sure that you have the exact lot location and specifications when you close.

Have a title search done before purchasing, and make sure you have clear title to the land. Get everything in writing. It should go without saying that you NEVER, NEVER, NEVER, buy land without seeing it first.

COVENANTS AND RESTRICTIONS

Assume nothing regarding covenants and restrictions. I looked at land that had some restrictive covenants regarding livestock, yet one of the landowners had horses in a corral next to his cabin.

I asked the Realtor about it, and he shrugged his shoulders and said evidently the neighbors didn't mind. I asked him if it would be okay to have horses, and he said it was probably okay as long as no one complained. The thing is, though, that the horse owner would have no legal leg to stand on the first time someone complained about his animals. He purchased the property with the covenants in place, and he is legally bound to obey them. All it would take is one complaint from an angry or new neighbor and he'd have to find a new home for his animals (or himself). If it's in your purchase agreement, a county ordinance, or state or federal law, you are bound by it. If it's something you can't accept, then don't purchase the land.

Make a list of things you might want to do to make a living or live your life and find out if there are any laws pertaining to those activities. Check with the county for laws on road maintenance, livestock, pets, and target shooting and hunting. Look for restrictions on junk vehicles or "unsightly trash." Check on regulations regarding building permits and how they apply to homes, outbuildings, and fences. What are the rules regulating septic systems, wells, water rights, and irrigation rights? Are there ordnances pertaining to home business operations and related matters like signs and parking? What about selling produce or home-produced goods? Do you need a special license to make and sell food such as jams or jellies?

Septic and water are two big issues in some rural areas. Some places, for example, don't allow pit toilets or even composting toilets. In a neighboring county, the commissioners recently decided that all septic systems must have a pressurized drain field system. That means that instead of a gravity flow from your septic tank to your drain field, you have to pump the sewage under pressure to the leach lines. This isn't a big deal if you live on grid, but many people around here live off-grid, and the system requirements mean that they must either greatly expand their off-grid systems or use a generator to run the sewage pumps. Find out about these things before you purchase the land.

Find out what the laws are regarding utility easements. Do you have control over where they run the lines across your property? Can you be charged for installation costs for lines crossing your property to neighboring properties?

Find out who owns such things as mineral, timber, and water rights. How will these affect you? If you are obtaining financing, see if you are allowed to cut timber for your own use or for sale. Many who offer owner financing do not allow timber to be harvested for sale until after the property is paid for. The reason is because some people have bought land with a low down payment, then sold the timber and defaulted on the loan. The owner is left with a virtual wasteland for the next 20 or more years. On the same note, be sure that no one else can sell the timber on your land once you close the deal.

Access can be another problem. Find out what your rights and responsibilities are. How is your access guaranteed across neighboring properties to yours? What about landowner access to properties beyond yours? Is there a road running through your land? Is it going to be a problem? Think of the future here. Right now the only homes beyond yours may be vacation homes occupied a couple of times a year, but what happens if they're sold to someone with teenage kids who are in and out 20 times a day, driving fast and stirring up clouds of dust and endangering your pets, children, or livestock? Can you

Many parcels of cheap land have old buildings on them. Some just need to be burned to the ground. Others can be used for storage as long as they're water- and pack rat-proof.

When you're looking for cheap land, be aware that you'll probably be doing a lot of building or renovating. Find out what's included in the deal before putting your money down. Do not assume that such systems as wells, septic, and power are functional. I once rented a place that was six miles beyond the last power pole. The house was wired for electricity, but the power lines had been removed 20 years earlier.

move the road without their permission? If so, who pays for it? Can other landowners move the road to your property? What about road width and condition? Whose responsibility is it to maintain the road? Are you required to maintain the road to specific standards? What about the road into your property? Who maintains it?

Access can be a critical issue if you must cross public land to get to your property. Make absolutely sure you have legal access. Dealing with the government on this issue is not fun. They may have more

Sometimes it pays to buy a cheap camper or motor home to live in while you build your house. You'll get more work done after a good night's sleep, and most come with a bathroom, shower, refrigerator, and cookstove. When the house is finished, sell it or use it for its intended purpose—camping!

laws and restrictions than you can imagine. It's possible you'll need to have an environmental impact statement submitted and approved to do even minor repairs or changes to a public road. Be clear about who maintains the road. Will you be allowed to make improvements if the government won't? We've been through this locally. A section of our road goes through national forest land. You need permits from the U.S. Forest Service to even grade the road. It might be an issue you'll have to deal with.

Learn what laws apply to livestock and pets. We've had people move near us who thought they could let their dog run free just because they lived in the country. It doesn't work that way. The dog can run free as long as it stays on its own property, but that's the *only* place it can run free. (Check local regulations to be sure!) You will be held responsible if your pets chase, harass, or kill wild or domestic animals. Many rural residents will shoot a dog that chases deer or livestock. Moving to the country does not relieve anyone of being a responsible pet owner.

Livestock can be another problem. In most instances you'll be required to properly confine your livestock, and you may be held responsible for damages your livestock cause if they do escape. That can be a big expense if they get hit by a vehicle.

There are exceptions, however. Montana is an "open range" state, meaning that livestock do not have to be confined. If your neighbor's cattle or horses are trespassing on your property, it's *your*

responsibility to build a fence to keep them out. That doesn't mean you can't contact the owners to seek a solution, but it does mean that they have the law on their side.

Also check subdivision requirements. First, if you desire space, the last thing you'll want is a nearby landowner building a subdivision next to your property. Second, if for some reason you want to sell part of your land, you'll need to know if subdividing is an option.

Be aware that many properties are advertised with "power to the property." Be sure you know what that means. Does the power run to the building site or just to the property boundary? Find out how much it would cost to hook up to the grid.

We had a neighbor run power lines to his place. It cost him over $30,000. However, there was a way for him to recoup some of his investment. If someone else hooked up to that line within the ensuing five years, they would have to pay half his costs (which the power company reimbursed to him). So if he ran the power line a mile and it cost him $30,000, then you hooked up later, you would have to pay $15,000 to hook onto that line, plus whatever extra it cost to run power from the line to your house. After five years, the extra fees would no longer apply and you only would pay to run power from the existing line to your home. So, even if the power is to the property line, you may be required to pay extra to hook onto it. Find out how much the total cost will be before you purchase the land.

TAXES

Find out how much you'll be paying in property taxes. Do not just go by taxes paid by the previous owner. Call the tax assessor's office and talk to them. They may not be able to give you an exact figure, but they should be able to give you a general idea of how much your taxes will be after you close. Be honest with them when you describe any improvements you plan on making to the property. They cannot give you a realistic estimate of future taxes if you misrepresent your intentions. The taxes on our land went up considerably after we moved onto the property. Prior to that it was all classed as agricultural/timber land, so the rate was very low. When we began living there, the acre on which our home was located was taxed at a substantially higher rate. It wasn't exorbitant, but it was an expense we hadn't anticipated.

Some states reappraise properties at a much higher rate after they're sold. This is usually to protect long-time residents from skyrocketing real estate values, which push their tax rates higher as well. Many of these people are on fixed incomes and would be forced off their land otherwise.

To clarify this: In some areas, the rate that property taxes can increase is limited by law. Once you purchase your property, no matter how much nearby values escalate, your property taxes cannot go up more than a specified amount each year. That's what protects the current owner from hefty tax increases. However, when the property is sold, the new owner is taxed at the current market value and may end up paying substantially more in taxes.

Be sure you find out about any sales taxes, special levies, or hook-up fees to local utilities you may have to pay. The government is not very forgiving. If you don't pay up, they will take your land from you.

NEIGHBORS AND NEIGHBORHOODS

Learn as much as you can about the neighbors and neighborhood. This includes not only looking up crime statistics but getting a general understanding of the people who live there.

Does the neighborhood look run down or have other signs of decay? Are there junk vehicles in evidence? Does that bother you? One of the fastest ways I know of to wear out your welcome in rural areas is to move there and try to change everyone around you. I know of an instance where people bought property, then tried to coerce the neighbors to pay for improving the private road they all shared. At one point the newcomers threatened to have the county take over the road and tax everyone for the improvements. They were laughed at and ridiculed, and some threats were made as well. The neighboring landowners refused to assist them in any way and generally made life miserable for them during the time they lived there. They didn't fit into the local community and should never have bought land there in the first place. What you see when you view the property is what you're going to have to live with if you purchase it. (There is more on community relations in chapter 17.)

Is your home going to be significantly above or below neighborhood standards? If you have more money than the locals, there may be resentment. If you have substantially less, they may also resent you.

Are the locals mostly related to one another? If so, what happens if there's a problem with one of them? Will you find the entire clan against you? What about racial tensions? Are there any unusual religions or cults in the area? Drug labs or marijuana fields? Is alcoholism or drug use a problem? Don't be naive about rural areas. They have their good and bad elements just like everyplace else.

In summary, determine whether this is a place where you'll fit in.

PUBLIC LAND ACCESS

This might be a big issue to some (it was to us). If you moved from a state that allowed motorized recreation on public land, check to see if it's allowed in the area you've targeted. Use restrictions are becoming far more common on public lands due to pressure from environmentalists and animal rights extremists. Some restrictions are necessary to protect high-use areas, but if one of your goals in moving to the country is unlimited access to public land to ride your ATV on, it's best to find out if that's even an option before you purchase land.

On this issue don't just listen to the locals. Some have been breaking the laws for years and no one has cracked down on them, but if the laws exist, assume that they will be enforced at some point in the future. Sometimes locals don't even know there are laws against certain activities.

Another thing to check is access across your land to public land. And not just the legalities. Do the locals have a trail beaten across your land? If so, what's going to happen if you close it off? Lawsuits? Trespassing violations? Vandalism? Resentment toward you? Remember, the people you're taking to court will be your neighbors. Is it worth it to stir up a lot of problems with them?

Address as many of these issues as you can before you make any purchases.

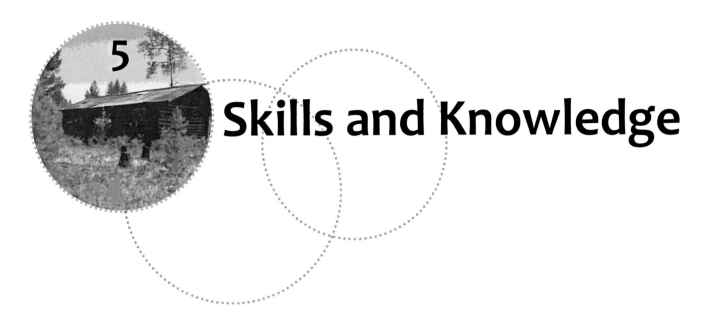

Skills and Knowledge

One of the blessings in my life has been a lack of financial resources. I never had the money to hire a plumber, so when a drain was plugged, I went to the library and found a book on plumbing and learned how to clear the drain myself. When I needed a room remodeled, I couldn't afford a carpenter, so I went to the library and checked out a book on home construction and remodeling and learned how to do it myself. The same with house wiring, cement work, septic systems, and everything else having to do with home construction and maintenance.

I was also blessed with relatives who farmed. At a young age I learned how to drive and maintain tractors, farm implements, and pickups; cut, bale, transport, and stack hay; prepare fields; plant, cultivate, and harvest both gardens and fields of corn, soybeans, milo, and wheat; and use a chainsaw properly. I also learned basic animal care, how to build fences and corrals, and how to milk cows by hand and by machine.

My father took me small game hunting when I was growing up, and I improved my skills by reading books and magazine articles on the subjects. In the same way, I learned how to fish. A neighbor introduced me to ammo reloading in his garage using an ancient (by today's standards) press with felt wads to reload paper shotgun shells. Later I graduated to reloading metallic cartridges with my first Lee Loader. I'm still improving these skills today.

A few years in the Boy Scouts of America taught me how to camp, plus such other outdoor skills as fire starting, knots and lashing, first aid, and more.

I took two years of auto mechanics in a local trade school my junior and senior years of high school and continued in that trade more years than I care to remember.

After graduation from high school, I enlisted in the U.S. Marine Corps. There I learned infantry tactics, marksmanship, discipline, close order drill, more first aid, how to drive trucks, how to type (not by choice!), and too many other things to list here.

In life after the USMC, I owned a couple of businesses and expanded my skills in welding and metal fabrication, learned automatic transmission repair and rebuilding, acquired basic bookkeeping skills, and became an avid gardener and trapper.

Later in life I earned a BS degree in Bible ministry and spent several years in the ministry pastoring two different churches. While there I learned (in addition to Bible knowledge) business administration, writing, speaking, and teaching skills.

I've taken correspondence courses in photography and auto body repair.

When we got our first solar panel (by barter), I went to the library and Internet and learned what I needed to know for setting up an off-grid power system.

I've also spent time as a camp administrator, security guard, and janitor. All these skills have been put into use in some way on the homestead.

I would have never learned many of these things if I'd been good at accumulating money,

I learned how to sharpen a chainsaw by purchasing a jig that clamped to the bar and had a file guide that allowed you to precisely set the angle of the file against the chain's teeth. Eventually I graduated to just using a file (which is faster because there's no set-up time).

This water pump was free because the housing was cracked. A few minutes brazing using a $60 oxyacetylene welder purchased at a pawnshop fixed it up as good as new. Don't know how to braze or weld? I learned how at a night class in a local high school. It was part of an adult education program sponsored and paid for by the school district. The only cost to the student was for the textbook. Many colleges, universities, vocational schools, and school districts will set up adult education classes if there's enough interest. Usually the cost to you is minimal.

because I'd have paid someone else to do it all for me. I'm not going to say that poverty is a blessing (there's nothing good about true poverty), but being short on money can certainly lead to a more self-sufficient life, so don't become discouraged over a lack of finances or knowledge. There are a lot of ways to learn the things you need to know without a pile of cash to draw from, but it will take some diligence on your part. If you're going to be a low-budget homesteader, you're entering a life of learning new skills and improving existing ones.

WHAT YOU'LL NEED TO KNOW

It's hard to imagine a self-sufficient homestead or retreat without having at least some basic knowledge to draw from. Some of the skills we've used in the last seven years include plumbing, carpentry, building and remodeling, roofing, log home construction, ammunition reloading, archery, hunting, fishing, trapping, butchering, lard rendering, hide tanning, gardening, foraging, canning and dehydrating food, root cellar food storage, solar and

Canning is one of the best ways to preserve food if you don't have a freezer available. Canning is not difficult to learn, but you must pay attention to the details. The Ball Blue Book *tells you everything you need to know in an easy-to-understand format.*

New construction never stops on the self-sufficient homestead. Learn as much as you can before you make your move.

Welding and auto repair skills are good for your own use or to make some money on the side. If you're not an auto mechanic or welder, look around until you find someone who's willing to barter for their services.

Roofing is not rocket science. There are a lot of good books out there that'll teach you all you need to know for those simple jobs. Don't be afraid to try new things, but do be careful. I fell off this roof about a week before this photo was taken and sprained my ankle. I was very fortunate that the sprain was the extent of my injuries. That's my wife helping to the left of me.

wind power generation, electrical wiring, automotive and small engine repair, welding, cement work, wood cutting, writing, and dozens more.

If you're completely new to this, don't be overwhelmed. Start with what you know or can learn quickly and continually add to your knowledge and skills as you go. Initially you'll want to pursue those skills that will keep you fed, sheltered, and secure before doing anything else. There are chapters in this book dedicated to each of these subjects. In fact, this entire book is about what you need to know to pursue your dream of self-sufficiency.

The most important thing to do is break things into bite-sized pieces. Even if you know nothing about gardening, you can learn enough in a short

time to grow peas, potatoes, onions, carrots, and tomatoes. With the exception of tomatoes, these are cold season crops that will grow almost anywhere and are basic ingredients for many fine meals. All can be stored for quite some time by dehydration. Electric dehydrators are cheap and easy to use, and the dried food can be stored in anything from plastic bags to old glass jars. Nonelectric food dehydrators can even be made from very simple materials if you don't want to go the electric route. (More on food preparation in chapter 8.) All are relatively easy to save the seed from, so you won't ever have to buy seed for these vegetables again if you use nonhybrids from the start.

The point is, that you can begin your journey to self-sufficiency with a very minimal investment in time, knowledge, and money. Do not get stuck on equipment or tool requirements. Very few things essential to life require expensive tools and gear. Mankind has survived thousands of years with nothing beyond what he could manufacture from local materials. You can too.

Raising animals can be done the same way. Start with something easy like chickens or rabbits. Go to the library or get online and learn what you can about choosing varieties, shelter and space needs, and food requirements. As you become familiar with them, go on to the next critter or skill and repeat the process.

Every skill you need to learn can be done this way. It also helps to read journals and books about life in the 1800s and before. Study the lives of people in third world nations today as well; they've survived without dependence on electricity or modern gadgets and conveniences. We hope things never reach that point, but if it does, you too can survive.

Remember, food, water, shelter, and security are your most important concerns. You don't have to know everything, but if you're new to this, concentrate on those areas first.

Above all, shut off the television and video games and start now! Do not wait until you make your move to learn how to grow a garden. Do not wait until you buy rabbits to learn how to care for them. The same is true for construction projects, cutting firewood, and the other tasks that are a part of self-sufficient homestead living. Start accumulating the tools you'll need at least a year in advance. That'll give you time to hit yard sales, auctions, and the want ads to get the best value for your money.

Also realize that you probably have more time and money now than you will after you make the move. Use them both wisely!

6 Pets and Livestock

Anyone who owns an animal is a slave to the animal. Many entering this lifestyle just assume that animals are a "must have." That's not necessarily so.

QUESTIONS TO ASK

In our lives, we've owned sheep, cattle, pigs, goats, rabbits, chickens, turkeys, ducks, and horses. We like animals and usually enjoy having them around, but animals also bring extra responsibilities such as shelter, feed, fencing, veterinary bills, and someone to care for them when you take a vacation. These are the reasons we ask ourselves a few questions before we acquire any.

Are They Useful?

This is a tough one, because many times desire overwhelms logic. We've owned several horses and every time we bought one, we did so with the idea of the things we could do if we had one (or more). In almost every instance we sold them later at a loss because they did not provide the amount of work or recreation we had anticipated. Now we try to be a little more ruthless when answering this question. The very first thing to decide is whether the animal(s) in question will make a positive contribution to your life.

Even pets should be evaluated as to their usefulness. We have a dog and a cat. They're more than just pets. When we didn't have a dog, the coyotes would come right up into the yard looking for ways to get to our chickens, and we had pack rats invading our outbuildings. The dog doesn't have to be outdoors all the time. Just having her scent around keeps the vermin away. She barks a warning when people come to visit.

When we were without a cat, the mice were everywhere. Now we have a fat cat and no mice. However, we have only one cat and one dog!

What you don't need is a critter (or a bunch of critters!) that demands your time, money, and attention and offers nothing in return or, worse, is a drain on your resources.

Do They Have Multiple Uses?

This is about getting the best return on your money and time. We've raised and butchered rabbits for sale and for our own use, but the next time we acquire them we're also going to tan the hides for sale or personal use after butchering them. We've heard that worms can be grown in rabbit manure, then fed to fish or chickens and the manure used as compost, so we'll be trying that next time too. Our chickens produce eggs for home use and occasionally for sale, but they also reproduce themselves. Their young can be kept for more eggs, raised and eaten, or sold. We've considered getting sheep because they provide wool and meat, and the extras can be eaten or sold. When we raised turkeys, I saved the feathers to use as fletching on my arrows. Horses, rabbits, chickens, and every other animal provide manure for compost. A milk cow or goat reproduces itself in addition to providing milk, and with milk you can make cheese, butter, and yogurt.

Hogs can eat leftover or spoiled garden produce and be housed in portable pens and used to clear and fertilize ground for gardening or other uses. People used to put a fence around a field with stumps, then dump grain around the bottom of the stumps. The hogs would root out the grain and the stump at the same time. In some places, hogs were free-ranged to forage on acorns and other natural foods, but that's not a good practice anymore. If left in the wild, they can multiply to the point of destroying habitat that's essential for native game species.

In essence, we try to get the most out of every animal we raise.

Are They Cost Effective?

This is primarily a financial issue, but the cost of animals should also be tempered by the quality factor. How much will you be paying for a dozen eggs after purchasing, feeding, and housing your chickens? If you use a straight dollar-per-dozen comparison, you'll usually find that it's cheaper to buy your eggs at the store, but there are other things that come into play here. Homegrown eggs, for example, taste better and are usually larger (and always fresher!) than those bought at the store. Plus, on a homestead you can free-range your chickens and feed them leftovers to bring your feed costs down. (Chickens make great garbage disposals!) You should also consider the rich, organic fertilizer they contribute and the amount of bugs they'll eat.

To further reduce costs, try bartering for animals and feed from your neighbors. We once worked out a deal to trade four tires for a couple of hogs. We've incubated eggs for a percentage of the chicks that hatched. Rural people tend to like bartering. See what you might have available for trade in either goods or services. It'll cut back on your total cost and might make an iffy proposition cost-effective.

Are They Sustainable Over the Long Haul?

Our goal is self-sufficiency. Even though it might be cheaper financially to go to the store, the idea of *self*-sufficiency is to provide things for ourselves. That means we want critters that can feed us and that can reproduce themselves indefinitely.

Cats are important for keeping rodent populations in check. Get them spayed or neutered so they stay close to home. Otherwise the coyotes will get them.

Dogs are indispensable on the remote homestead. Just having their scent around helps keep predators away. This is Bear, and she just came back from running my trapline with me. It was about 10 below zero that morning and we were both frosted over pretty good.

If you look at the livestock chosen by the poor in developing nations, you'll find mostly chickens, pigs, and goats. Why? Their space needs are small and they'll eat almost anything, including garden waste, weeds, brush, and stale or spoiled food.

Now, why did I bring that up here rather than in

Chickens are a good choice for homestead livestock. They provide meat and eggs and can replenish themselves. The two on the right are sitting on eggs to hatch them out. This is a trait that's been bred out of most chickens. If you have broody hens, take good care of them!

This chicken is now the proud momma of . . . baby ducks? Okay, we switched the eggs when she wasn't looking! One of the best things about homesteading is seeing life at its basics. How many people have ever seen a baby duck or chicken struggle to break free of an egg?

The white egg on the far right is a grade A, large from the store. The brown eggs are from our chickens. The extra large one on the far left is a double yolk egg. It has two yolks instead of one. Homegrown eggs taste much better than those you purchase at the store.

the section on cost effectiveness? Because on the self-sufficient homestead or survival retreat, you'll have to produce food not only for yourselves but for your animals as well. We know from experience how much work it is to grow and preserve a year's supply of food for a family. It pays to remember that with animals, you'll also have to grow food for them. Under these circumstances, it might be best to have animals that can live on the things you can't. That way there's not as much competition for available food or resources.

Small animals are easier to care for and have higher reproduction rates. Cattle generally have one calf but sometimes have twins, while goats often have twins and triplets. Rabbits are very prolific, as are chickens. If you're unfamiliar with livestock, small animals are less intimidating to be around. It's cheaper and easier to build shelters for small animals as compared to larger livestock, and it takes less space to store their food. Additionally, smaller animals give birth easier with fewer complications and avoid many of the medical costs associated with larger livestock. Plus, if they die you aren't out as much money.

We have nothing against owning large animals or lots of animals or even lots of large animals, but pets and livestock are dependents, and as long as you have them you'll have the responsibility of caring for them. Make your choices wisely!

Which Variation Fits My Needs Best?

Critters are like cars—you can choose the make and model that best fits your needs or desires. Just remember that homesteading is different from farming. A farmer is concerned primarily with making money. He has overhead to pay, along with equipment costs and other expenses related to the business of farming. The homesteader isn't concerned as much with the bottom line as he is with quality. When a farmer makes his money selling eggs, he's going to want chickens that lay consistently and prolifically, and he's going to use methods that push the chickens to maximum production. They're basically egg machines. They live in climate-controlled buildings and are given food mixtures designed for maximum egg-laying efficiency. Artificial daylight is preprogrammed to keep chickens at their optimal egg-laying potential. When production slacks off, they're sent to the slaughterhouse to become the canned chicken you buy in the grocery store.

This is not a diatribe against farming or farmers; it's just to point out the difference between farming and homesteading. Farming is a business whose goal is making a profit. Homesteading is not business; it's a way of life that stresses self-sufficiency and quality of life.

When we buy chickens, we buy breeds selected for our climate and the quality of their eggs. We like Barred Rocks because they can take the cold and they lay large, delicious eggs. We've also found out that they make good "setting hens" for hatching out their own eggs (a trait that's been bred out of most varieties of chickens). When we bought chickens for canning, we purchased 50 Cornish Cross meat chickens. They're bred to grow fast and large. There are probably hundreds of varieties of chickens available, but the point is that each one has different traits, making it better for some things and worse for others. As a homesteader, you'll want to pick a variety that best fits your needs.

Virtually every domestic animal you can think of has strengths and weaknesses. Some breeds of milk cows produce a higher ratio of cream than others. Some produce larger quantities of milk, some less. Some breeds are larger and some smaller. A commercial farm will tend toward breeds that produce larger quantities of milk with

Goats provide meat and milk. You should probably try goat milk before you buy a goat. It tastes different than cow's milk and some people don't really like it. I like it best with a little Nestle Quik mixed in to give it a chocolate flavor.

Baby animals (and goats in particular!) are cute, but don't forget that they eventually grow up. If they're male you'll probably be eating them, so don't get too attached! Try to avoid impulse purchases.

This is Peaches, our Belgian draft horse mare. She weighed approximately 1,500 pounds, measured almost six feet tall at the withers (shoulder), and was as gentle as any horse I've ever seen. Our youngest daughter spent hours with her, braiding her mane and sitting (or sleeping) on her while she grazed. But she was never more than a family pet that ate prodigious amounts of hay and made even larger amounts of compost. She drank about 10–15 gallons of water per day, which we melted from snow in the winter. (That was a full-time job!) We eventually sold her.

HEALTH AND MAINTENANCE ISSUES

Have you ever tried to bury a dead horse? Once you acquire an animal of any type, it's now your responsibility to care for its every need from the day you get it until the day you dispose of it. That can be quite a task.

Before you purchase livestock, be sure you can care for it properly. One thing you don't want is to have the county sheriff knocking on your door because someone turned you in for animal abuse or neglect, and you certainly don't want animals in your care to suffer needlessly. Almost as bad is being saddled with critters costing you as much to feed as it does your family and you can't even give them away. (The animals, I mean, not the family.)

Most livestock animals need periodic care, like worming and vaccinations. If you don't have a male of the species and you want your females to reproduce, you'll need to make arrangements for breeding through a veterinarian or someone who has a suitable mate. (Or you can do like one old farmer I know who just kind of let a few strands of the fence down and allowed the neighbor's bull do his thing.) Livestock like horses, mules, donkeys, goats, and sheep may need regular hoof care, such as trimming and/or shoeing. You'll either need to learn how to do it yourself or pay someone else to take care of it for you.

If they get sick, you'll need to take proper action. In the case of chickens, ducks, rabbits, and other small animals, you might just have to let them die and take your loss. (Often they die before you even knew there was a problem.) If it's something you have a lot of money invested in or replacement costs will be expensive, you'll need to contact a veterinarian.

And finally, if they die in your care, you're accountable for disposing of the body. With small animals it's much easier than large ones. If you have a horse, cow, or other large creature die, disposing of the carcass is more work. In our very rural neighborhood, it means you drag them off into the woods and let nature take its course. In more populated areas, you may have to employ other, more costly, measures.

In any case, these are issues you need to think about before you purchase livestock. Once it's yours, it's yours in sickness and in health and possibly yours until death.

a lower fat (cream) content. The homesteader may be best served with a breed that produced less milk with a higher fat content, which is better for making butter and cheese. Milk goats can be selected the same way.

When choosing a homestead animal, you'll want one that is hardy for your climate, easy to care for, reproduces itself well and with minimal complications, doesn't need a special diet, and is best suited for your intended use. Size matters as long as it doesn't sacrifice effectiveness. Smaller animals eat less and need less space. There are so many variations of animals of the same species that making a choice can have you pulling your hair out in frustration. One of the things you can do is call the county extension office and ask for their advice. Tell them what qualities you're looking for and they should be able to give you some suggestions to follow up on.

FEED AND WATER

Have you ever thought about what it will take to feed your animals all year long on a homestead that is self-sufficient ? That means that not only will you have to grow and store enough food for you and your family, you'll have to do it for your livestock and pets as well.

What will you have to grow to feed a horse or cow all year from your own resources? Do you have adequate pasture for grazing? What about a field of alfalfa and grass for cutting and storing a sufficient amount of hay for winter? Do you have the equipment and knowledge to cut, cure, transport, and store the hay? Can you grow enough grain to supplement your livestock's diet without putting your family at risk?

Can you support chickens, rabbits, goats, sheep, or any other livestock you might have? They need to eat all year long, just like you do, and if your goal is self-sufficiency, they'll need to be fed from food grown by you. That's one reason third world people tend to acquire animals that don't compete with their own food supply.

What farmers did at times in the past was hatch chickens in the early spring, let them run free (so they'll scrounge for their own food) all summer, then butcher them in the fall. Rabbits and pigs got the same treatment to save money. That way they didn't have to feed them over the winter.

Water is another consideration. We kept a 1,500-pound Belgian draft horse one winter. Not only did she give real experience to the quip "eating like a horse," she also drank like a horse. We live off-grid with solar power and no running water. There was no way we could keep the water in the horse's tank thawed out, so I ended up carrying five gallons of water to the horse twice a day. We had to haul water for ourselves to begin with, and now one horse was drinking more than the entire family used for drinking, bathing, and washing dishes. That was a lot of work, and we sold the horse the next summer.

Do you have a good source of water for yourself and your livestock all year long? In winter, will you be able to keep the water from freezing? One of the reasons we only have chickens now is because they don't drink a lot of water over the winter. We fill their water bowl twice each day. I bring it in and set it beside the woodstove to thaw the leftover ice, fill the bowl with water, then take it out to the henhouse and swap it with the bowl I left there earlier. I then repeat the process by thawing out the ice in that water bowl. We can easily melt enough snow to keep the chickens, cat and dog, and ourselves in water, but that's about all we want to do at present.

SHELTERS AND FENCING

This is another good argument for small animals. It's much easier and cheaper to build rabbit hutches than to build a shed and fence in 20 acres of pasture for a horse. I'm not going into a lot of details on this because it could become another book within the book. Part of your research before you acquire any livestock should include fencing and shelter needs for the animals in question.

One thing to keep in mind is that fences are not always to keep your animals in; sometimes they're there to keep other animals out. Small livestock in particular needs protection from predators. Virtually every predator on earth likes chickens, rabbits, and mutton for dinner. When we shut our chickens up at night, it isn't to keep them confined but to keep the weasels, skunks, badgers, raccoons, owls, foxes, coyotes, wolves, bobcats, mountain lions, bears, and stray dogs out.

Tool and equipment needs for building fences are minimal. All of it can be rented, but I'd advise reading up on fence building before you make any purchases or sign any rental agreements. Electric fences are usually the easiest, fastest, and cheapest fences to build. They work great on anything larger than sheep. Fence chargers can be powered by 120-volt AC electricity if you're near a power source, solar powered for remote or off-grid applications, or battery powered (these use a 6- or 12-volt automotive battery that must be recharged occasionally). Be sure that any fence you build is within your property boundaries.

Again, check the fence recommendations for the animals you intend to own.

• • • • •

As I said at the beginning of this chapter, anyone who owns an animal is a slave to the animal. Enter into the arena of animal husbandry with caution.

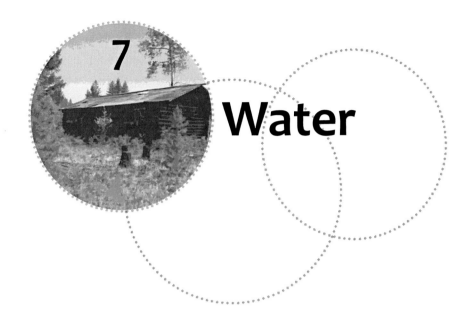

7 Water

Water is the Achilles' heel of cheap land. Occasionally you'll run into a deal on land with water on it, but not often. If there's a natural source like a stream, spring, or lake, the price goes up considerably. If there's a drilled well, the price goes up to cover the cost of the well. If you buy land and drill a well, you'll have to fork over the dough to get that task done, so water is a major consideration for the low-budget homesteader. This doesn't mean you should give up or reject any land without a source of water. It just means you need to be aware of the importance of water and have some alternate ways of obtaining it.

There are two types of water we'll concern ourselves with: potable and nonpotable. Potable water is pure enough for drinking. Most surface water such as lakes, rivers, and ponds are not potable unless you treat it through boiling, filtering, or chemical means. Most springs fall into the same category, as do many shallow wells. Most deep wells are potable without treatment because the ground filters out contaminants as the water seeps down into the aquifer. That being said, you should always have any water you plan on drinking tested for contaminants. Even deep wells can sometimes be contaminated.

If you plan on having a well drilled, check with neighboring landowners to get an idea of how deep they had to go for good drinking water. Well drillers charge by the foot, and few, if any, give guarantees of hitting water. We have one acquaintance who

spent more than $12,000 and never did hit water on his property.

Know your rights regarding water acquisition before you purchase property. You may be subject to local, county, state, and even federal regulations concerning water use on your land. Even if you have lake frontage, you may not be entitled to use that water for drinking or nonpotable purposes.

Let's take a closer look at ways to get water for the homestead.

WELLS

Wells are generally classed as shallow or deep, depending upon how the water must be pumped to the surface. A jet pump used for shallow wells can draw water from about 25 feet below the pump. They work by creating a vacuum above the water so that atmospheric air pressure will "push" the water up the pipe to the pump. Thus the 25-foot limit is set because of the physics involved. The amount of atmospheric pressure available to push the water up the pipe is the limiting factor. It's much easier to push water than to pull it, so you always want your pump to be located as close to the water as possible. Jet pumps are available that will bring water up from deeper wells, but they are very inefficient compared to submersible pumps. If your well is over 25 feet deep, get a submersible pump. The only limiting factor when using a submersible pump is the size of the well casing. Usually a four-inch inside diameter is minimum.

We haul most of our drinking water in plastic jugs. There are several sources we can draw from, including one artesian well at a neighbor's house.

There are hand pumps available that will draw water from depths of 350 feet and more. They are expensive but reliable and can be converted to wind power using equipment like the old-fashioned windmills you often see in farming country. These windmills have a gearbox at the top that converts the rotary motion of the wind vanes into vertical movement at the pump. As the impeller rotates, it moves an arm at the other side of the gearbox in a circular motion. The arm is connected to a long rod hooked to the top of the pump shaft, which is moved up and down to pump the water. These are very low tech and need very little wind to function. In high wind they have a governor that turns a tail fin so that the vanes are twisted perpendicular to the wind. The impeller then slows down, protecting the mechanism from damage.

The best book I've seen on home well drilling is a United Nations publication, *Self-Help Wells*, available through the UN's Food and Agriculture Organization (FAO) (www.fao.org; just enter the publication title in the search box). It's designed for use in low-tech applications in third world countries. Be sure to look over the photos at the back. Third world people are amazingly resourceful

(much like the early pioneers in the USA). Many of the tools needed were manufactured from locally available materials. It's also available for downloading in PDF format at www.watersanitationhygiene.org.

Be advised that there's more to drilling a well than boring a hole in the ground and pumping water out of it. When you pump water out of a new well, it's normal for the water to appear cloudy. Most drillers will pump a lot of water out of a well before it clears up. However, there are some types of water-bearing strata that will never clear up no matter how long you pump water out. A professional driller will know the difference and advise you accordingly. If you don't know what to look for, you'll just have to take your chances. If the intended use of the water is for livestock or irrigation, it might not matter if it's a little cloudy. If you want it for drinking and washing clothes, you'll either have to try again or run it through a filtration system.

The ideal for the self-sufficient homesteader is to hit an artesian well. This is water that's under pressure. You don't need a pump because the water will flow up the well casing and out the top. Be careful sealing these because if you try to stop all flow, the water often erodes around the well casing, sometimes pushing the casing itself out of the ground. Most artesian wells that I've seen have valves on top of the casing that allow water to constantly flow, thus relieving pressure and keeping the well intact.

It's always a good idea to have your water supply tested, but be especially diligent with shallow wells. Nitrate contamination from inorganic fertilizer and animal manure is a common shallow well pollutant in farm country. You can still use the water for irrigation, but don't drink it.

Driven Wells

Perhaps the simplest way of reaching water when conditions permit is the driven well. To drive a well, you start with a "drive point," which is basically a section of porous pipe with a pointed end. You attach a hardened cap to the top of the pipe and drive the pipe into the ground with a post driver. Keep adding new sections of pipe as you go deeper into the ground. When you think you've reached the water table, attach a weight to a string and lower it to the bottom. If the string is wet, drive the pipe down another 20 to 30 feet and start pumping water!

This method works best in sandy or loose soil. If you have rocky ground, it's less effective. Buried rocks will either deflect the drive point (making the well shaft crooked) or stop it altogether. It won't work at all in solid rock. Under ideal conditions, you may be able to hit 150 feet if you're doing it by hand.

Hand Augers

Wells can also be bored with hand augers. These are a smaller version of a posthole auger, designed for taking soil samples by drilling a hole about three inches in diameter. You can use a posthole auger if that's all you have. Try to find one that is adjustable, and use the narrowest setting. When you get down a few feet, it becomes much more difficult to turn the shaft. The larger the diameter, the harder it will be.

A hand auger is more work than a driven well but will go through compacted soil better than a drive point. With a hand auger, you twist the handle, making the shovels on the bottom bore into the ground. When you've gone down about a foot or so, you'll have to bring the auger back out of the hole and dump the dirt out of it. As you go deeper, keep

We bring the water to a boil to sterilize it, then pour it into our storage barrel in the house. From there it's pumped into a tank that's above the sink. It flows by gravity from there to the sink.

adding sections of pipe. It's kind of a slow process since you'll have to unscrew the additional sections of pipe each time you bring the auger up to dump the dirt out of it. To expedite things, you can build a platform above the hole and have a friend help. The increased elevation of your partner will enable you to pull up longer segments before you need to uncouple them. A tall stepladder (anchored solidly!) can help. I once stood on the roof of a garage to accomplish the same thing.

Another method is to build a tall tripod over the hole with a pulley at the top. Run a rope through the pulley and back down to the ground. When you need to remove the auger to dump it, tie the rope to the pipe and pull the entire section out of the ground. If your tripod is 15 feet tall, for example, you should be able to pull up a 14-foot section at a time for cleaning.

Stay clear of any overhead power lines! You do not have to physically touch a power line to be electrocuted. Electricity will jump the gap from the line to any metallic object just like the spark will jump the gap on a spark plug.

Even with the extra work of constantly dumping the dirt and uncoupling the pipe, it isn't difficult to bore a hole 25 feet deep in an afternoon.

When the dirt you dump out of the bit comes up muddy, you'll know you've begun to hit water. When you think you're deep enough, run a pipe down the hole, attach a pump, and see how much water you can get. Fifty feet is about maximum depth using this method. If you hit a rock, you'll have to start a new hole elsewhere.

With both driven and augured wells, it's important to pump water out of them for awhile to clear out the sediment so that the water underground will flow more freely.

Hand-Dug Wells

There are few tasks more dangerous than hand digging a water well. It was done in the past because no other method was available, but a lot of well diggers lost their lives when walls collapsed on them or they were overcome by poisonous gases. They also needed to be careful that they didn't run out of oxygen in the bottom of the hole. When they reached the water table, they kept digging deeper until the water was flowing in faster than they could pump it out. At that point, they had to shore up the sides with stacked rock at the bottom and mortared rock or bricks above the water level. Most wells dug by hand are about four or five feet in diameter, because this is as small an area that a person can work in. I would never recommend hand digging a well and only mention it here for information purposes.

Motorized Well Drilling

There are a couple of options here. I once used a home-built drill rig powered by a 10-horsepower gasoline engine. It worked okay until I hit a rock. The drill point worked around the rock, then slid back under the rock and continued downward. There was a kink in the hole I couldn't get a pipe through, so even though I hit water, I couldn't pump it out.

There are companies that sell portable, gasoline-powered rigs for drilling your own wells. Those I'm familiar with advertise reaching depths of 200 feet or more under good conditions. I've never used one, so this is neither an endorsement nor denunciation. My advice would be to get references from people who have used them.

Motorized drilling requires a water source and pump to push water through the drill shaft. The water cools the bit and forces the displaced soil up and out of the hole. If you didn't do this, the dirt would fill in the hole above the bit and all you'd accomplish is drilling the bit deep into the ground like a 200-foot-long lag bolt.

Jetted wells are another option. This works by forcing water through a pipe. The water actually erodes the soil ahead of the pipe and the pipe slowly sinks deeper into the ground. There are normally some kind of teeth on the bottom of the pipe to help break up the soil and speed the process. You need to keep turning the pipe and pumping it up and down as you work. Otherwise the pipe will eventually stick in the hole and all you'll end up with is a 50-foot-deep posthole with your drill pipe stuck in it. Jetted wells can reach depths of 300 feet or more depending upon soil conditions and the strength of your pump.

SPRINGS

A spring is a place where water in underground aquifers reaches the surface. Springs come in all sizes, from miniscule, seasonal springs that may only create patches of boggy ground at certain times of the year to the gusher flowing nearly 10 million gallons of water per hour at Mammoth Spring, Arkansas. Many lakes are fed by underground springs out of aquifers located miles away.

In most cases, you'll have to do some developing to get the water where you want it. Developing a spring means that you find a way to build up a reservoir of water and/or channel it through pipes to get it where you want it. Sometimes this can be as simple as pounding a drive point into the spring's outlet. Other times you may have to excavate an area and build a tank out of stone or cement to capture the water. If the spring is above your home and garden, you can pipe it downhill and have running water without needing a pump of any kind. If it's below your home and garden, you'll have to pump it to where it's needed. In either case, developing a spring is much cheaper, faster, and easier than drilling a well.

Again, be sure to check the water for contaminants. Some springs flow from deep underground, and if surface pollutants are kept clear where it emerges, the water may be pure. In many cases, the spring may flow underground yet near the surface and pick up contaminants along the way. You won't know until you have the water tested. It's wise to build a fence around the spring's outlet to keep animals away. Otherwise, the water may be polluted by feces.

RIVERS, LAKES, AND CREEKS

Surface water is seldom pure enough to drink. There are just too many possible sources of contamination. It can, however, provide water for irrigation, livestock, and washing. In most cases, all you'll need is a pump to get the water where it's needed. You'll need to filter and purify it for drinking.

If you're depending on these sources for water, do some research on flow rates for the entire year. Many creeks and some rivers dry up during the hot summer months. You'll also need to be prepared for spring or fall flooding.

Be sure you can legally tap into this source for your own use. (This also goes for springs.) Don't just assume that because the water touches your property it's yours to use as you desire. There may be farmers or ranchers that have irrigation rights preempting yours, or nearby cities that own the water and use it for their municipal water supply. If anyone upstream from you has rights to the waters, you might see "your" stream or even lake going dry when the farmer above you powers up his irrigation pump to water his crops.

PONDS

In places with adequate rainfall, ponds can be a great water source. If there's an existing pond, check to see how old it is. If there are trees growing in the pond dam, they'll give you a hint at its age. The larger the trees, the older the pond. Check water depth as well. Sometimes silt buildup over the years can fill in a pond so that even though the pond may appear deep, it isn't. If silt buildup is a problem, you may be able to revive the pond by dredging it out. Be sure to check with local authorities regarding the legal issues involved.

You can build your own pond if there's a depression with adequate drainage leading into it. If you want a large pond, you can hire someone with a dozer. Smaller ponds can be dug by hand if you have the time and energy. Contact the county extension office to see what your options are for building a pond. In some cases they may know of ways to have it done free. In one county where I lived, the government built ponds on private land to aid in flood control.

If you have a pond, use it! Stock it with fish for recreation and a steady food supply. They also make nice places to swim in summer and ice skate in winter. Just remember to be safe when in, on, or around the water.

COLLECTING RAINWATER

It wasn't that long ago that many farmhouses had a rainwater collection system of some type. Hand-dug wells sometimes went dry in the summer and many didn't have enough flow for times when company came, so it was nice to have a few thousand gallons stored in cisterns. Depending on the surface area of your roof and the amount of rainfall you receive, rain may supply all your water needs.

Even if it doesn't, it might still be worth the investment. If you're on rural or city water supplies, you'll be charged by the gallon for every drop you use. Rain is free, and whatever falls on your roof is caught by the rain gutters and dumped on the yard. Why not let it run into a tank and use it for livestock or to water your garden? All you'll need is a small electric or gas-powered pump and a hose, and you can have water as far away as the hose will reach.

One inch of rain will add up to .623 gallons per square foot of surface area. Remember, this is on a flat roof. Most homes have sloped roofs, so you'll need to figure the square footage as if the roof were flat. For example, if your home's outside dimensions are 30 by 30 feet and your roof overhangs the outside walls by one foot on every side, the actual surface area for rainwater collection is 1,024 square feet. Again, the pitch of your roof doesn't matter; the only thing that matters is the amount of ground covered by the roof. Now take 1,024 times .623 and you'll have the potential of collecting almost 638 gallons of water for every inch of rainfall you receive.

We collect rainwater in 50-gallon barrels under the downspouts of the rain gutters. We put a siphon hose in each barrel and siphon the water from the barrel to a storage tank behind the house. We use an electric pump to move water from the main tank to the tanks in the garden and for watering the garden with the hose.

Note: Be sure that collecting rainwater is legal in your area. In some states it isn't; in others it's restricted to small-scale systems.

MELTING SNOW

If you live in snow country, you can melt snow to obtain water. If you've ever melted snow, you'll know it takes a lot to make a gallon of water. Cold, fluffy snow has the least water content by volume, while warm, wet snow has the most. We still advise treating it by boiling, filtering, or chemical means before drinking it.

The easiest way to get an idea of how much water you'll get out of the snow is by weight. We've melted so much snow that we can tell how much water it will produce by the weight of the bucket when we bring it into the cabin. A pound of snow will produce a pound of water. The thing is that fluffy, cold snow is less dense so even though the bucket might be full by volume, the weight is relatively low. A bucket full of wet snow will have the same volume of snow, but the water content is much higher. No matter how wet the snow is, though, it will still take a lot of it to make a gallon of water.

The way we melt snow is by leaving about a fourth of the kettle filled with hot water, then fill it the rest of the way with snow. As that melts, we add more snow until the pan is full of water. We then dump the water into the tank, leaving some water in the pan to start the entire process over again . . . and again and again and again!

You may need to filter the melted snow when you transfer it to your storage tank. At home the wind blows dirt and lichen off the trees, and there's usually a little soot from the chimney as well, so we use a canning funnel and coffee filters to filter the snow water when pouring it into the storage tank.

I've heard that you can scorch snow, but I've never seen it happen. You can, however, seriously burn your pan if the heat's too high. The actual moisture content of snow is low, so the base layer contacting the heated pan bottom may melt and turn immediately to steam. The steam is quickly absorbed by the snow above it, and you end up with a cave of sorts in the bottom of the pan. This is dead air space, and air is not as efficient at conducting heat as water. The result is a pan bottom that may become red hot in places while there is still unmelted snow only an inch or so above. Keep the heat low until you have at least a couple of inches of water in the pan.

GRAY WATER RECOVERY

Some states are finally lifting restrictions on gray water use around the home. All I can say is it's about time! Gray water is defined as the leftover water used for other purposes, such as bathing and washing clothes and dishes. Never use black water, which is water used in the toilet or water contaminated with toxic chemicals like paint or solvents. Water laced with salt or heavy detergents is also unsuitable for reuse in the garden.

If you plan on using your gray water in your garden, avoid using bleach and/or detergents

In the winter we melt snow for water. We keep a large kettle on the woodstove at all times.

Even though the water has been purified by boiling, we filter it through a coffee filter to strain it. No matter how clean it looks, there is always bits of lichen and other debris in the water.

containing boron. Gray water tends to be alkaline, so don't use it exclusively in any single area. It's not good for seedlings, but it should be safe for established plants. If you have any doubts about using gray water on food plants, reserve its use for ornamental flowers and shrubs and the lawn. There is conflicting information on the use of gray water for food crops, so do some research and make your own decisions.

We use baking soda in our wash water (for both clothes and dishes) in place of detergents. We use white vinegar in the rinse water. The wash water containing baking soda (being alkaline) is used to water plants like cabbage, asparagus, and our plum trees. The rinse water containing white vinegar (which is acidic) is used on our blueberries and strawberries.

In our case, it's easy to capture the wash water because the tubs have drains with hoses, so we just drain the water into buckets. It might take a little more resourcefulness in the average home. Most dishwashers and automatic washers pump the old water out with considerable pressure. If you're serious about reusing it, you can adapt the drain hose to accept a garden hose and pump the gray water to an outside tank for further distribution later. With wringer washers, just drain them into a bucket and dump it where it'll do the most good.

CONSERVATION

At one time, buffalo (bison) roamed the prairies in herds so large the beginning and end couldn't be seen from the same location. Those days are long gone. Large-scale market and hide hunting and a government desire to eradicate the food source of the Indians left buffalo carcasses rotting in the sun in numbers too great to count. The relentless destruction of this "endless" resource by shortsighted bureaucrats and the sheer greed of humanity has left only remnants of these magnificent animals scattered about in small, protected herds on public and private land.

Our nation's water supply is on the same road to destruction. Even if you live in the city with unlimited water availability, water conservation needs to become a way of life. Water is one of the most precious resources we have . . . and also one of the most abused.

In our society we take water for granted. According to the Environmental Protection Agency (publication EPA 810-F-95-001), a single person needs 2.5 quarts of water from all sources (water, food, etc.) per day to maintain health, yet the average consumption per day is 50 gallons. Where does it all go? Between two and seven gallons are used each time a toilet is flushed. Between 25 to 50 gallons are used in the average five-minute shower. Two gallons are used to brush your teeth. Washing dishes with an automatic dishwasher takes between 9 to 12 gallons, while washing dishes by hand uses on average 20 gallons of water. When you add all the other times water is used, the average American residence goes through 107,000 gallons of water per year. The average American pays 25 cents per day for water.

Don't let our water supply take the same route as the American bison did. Don't deprive our children and grandchildren of this most precious resource through wanton waste.

Conserving water is a good stewardship of resources even when you have lots of it available. When it's in short supply, conservation is even more important.

We live in an arid climate. From the first of April to the end of October, we capture about 3,000 gallons of rainwater. We normally water the garden approximately 10 times per year using about 900 gallons each time. Add in approximately 30 gallons per week for household uses and it totals approximately 10,500 gallons of water per year that we use for cooking, canning, washing, and gardening. We grow and preserve our own food, water the garden, keep up with all our household cleaning, and meet our drinking and cooking needs on less than 10 percent of the water used by the average American household.

We don't claim to know everything about water conservation, but in the last eight years especially, we've modified our lifestyle to conserve every drop we use without sacrificing cleanliness, health, or food production.

Now that you have your water, let's examine ways in which you'll manage and use it.

HAULING WATER

We haul water for drinking using plastic water jugs. We currently have one six-gallon jug, two seven-gallon jugs, and two that hold five gallons. If you're going to buy water jugs, we recommend purchasing the smaller containers. Water is heavy, and five gallons is about right for us. These supply enough water for drinking, cooking, washing dishes, and bathing for about a week on average.

During the spring, summer, and fall, we use rainwater for bathing and washing clothes and for our garden, livestock, and pets. In the winter we melt snow. By late summer, when we've used up the water in the cistern, I haul water for the garden using the pickup with six 50-gallon barrels. This way I can get 300 gallons on each trip. We have neighbors who have tanks mounted in their pickup to haul water. While it's inconvenient at times, hauling water is not a big deal if you use the water wisely.

Hauled water can be stored in a tank inside the house if you have room. If the tank is at ground level, you'll need a pump to run the water through the lines when you turn on a faucet (like most camp trailers). Just remember that if the batteries are dead, you won't have running water! If you use an overhead tank inside, you can let gravity do the pumping. We do this for our kitchen sink and plan on hooking up the shower this way too.

We once stayed at a cabin that had a 300-gallon water tank mounted outside on stilts. The water was pumped into the tank, which was plumbed into the house. All you had to do after that was turn on the faucet and you had running water (although the supply was limited, so you still had to use it frugally). In the winter the tank had to be drained to keep it from freezing. Since the cabin was only used in the summer, this wasn't a problem.

You can also bury a water tank on a hillside above your home. You can then run the plumbing from the tank to the house to have running water inside. Again, remember that the supply is limited. The advantage here is that as long as the tank and pipes are buried below the frost line, they can be used year-round because the ground will insulate them and keep the water from freezing.

One thing to remember when it comes to storing water and heating entirely with wood: if you leave in the winter for more than a day or two, you'll have to drain any aboveground tanks to keep them from freezing, or you'll have to leave someone around to keep the fire in the woodstove going. Some people solve this problem by having a propane heating stove to keep the house above freezing when they are away. My personal opinion is that the best way to store water is in an underground tank. It's on our "things to get when we have the money" list.

WASHING CLOTHES

Washing clothes is accomplished using two washtubs and a hand-cranked wringer. It's time consuming, but not as difficult as some imagine. If you don't want to take our route, get a wringer washer. The difference between a wringer washer or washtub compared to an automatic washer is that an automatic washer uses a new load of water for each wash and rinse cycle (about 35 gallons on average). With a wringer washer or washtubs, you don't change the water until you're finished. Washing four loads of laundry per week in an automatic washer will use approximately 7,300 gallons per year. With a wringer washer using about 20 gallons per week, you'll use approximately 1,040 gallons of water. That's a difference of over 6,000 gallons of water per year.

If you're using a wringer washer, fill the washer with water, add detergent, and wash your laundry. Usually about 10 or 15 minutes is enough. The first load should be the cleanest clothes (usually white and/or light colored). Once these are clean, you run them through the wringer into the rinse tub. Now put the next load of dirty clothes into the washer, still filled with the same water. While these are washing, agitate the clothes in the rinse water with a plunger, stick, or similar implement to rinse out the detergent residue. When they're rinsed adequately, turn the wringer 90 degrees and run the rinsed clothes through the wringer, letting them drop into a clean laundry basket below. Now hang them to dry and continue this process until the laundry is all washed and hanging on the line.

You may have to add more detergent to the wash water at some point along the way as you wash progressively dirtier clothes, but don't use too much or it becomes difficult to rinse it out of the clothes. Some people use two rinse tubs. We prefer to use less detergent (or baking soda). It's very important to sort the laundry from the cleanest to the dirtiest (usually my work jeans) and wash it in the proper order. If the water gets too dirty in either the wash or rinse tubs, change it. At the end of the day's laundry, drain and rinse the washtubs. Most

When using the washtubs, always wash the cleanest clothes first and the dirtiest clothes last. That usually means my work jeans are the last to get washed.

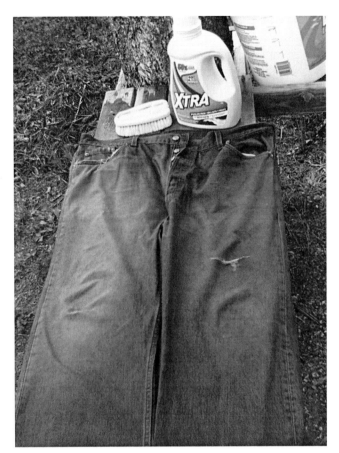

The best way to clean extra dirty clothes is by laying them on a bench, sprinkling them with liquid detergent, and scrubbing them with a brush. We've used washboards, but they don't do as good a job and are much harder on clothing.

people I know who've used wringer washers believe it gets their clothes much cleaner than automatic washers.

The washtub method is similar to the wringer washer except you agitate the clothes by hand in both the wash and rinse tubs, and it doesn't need electricity. You fill the tubs about two-thirds full with water, and plunging time will vary according to how dirty the clothes are (experience is a great teacher on this). You may have to do some scrubbing on extra dirty clothes to get them clean. We lay the clothes out on a washboard, clean bench, or table (anything with a clean, flat surface), pour on a couple drops of liquid detergent or rub some bar soap into the stain, and then scrub it out with a brush. It will take out the most stubborn dirt or stain. Once the clothes are clean, we run them through the wringer and into the rinse tub, put the next load into the washer, agitate them a bit, and then let them soak while we agitate the rinse load. When the soap

is rinsed out, we run them through the wringer and hang them and then repeat the process until the laundry is finished. Add more detergent to the wash water as needed, but again, less is best.

If you do laundry by hand like we do, we'd advise getting two items to make the job easier and faster. First is a tool called a "Rapid Washer." It looks like a stick with an upside-down metal funnel on the end. It makes a much better agitator than anything else we've tried. Second is a hand-cranked wringer. Wringing the water out of the clothes by hand is much more labor intensive than you'd think. The wringer makes the job easy.

Other Low-Tech Laundry Methods

If you're going anywhere and have room, you can put your laundry in a bucket or barrel that has a watertight lid on it, add water and detergent, seal the top, and set it in your vehicle. Drive around doing your errands, then dump the soapy water, squeeze as much soap out of the laundry as you can, add clean water to the barrel, reseal the top, and drive home. When you get home, take the now clean and rinsed laundry out of the bucket and hang it to dry. This works particularly well when doing large, bulky items like winter coats, blankets, sleeping bags, and rugs.

Laundry can also be washed using just a bucket. Follow the same procedure as used for the wringer washer, only do the agitating and wringing by hand.

A note on scrub boards: We have a couple, but we don't use them like the old-timers did. We lay them flat or at an angle into the washtub, lay the clothes across the corrugated surface, and use a soft-bristle brush to scrub the clothes. It's easier and faster than the traditional method of scrubbing the clothes across the board and much, much gentler on your clothing.

WASHING DISHES

This is easy: wash dishes less often using less water and soap. If you have a large sink, use a dishpan so you won't need as much water. It also helps to clean your plate better after eating. Use a plastic spatula or rubber scraper and squeegee off leftover food and put it in the compost bin or feed it to the chickens, pigs, or dog. Your wash water will stay clean longer, and you'll need less of it if the dishes don't have a lot of leftover food stuck to them. Put the dirty dishes out of sight if it bothers you to have them in the open, and wait to wash them until you have a decent load set aside.

WASHING PEOPLE

If you have running water, take a "navy shower." Get wet, turn the water off, soap up, water back on, rinse, water off, dry off. Use as little water and soap as you can. If you use too much soap and have difficulty rinsing off, try a quick rinse over the soap, squeegee off the excess with your hands, then rinse off the residue.

If you don't have running water, you can use a solar shower designed for camping. These are plastic bags holding about five gallons of water that you hang in the sun to allow the sun to warm the water. They'll have a small plastic hose with a showerhead and a valve that lets the water out. You can use it without the sun by heating water on a stove and

When there's no running water, showers are taken by putting water into a kettle and then pouring it over yourself with a cup. You get wet, soap up, and rinse off. Anyone who's ever been in the Navy knows the drill. In most cases we need less than two gallons of water to take a shower.

pouring it into the plastic reservoir. If you use the entire five gallons to shower, you're using too much.

Another method is to put warm water in a bucket, then dip the water out with a cup and pour it over yourself. First get wet and soap up, then rinse off. Start at the top and work down.

You can also take a sponge bath. Put some soapy water in a bucket or basin. Using a sponge, start at the top and wash down. Repeat the process with a basin of clean water to rinse off.

It isn't always necessary to bathe daily. Even after a day of hard labor, you might just need to rinse off with a basin of water and a sponge. If you have access to a pond or creek, a quick dip is often enough to remove the day's grime.

You can also use a body brush for a periodic scrubbing. These aren't meant to take the place of showering, but they allow you to shower less often. They're easier on your skin because you don't have soap washing away your body's natural oils.

Bathing doesn't have to take a lot of water. Every method above can be done with less than a gallon of water. The key is to use as little soap as possible and to squeegee as much soap residue off as you can between rinses.

It's even possible to wash your hair in just a single cup of water. I didn't believe it until my wife showed me how to do it. I gave her a measuring cup with precisely one cup of water in it just to prove to me it could be done.

I insisted she use our middle daughter to demonstrate because she had thick, waist-length hair. She sprinkled the water into her hair and slowly began working in small amounts of shampoo. She continued until her hair was saturated with suds. When her hair was clean, my wife began to squeeze the suds out of our daughter's hair. She continued this process, adding a few drops of water at a time and squeegeeing until all the shampoo was gone and her hair was squeaky clean. You may not want to go to this extent to conserve water when washing your hair (and we seldom do), but it's good to know it can be done.

WATERING THE GARDEN

First rule: get rid of the sprinklers. Even on a cloudy, cool day, evaporation takes a lot of the moisture away before it ever reaches the ground. Additionally, sprinklers put too much water between the rows, which merely gives the weeds a drink. Any gardener knows that weeds don't need any help growing. They do quite well stealing nutrients and water from the rest of the garden.

If you have a pressurized water system (including gravity flow), soaker hoses or a homemade equivalent placed on the ground next to the plant's roots works very well. There's little evaporation, and the slow application of water allows it to soak into the soil instead of running off where it's not needed.

We usually water each plant by hand using a low-pressure sprinkler head on the hose when we have the pump running. In dry times we may water twice a week. It usually takes about three hours, but this is how we get the best results using the least amount of water. That may sound like a lot of time, but remember that this is our job. It's just part of our work routine. Some water-dependent plants like tomatoes get more frequent watering by dipping the water can into the water tank and

hand-watering each plant. We often build small dikes around plants to help contain the water and give it time to soak into the ground where it's needed most.

I've seen elaborate systems of plastic pipe routed to raised beds. It looks like a great system and we plan on doing that eventually. Right now it's a money thing holding us back. It takes a lot of pipe to reach every bed in a garden the size of ours.

Rule two: plant intensively, meaning grow more in less space. Intensive gardening is most commonly found where space is limited. It's also a great way to conserve water.

When I lived in Kansas, I had a couple of acres of tillable ground and a good well from which to pump water. I had a tractor for preparing the ground, a push planter for rapid planting, and a large tiller for keeping down the weeds. Here we have none of those benefits. Our ground is poor, rocky, and congested with stumps. We have to fight for every square inch of tillable ground. To top things off, our growing season is short, and we haul the water we use for watering the garden. If it wasn't for intensive gardening, we'd never be able to grow enough to provide for ourselves. Between the efficient use of space and water conservation, it's the only way to grow what we need here.

Rule three: mulch, mulch, mulch! As soon as the ground warms and the plants are up, we begin applying mulch. We'll use old hay, straw, leaves, newspaper, and even old rag rugs. Anything that will safely cover the ground to keep moisture in the soil is fair game. In the corn patch (and other crops planted in straight rows), we mound the dirt between the rows and cover the mounds with old newspapers. Then the water is channeled directly to the roots of the plants.

Rule four: shade the plants during the hot days. This might be a surprise considering that in northwestern Montana we don't have very many hot days! We found this out because we often need to cover our plants due to frost danger. As an aside, we discovered that by providing some shade to our plants, they needed less water. It made sense once we thought about it. Plants, like people, lose a lot of moisture on hot days, but unlike people they can't move to a shady place. So we provide some shade for them. We use row covers sold in large rolls by seed companies or thin, light-colored cloth material (bought on sale from sewing and craft stores) spread over frames to cut down on the sun during the hottest part of the day. Both diffuse the sunlight while letting the rain and dew through to the plants. We build frames and suspend the material like a tent or lay it directly on top of the plants.

Don't overdo it, though. If the plants don't get enough sun, it will inhibit growth.

Rule five: give more water but less often. It's generally recommended that you water your garden once a week instead of daily. The reason is that as the ground dries, the plants will send their roots deeper into the soil. Shallow watering tricks the plants into sending their roots out just below the surface; then when the ground dries up later in the year, they can't draw from the moisture deeper in the ground. We usually water once a week unless it's extremely dry, but when we do water we make sure the ground is thoroughly soaked beneath the mulch.

If your soil is sandy or extremely porous, this may not work for you. In this case, a heavy layer of mulch is especially helpful.

Rule six: drought-resistant plants can save you a lot of water and work. If the option is available, it just makes sense to go with varieties that are drought tolerant. It's in their genes. They just need less water than their peers.

• • • • •

Having water on your property—whether it's a pond, lake, stream, spring, or well—makes life a lot easier. But don't let the lack of water stop you. There are ways to survive without endless amounts of water, and even if water is plentiful, be a good steward of it. Future generations will thank you for it.

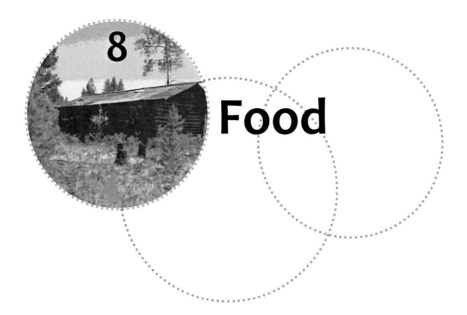

8 Food

Shelter, water, security, and food are the most important aspects of self-sufficiency. Out of these four essentials, food will probably require the most effort. In this chapter, we'll look at six methods of procuring food and then we'll examine some low-tech, low-budget ways of preserving, storing, and preparing it.

THE SELF-SUFFICIENT GARDEN

One of the most difficult tasks we've faced is growing enough food to provide for ourselves. We've been gardening for over 30 years, but gardening for self-sufficiency is different than our hobby gardens of the past. Self-sufficient gardening has broader focus, to include such issues as productivity, reliability, harvest time, storability, and self-perpetuation.

With that in mind, we've come up with 10 rules for self-sufficient gardening.

Rule Number One:
Plant What You Eat

Self-sufficient means you live off what you produce. So, the first rule is to plant what you like to eat. We love carrots, potatoes, rutabagas, turnips, squash, tomatoes, and peas, so we plant lots of them. We also plant broccoli, celery, lettuce, and brussels sprouts, but in lower volumes to reflect our usage. We grow a lot of herbs and spices as well.

Gardening for self-sufficiency isn't about money. For years I didn't plant potatoes because they were cheap at the store, but that attitude defeats the purpose of gardening for self-sufficiency. The idea behind self-sufficiency is to provide for yourself. We ask ourselves what we would grow if we were Robinson Crusoe and there was no place to purchase food.

Rule Number Two:
Plant What You Can Reliably Grow
Under Adverse Conditions

The key phrase here is "reliably grow under adverse conditions." If self-sufficiency is the goal, you don't want to depend on undependable crops.

We order varieties rated at least one (often two!) zone(s) colder than the seed companies recommend for our area. We live in the mountains, so our weather is fickle. Last year we had frost every month of the year, so we want our plants to be frost hardy. We try to cover them when cold nights are forecast, but what happens if we're gone? It isn't just about the number of frost-free days either. While the number of hours of sunlight here can be long and the summer days can be warm, our nights tend to be cold, which retards the growth of many plants. Plus, with a short growing season, we get no second chance. If a frost takes out a crop, it's finished for the year. Done! Over! We do without until the next year. It's just proven best for us to order seed for a colder zone than those recommended by the seed companies.

Because of our climate, our mainstays are cold weather crops. That means the prime spots are devoted to root crops like potatoes, rutabagas, turnips, onions, and carrots. We also plant peas, celery, asparagus, brussels sprouts, and broccoli.

We grow tomatoes, peppers, beans, and squash. These aren't frost hardy and take a lot of extra care, but we like eating them. In order to meet the "reliably grow under adverse conditions" clause, we grow them in hoop houses for frost protection.

We plant more varieties than those listed here, but these are the vegetables we depend on year after year.

Rule Number Three:
Diversify!

Potatoes are our favorite root crop and usually reliable. However, last year the potatoes were hit hard by several late frosts, so production wasn't up to par. The good thing was that our rutabagas, turnips, and carrots had a great year and made up for the shortage of potatoes. Since we often use turnips and rutabagas the same way we use potatoes, we'll still be okay for the year. Next year our potatoes may do great and the rutabagas may falter, but we've never had a year when everything floundered.

One year we had cane borers in one of our raspberry patches. We cut out the infected branches, but it greatly reduced our harvest the next year. We did, however, have other raspberry patches that were not infected because we plant them in different areas just in case of problems like this. We do our other crops the same way. We'd rather have five smaller potato patches scattered around than a single large one.

If you're blessed with a long growing season, you can plant early and late season crops. When I lived in Kansas, I planted late and early varieties of corn, beans, squash, and tomatoes. Not only did I begin eating out of the garden earlier, but if we were hit with a summer drought or excessive heat that baked the garden, I still harvested the early season crops. Always plant a late season or cover crop as you harvest the early varieties. We planted turnips as a fall cover crop. We could harvest the greens and the turnips; plus, by broadcast sowing them, they provided weed control and kept the ground cooler.

As the saying goes, "never put all your eggs in one basket."

Starting a garden on raw land is a lot of work. In most cases the land must be cleared of brush, trees, and old stumps. Usually the soil will need tons of compost, peat moss, or other organic matter before it's fertile enough to grow decent crops.

We've added a new section to our garden every year since we moved here. It generally takes three years of tilling, composting, and planting before the ground is at its best. The stumps eventually rot and we pull them up. If you have access to a backhoe, you can remove the stumps with it.

Our climate is harsh, so we use "wall of water" towers for our tomatoes and hoop houses covered in plastic to give the warmer season crops a head start.

Rule Number Four:
Plant More Than You Think You'll Need!

Last summer we had frost every month of the year and lots of cold, cloudy days. We lost a few things to frost, but the greatest damage was to overall yields. The cold nights stunted growth and harvests. We still had enough to live on, but only because we always plant more than we think we'll need. If you have extra, you can sell it or give it away, feed it to the livestock, compost it, or preserve it for use in the lean years.

Remember, the idea is to be food self-sufficient for the entire year. That means you should have enough stored to get you through to the next harvest. With a long growing season, that may only be a few months in the dead of winter. In our case it means that food harvested in the fall needs to last us until the next harvest a year later.

Rule Number Five:
Save Your Own Seed

Why save seed? Because if you can't get seeds from other sources for some reason, you'll be right back to depending on the grocery store for your food. We didn't take this seriously until a few years ago. Every year we ordered our corn seed from a major supplier, but that time we received word back that it would be shipped "in season." What we didn't know was that the supplier was low on seed and was shipping the available stock to warmer zones first since they could plant it earlier. The idea was that they'd have more seed later to ship to the more northern gardeners. A couple of months later we got a notice that they were out and we wouldn't be getting our seed, and we should "feel free to order it from another company." By then no one had any seed corn varieties that would grow in our zone. Now we specify that anything we order except trees and shrubs be shipped immediately.

Since then we also grow only heirloom varieties so we can save our own seed. Now our seed catalogue orders are for new varieties we're trying for the first time, not for crops we depend on!

We also save a pile of money. We used to order over $100 worth of seed and plants every year. We still spend quite a bit, but our orders are different. We now have the money to purchase fruit and nut trees, berry bushes, and other things we couldn't afford before. Saving money is much easier than making money on the low-budget homestead.

Rule Number Six:
Don't Forget the Specialty Items

Specialty items are those things we don't usually associate with gardening. We grow a lot of mint because we like mint tea. We also grow such herbs as oregano, basil, sage, and thyme. We grow grains like wheat, oats, and barley on some plots outside the fenced garden area. They are labor intensive to harvest, so we grow just enough for our own use.

We also have strawberries, raspberries, and blueberries. We planted grapes last year, so we'll see how they do this year. Years ago we planted apple and cherry trees in the garden; then a rabbit killed most of them by chewing the bark off the trees over the winter. We did get some apples from our two remaining trees, and we planted new ones to replace those that died.

Rule Number Seven:
Stay Organic

We are 100 percent organic growers. No pesticides or herbicides or chemical fertilizers. We have few problems with insect pests. Part of it is due to our cold climate; many garden pests simply cannot survive the winter here. Another thing is that pesticides destroy both the bad bugs and the good bugs. We've found over the years that without pesticides, you get a few bad bugs but you also get good bugs to eat the bad bugs and keep them in check. We also work hard to enhance soil health, believing that good soil produces strong, bug- and disease-resistant plants.

The truth is that you must stay organic to be self-sufficient unless you happen to have an oil well in your backyard and the capability of turning crude oil into fertilizer. We've put ads up for old hay and manure to compost. Some of our kids own horses, and we get manure from them as well. We feed a neighbor's buffalo during the winter and clean up the feeding area every spring for some of the best compost material you can get. We also utilize manure from our chickens and rabbits (when we have rabbits). All kitchen waste that's not fed to the chickens goes to the compost pile. I'd estimate that we add about three to four tons of compost to our garden every year. In our "old" garden sections, the soil is so friable that we no longer need a shovel to harvest potatoes or carrots. We simply dig into the soil with our hands. We have very few problems with either bugs or disease.

We water the garden with a hose instead of sprinklers, which lose too much to evaporation. If you have a well and pump, you can use soaker hoses to accomplish the same thing with less labor.

We cover the garden at night to protect it from frost. Last year (2011) we had frost every month of the year. You don't take chances when you depend upon your garden to feed you. If you live in a friendlier climate, you won't have to go to the extremes we do to protect your crops.

Part of the harvest! Our staples are potatoes and carrots. Both tolerate cold well and produce prolifically in our climate. They're also easy to store in the root cellar.

Rule Number Eight:
Don't Try to Do It All the First Year

This might seem to clash with rule number five (plant more than you think you'll need), but if you're new to gardening, you'll get more food out of a small, well-cared-for plot than a large garden with poor soil that's choked with weeds. Gardening is hard work and if you're working with new ground, you'll be fighting weeds, grass, and soil fertility the first year or so. Our ground here consists of poor soil with a lot of clay. It takes us about three years, applying thick layers of compost every year, before the soil improves measurably. Add in the time it takes for planting, weeding, watering, harvesting, storing crops, and putting the garden to bed each fall and you'll have a lot of time invested. So, if you're new at this, start small and add more as you become more proficient.

Rule Number Nine:
Time Is Your Friend *and* Your Enemy

Many if not most people reading this live in a much more forgiving climate, with longer growing seasons and less dependence on storability. But always remember that the goal in having a self-sufficient garden is food self-sufficiency. And that takes time—time to build up the soil, time to grow the crops, time to preserve them, time to learn the craft. But the best time of all is when you look in your pantry and root cellar and realize it's time to kiss the grocery store good-bye.

Very few people are going to grow enough food the first year, but by following these guidelines, you'll be well on your way to producing all of the fruits, grains, vegetables, and berries you'll need to feed you and your family for the year.

Rule Number Ten:
Animals Are Not Your Friend

The fuzzy little rabbit that was so cute hopping around in the garden and playing with the kitten last summer killed several of our fruit trees the following winter. These were trees that we'd been nurturing for the last five years. Deer broke through a fence one night and in a matter of hours ate all of the field peas and soybeans on one plot. They came back the next night to break through the repaired section and eat all of the corn we had planted.

I've heard dozens of ways to keep deer out of a garden, but the only one I know of that consistently works is a good fence. Our new fence is six feet tall with electric wire at the top and bottom to keep the deer, elk, moose, and bears out. Rabbits, chipmunks, red squirrels, and ground squirrels are trapped or shot (I use a high-velocity air rifle) if they're found anywhere near the garden. Mice and moles can also wreak havoc on your garden if left unchecked. If you can't bear the thought of killing the animals, build a good fence to keep out the large critters and use a live trap to catch the small ones. Just be sure to release them miles away from your garden or they'll probably be back before you are. Also be sure that you don't release them where they'll be someone else's problem. As for me . . . squirrels and rabbits taste mighty good fried or in potpies.

HUNTING

If you haven't already been through a hunter safety class, the first thing you should do is take one. Most states require it before they'll sell you a hunting license, so contact your state's Department of Fish, Wildlife, and Parks (or whatever agency regulates hunting in your state) and enroll in a hunter education course. They will not only educate you on safe gun handling but on hunting and survival techniques, game laws, hunting ethics, and suitable weapons to obtain and use.

Hunting Basics

When the earliest European settlers arrived on the shores of North America, they nearly starved to death. Growing food was more difficult than they'd imagined, and game animals, while abundant, were in their words "exceedingly wary." Life was harsh in this new land, and illness and starvation haunted them through the long winters. If the natives hadn't shown them how to grow and hunt their food, many more of these immigrants would have starved.

Historically, hunting skills were passed from one generation to the next. In our modern world, that's often not the case. But hunting is a learned skill. It doesn't matter if you've never hunted anything more elusive than a television remote control: with some basic knowledge and practical field skills you can "make meat" with the best of them.

To be a successful hunter, you must do two things: (a) find the animal, and (b) kill it. (Butchering, cooking, and eating it are separate subjects.) Let's take a look at what each task requires.

Finding the Animal

Step one is to narrow your focus. If you've never hunted before, it's usually best to start with small game (rabbits and squirrels); upland birds like quail, pheasants, and grouse; and/or waterfowl (ducks, and geese). These are more abundant and have longer seasons; plus the methods you use to bag small game will also apply to big game.

The first thing to do is contact your state's Fish and Game Department and request hunting regulations. Most have them available for download at their website. These will tell you what animals are available to hunt, the season dates they can be legally hunted, and the weapons you can use to hunt them. They may also have information on public land that's open to hunting.

Don't overlook nongame species. These can usually be hunted year-round and will offer valuable practice for honing your hunting skills. Once you've seen what's available, narrow your focus to one or two animals. My recommendation is rabbits or squirrels. These are plentiful almost everywhere, and the same skills you use to hunt them will be helpful with other game animals as well.

Step two is to know the animal. You must have an understanding of an animal to find it consistently. Once you've identified your target species, go to the library or get online and do some research. Answer the following questions: What do they eat? Where do they find water and how much do they need? What do they need for shelter from weather or predators? What kinds of habitat do they prefer? Do they have any seasonal traits such as migration or hibernation? Are they solitary or herd animals by nature? Are they most active during the day, night, or in between? What kinds of "sign" (tracks, droppings, scrapes, rubs, wallows, etc.) do they make? How well do they see, hear, or smell? What are their reproduction characteristics?

By knowing the needs of an animal, you can find where it lives. By knowing what kind of sign it leaves and its preferred food, you'll be able to locate its home territory and travel routes. By knowing its habits and sensory abilities, you can narrow down hunting methods and times.

All these things help you to locate the animals you intend to hunt.

Killing the Animal

Once you know the characteristics of the animal you're going after, you need to formulate a plan to kill it. Hunting methods include stand hunting, still hunting, spot and stalk, walking, using dogs, baiting, calling, and combinations of the above.

Stand hunting (usually done by sitting) refers to finding a place where well-used game trails intersect and setting up a comfortable stand where you can watch for animals to pass within range of your weapon. Stands may be ground level or elevated. A ground stand, or "blind," is where the hunter stays on the ground. He may stack or weave brush or limbs for concealment or maybe just sit with his back against a tree.

Elevated stands position the hunter above the

Hunting plays a large part in our meat acquisition. Here is a fine whitetail doe that Susan harvested the first day of the season.

ground anywhere from a few to 15 or more feet above the earth's surface. They may be in a tree or built on stilts. The advantages to elevated stands are that you can see farther and, since you are also above the animal's line of sight, it's not as easy for it to see you. When using elevated stands, your scent is often carried above the game animals instead of directly to them. The disadvantage is that, should an animal take a different trail, you can't get down to follow it without being seen. Ground blinds offer a chance to do some stalking if the opportunity presents itself but increase the odds of being smelled or seen. *Always use appropriate safety restraints when hunting from elevated blinds.*

Still hunting refers to quietly and slowly walking through the hunting ground trying to see the animal before it sees you. It's a very challenging way to hunt. The keys are, first, to be where the animals are; second, to move slowly; and, third, to see them before they see or smell you. The general rule for still or stand hunting is that you should be sta-

tionary when the animals are moving and be moving when the animals are stationary.

Spot and stalk is when you move from one place to another and look for game animals in the distance. It's a common method in the central and western states, where you can see long distances. Once you spot them, you stalk (like a cat sneaking up on a bird) to get within shooting range.

Walking is just that—walking through your hunting area hoping to scare up animals to shoot. It's the way people usually hunt upland game birds like quail or pheasants or small game such as rabbits. A variant of this is the deer drive, where people walk through a section of woods where deer are known to be hiding. Other hunters take "stands," setting up ambushes at places where deer are likely to go to escape from the drivers. You must be very careful setting these up to ensure the safety of everyone involved. Usually shooting is limited to those on the stands, and they are allowed to shoot only when a deer has passed them and is heading away from the drivers.

Dogs have been used to hunt deer, bobcats, mountain lions, bears, coyotes, raccoons, rabbits, squirrels, and virtually all game birds. Their job varies from retrieving downed birds, chasing the animals out of heavy brush, trailing them by sight or smell, or even distracting them until a hunter can get a shot. Using dogs to hunt is regulated by state game laws.

Baiting is when you draw animals in to your stand location by using food for bait. It's sometimes used when hunting bear or deer. This practice is also regulated by game departments.

Calling can be an effective way to hunt. To call in predators, you make sounds like a prey animal in distress. The predator comes in looking for an easy meal. Many calls mimic the sound of an animal calling in a mate. Calling methods vary according to the species being sought. I've used calls to lure in turkeys, squirrels, deer, elk, coyotes, ducks, geese, and crows.

These are all common tactics used to get close enough to an animal so you can kill it. No matter which method you choose, a key to success is to look for parts of an animal. For every game animal standing in the open, there will be ten who show only a foot or ear. Look as far away as you can see (not at your feet!). Watch for movement.

Weapons

Weapon choice is a highly personal matter. The standard advice is to use the most powerful weapon you can shoot comfortably and accurately. Bullet or arrow placement is always more important than the power of the projectile used.

Most game departments limit the types of legal weapons for hunting game animals to firearms, bows and arrows, and crossbows. Obviously the effective range of any firearm is much greater than that of a bow and arrow. However, a bow is relatively silent and in a survival situation in which stealth is important, a bow or crossbow might be a good choice.

Check state and local game regulations regarding any weapon before using it for hunting. Whatever your weapon of choice is, it's up to you to become proficient with it. You should always have enough respect for the animal to kill it as quickly and humanely as possible.

Hunting for Self-Sufficiency

Hunting plays an integral role in our life. Most of our meat for the year is shot during the fall deer season. In our state, you can purchase an "A" tag and several "B" tags for antlerless deer in selected hunting zones where overpopulation is a problem. We usually purchase two "A" tags (one each for me and my wife) and sometimes a couple of "B" tags. Depending on how many kids are at home, they usually purchase licenses too. We get about 40 to 50 pounds of extra lean venison off each deer taken. That's only 100 pounds of meat for a year. We also purchase elk and bear tags, but filling them is an iffy proposition most years. So, we plan on having a minimum of 100 pounds of venison for the entire year. That's not quite two pounds a week. With just my wife and me, a half-pound of venison is about right for most meals, so we have enough venison for 200 meals annually. So, if we want a serving of meat every day of the year, we need other sources.

Small game hunting adds not only to the amount of meat in the pot but also to the variety available. We often supplement our venison with grouse and sometimes snowshoe hare. If I wanted to, we could purchase licenses to hunt turkeys, ducks, and geese to add to the yearly meat supply and variety. If you happen to live where small game is plentiful, you may be able to add rabbits, squirrels, quail, pheasants, and other small game animals and birds to your diet.

Some of the advantages to small game hunting include availability (there are larger quantities of animals available and seasons are usually longer), accessibility (it's often easier to get permission from private landowners to hunt small game than large game; plus you can usually find small game near where you live), and expense (license fees, travel expenses, and equipment costs are usually less for hunting small game than large game).

It pays to remember that subsistence hunting is different than trophy hunting. I want to stress here that I am not against trophy hunting. It takes a lot of skill to find and kill a wise old buck or bull, but like the saying goes, "you can't eat horns." The person hunting for their meat supply is concerned about the size of the animal instead of the size of its antlers or horns. After all, if you only have a tag for one deer, elk, or moose, you'll get more meat from a large one. A true trophy hunter will pass up an animal whose horns won't make the record book. If you're a subsistence hunter, that may mean an empty freezer. A subsistence hunter may hold out awhile for a large-bodied animal, but when the season draws to a close and you haven't filled your tag, you should be prepared to settle for any legal animal you can ethically harvest. Don't forget, it's about meat for the pot, not social standing or bragging rights.

From a purely practical standpoint, hunting, for most people, is not cost effective. If you travel long distances to your hunting territory, you'll need to figure in travel, food, and lodging expenses in addition to license fees vs. the number of pounds of meat you procure. If you take it to a commercial processor, you'll need to add that expense into the cost as well. At the dollars-per-pound comparison, it might be cheaper to just purchase livestock and grow your own meat supply.

Remember that our goal is to live independent of outside resources, so we spend very little on travel to and from our hunting area. Once there we stay in tents and eat homegrown and preserved food. We stay at that location and fill as many tags as we can and process whatever we kill ourselves. We are fortunate to live where the hunting is difficult but good. What I mean by that is that we have a lot of different game animals available, but the mountainous and heavily forested terrain keep population densities low and make hunting a challenge. The opportunities are there, but you have to work to fill your tags. If hunting for meat is going to be a part of your homesteading or survival experience, it's important to learn how to do so efficiently and economically in your neck of the woods.

So, if hunting isn't economically viable, why hunt? We hunt for several reasons. First, wild game is extra lean meat, which is healthy meat. Wild game is cheap meat the way we hunt it. We've never purchased or grown food nor ever built or repaired a fence to contain wild animals. Wild game is organic in the best sense of the word. They haven't been force-fed antibiotics, growth hormones, or any of the other additives often given to commercial livestock.

Wild game is free ranging. I have a difficult time killing an animal that's never had a chance for freedom. Domestic animals are confined from their birth to the time of execution. Their owner may have nursed them back to health if they were ill and protected them from predators and most certainly fed and sheltered them, but all for the express purpose of killing them for money or food. I'm not saying anything is wrong with killing domestic animals. I've done it myself, but it's definitely not something I look forward to.

Wild animals at least have a chance of escape. If I do my part right, it never sees death coming and its death will be quick and painless. (Contrary to nature's way of killing, which is often slow and excruciatingly painful.)

Now, if you're the type who thinks killing an animal is wrong, you'd better be a vegetarian and live in a cave or grass hut and eat only food foraged from the wild. Otherwise you're a hypocrite. The meat, fish, or fowl you eat was once a living, breathing creature. If you didn't kill it yourself, you paid someone else to do it for you. The only difference between you and someone who kills their own food is that they at least recognize that for them to live, something else must die.

Final Notes on Hunting

Reading is not enough to make you into an effective hunter. You must get out and hunt to become good at it.

You can go to a park and observe animal behaviors, but animals in the wild are much more wary, and they often know when your intentions turn from observation to annihilation. Likewise, the deer you see standing peacefully at the side of the road will seldom act the same when you are hunting it.

In the same way, being an expert marksman on the rifle range doesn't mean you'll be able to hit the kill zone on a deer or rabbit in the hunting field. When shooting at a live target, many other things enter into the picture. Things like adrenaline, a pounding heart, rapid breathing, muscle shakes, poor sight pictures, shooting at the whole animal rather than picking a spot, and a dozen other factors will affect your shot placement. I've known people who were overwhelmed by "buck fever" and shot five times at a deer standing broadside at 50 feet and never touched a hair on it. I've seen accomplished skeet shooters miss when a covey of quail flushed at their feet.

We have a saying at our house that "you can't do it unless you've done it." What we mean is that many things that seem simple aren't, and unless you've actually done it enough to become proficient, don't count on being able to do it when the chips are down.

This is especially true when hunting. Reading this chapter is a start, a beginning. It's imperative that you get out in the woods and put these things into practice.

TRAPPING

Trapping is a timeless profession used in both ancient and modern times to provide food and clothing and as an effective means of predator and pest control. It's a shame it's received so much bad press from the politically correct and animal rights groups. Despite the bad rap, trapping is one of the most effective ways to feed and clothe your family and protect your homestead from furred invaders. After all, who among us has never trapped a mouse that had its sights set on our stored grain?

Trapping played a major role in every primitive culture I'm aware of. Very effective snares and deadfalls can be made from locally available materials with a minimum of fuss and no investment other than the time it takes to make and set them. Learning how and where to set them takes some skill, but it's no more difficult than learning how to hunt or fish. Traps have the additional advantage of working 24 hours a day, seven days a week in rain, sleet, and snow. If you're ever in a true SHTF or TEOTWAWKI situation, trapping may be the only reliable way to obtain meat.

The prerequisites of trapping are similar to those for hunting. Get to know the animals, know and obey the appropriate laws and regulations, purchase or make the required equipment, and start trapping.

Always know the laws regarding trapping and obey them. The only exception is if you find yourself in a survival situation, and even then you'll have to rest your case on the mercy of the court. Depending on the location, it may not be legal to trap or snare some of the animals I will discuss in this section. If so, this is for informational purposes only and is not an endorsement of illegal activities.

Equipment Needs

Traps fall into three categories or types: foothold, body grip, and live traps. All come in different sizes. The correct size is dependent upon what you're trying to trap.

Foothold traps have been around for centuries

Heading out to check traps.

and originally were used to trap people. They're designed to close on an animal's leg and hold it until you arrive. Modern traps differ little in appearance from those original traps, but there have been improvements made in the last few years. They can now be purchased with rubber padded jaws (required in some states), offset jaws, and double jaws in addition to the traditional models. Foothold traps are available in different sizes relating to the target

When we spend an afternoon cruising a lake in kayaks for pleasure, I'm also scouting out new trapping areas. If you look closely, you'll see a large beaver lodge next to the spit of land on the left side of the photo.

animal. Foothold traps are my favorite for ground sets because you can release animals you didn't want to catch. If the proper trap was used, they usually leave with nothing more serious than a bruised leg. I've had squirrels bound up a tree and scold me soundly after being released from a foothold trap.

Body-grip traps are designed to clamp around the animal's body, crushing its chest and killing it quickly. Be very careful with these. There is no second chance if you catch a nontarget animal. I use them on aboveground sets and water sets in places where I'm sure someone's pet won't stumble into it. They come in different sizes, and the larger ones used for beaver and otter are truly formidable. They are very effective traps, and the small ones can even be used to catch fish under survival conditions. Again, I'm not advocating illegal activities, only informing you that it can be done.

Live traps are usually wire boxes that simply shut a critter in. After that, you decide its fate. They

are especially effective with rodents like pack rats. They are best used in areas where there's a chance you might catch your or your neighbor's pet and you want the ability to release it unharmed. Be careful about liberating vermin and pests. You'll need to release most of them many miles away or they'll simply return home again. You don't want to release them where they'll damage someone else's property either. When we use them to trap pack rats, we just shoot the rat with a .22 rimfire shot shell while it's in the trap. It kills the rat instantly, and we don't have to worry about shooting holes in or otherwise damaging the trap as a solid bullet or pellet might do.

Snares are easy to make and use. They have the advantages of being cheap and light weight so you can make dozens of them and set them all over. They have the same disadvantage as body-grip traps when set to choke an animal. There will be no second chances, so don't set them where your neighbor's pets roam. I've made snares out of piano wire and guitar strings, picture-hanging wire, steel fishing leaders, military surplus trip wire, and stranded copper wire stripped from old extension cords. For larger animals like coyotes, make your snares out of small-diameter steel aircraft cable. All you need is a one-way slide and a flexible wire loop strong enough to hold whatever it is you're after.

Snares have been used for every animal you can name. In some cases they're set to catch an animal by the leg, and in other cases they grip them around the neck. Snares for larger animals should have a one-way lock so that when the snare tightens it won't reopen when the animal releases pressure. Be sure to check trapping regulations before setting snares.

Trapping for Food

In my opinion, snares are better than traps for small game like squirrels and rabbits. For tree-dwelling squirrels, set the snares in travel routes leading to where they eat. Sometimes leaning a pole against a tree or spanning a pole between two trees is a good plan since squirrels like to use them for travel corridors. It's better to have a dozen snares in good locations than two dozen scattered haphazardly in hopes a squirrel will stumble into one.

Rabbits will have runways and trails along the ground. Often the best way to find them is to lay down on the ground and look things over from the rabbits' viewpoint. Find places where the trails cross or merge. Sometimes at the edges of thick, tall patches of grass, the rabbit trails will fan out from a single opening in the grass. That will be a good place to set a snare. If there are a lot of trails, try blocking some off with stick fences to funnel the rabbits through the trails where you've set your snares. Scouting really pays off here. The more rabbits using an area, the more likely you are to snare some.

While I believe snares are the best way to catch rabbits and squirrels, there are other methods you can use. In my experience, foothold traps work well on squirrels but not so well on rabbits. Rabbits have thinner skin and their bones break easily. They may escape the trap, only to die an agonizing death in their burrow. Small body-grip traps work well on squirrels or rabbits, but you'll want to be sure they won't catch nontarget species.

Trapping for Fur and Profit

Fur prices fluctuate according to demand. It's kind of like farming: you never know whether you'll make money until you sell the crop. Trapping is one of those things you can do a little or a lot of. The choice is yours. Many farm boys made spending money running a short trap line before or after school, and many people today make their living trapping. If you're new to trapping, see if your state offers a trapper education course. You might also contact your state's trapping association for information.

If you like trapping, you should check into nuisance trapping. Nuisance trappers go after animals that have been deemed a threat or nuisance to local landowners. It might be trapping beaver that have built a dam that's flooding a golf course or killing trees in a subdivision. You may find yourself trapping skunks in a crawl space or bats in an attic. Contact your state's Department of Fish, Wildlife, and Parks to see if there are any legal hurdles to overcome, then run an ad in the newspaper, yellow pages, or whatever.

Trapping for fur can be an additional source of food as well as income. Many furbearing animals are edible. Muskrat (aka marsh rabbit), opossum, and raccoon are considered good table fare in some parts of the country, and if things get really bad, they'll be considered good table fare everywhere.

Trapping Pests

Sooner or later your garden and feed shed are going to draw in rats, mice, gophers, or other pests. Live traps have already been mentioned, but you'll want to keep a few rattraps and mousetraps nearby as well. The rattraps I'm speaking of look like mousetraps on steroids. They're big enough to kill rats and small rodents like chipmunks. One thing we've learned is that they don't always kill a rat quickly, so they'll need to be anchored firmly or the entire trap will be gone. We handle the situation in two ways. One, we drill a hole in the base of the trap and fasten a steel wire through it and tie it to a post or other solid anchor. The second method is to fasten the trap to a larger board that a rat can't drag away. Again, be careful with them. These traps can seriously ruin the day of any cat that happens along.

FISHING

I'll start this section off with a disclaimer: I'm not a great fisherman. Actually, I'm not even good at fishing. Sure, I catch fish sometimes, but I don't have the patience or knowledge to catch fish consistently. That being said, I do catch some fish and I thoroughly enjoy eating fish, but they aren't a big part of our homestead meal ticket.

Fishing is kind of like trapping. You need to know your quarry and the best methods of catching it, so begin by identifying the fish that are legal and desirable in your area. Once you've learned their likes and dislikes regarding water temperatures, preferred depths to hang out in at various times of the year, favorite hunting grounds when they're hungry, favorite foods, breeding habits, and temperaments, you can formulate a plan to catch them. While there are lots of ways to catch fish, you're going to be limited to those that are legal under your state's fishing laws.

Most people use reels mounted on fishing rods to cast fishing line with hooks baited with live bait, various kinds of meats and cheeses, corn, or some smelly concoction bought at a store or put together in their top-secret lab at home. (Okay, I'm exaggerating a bit here about the lab!) They go where they believe the fish are and go fishing. Those who are good at it often bring home lots of very high-quality food.

Some of the most productive ways to fish where it's legal to do so are jug fishing, limb lines, and trotlines. Jug fishing is done by tying your line, hook (or several hooks to one main line), and bait to an empty plastic jug or float of some kind and throwing it out into a pond or lake. If you don't have a boat, you'll want to tie another line to the jug and anchor the end to the bank so you can retrieve the jug later. If you have a boat, you can let the jugs float freely and retrieve them from the boat. You can also tie a heavy weight to the bottom of the line to anchor the jug in a specific fishing hole. I've done it all three ways. The idea is that as the jugs bob around on the waves, the fish will find the bait and swallow it. They're then hooked until you come to collect them. I recommend checking the jugs at least daily; twice a day is even better.

This method is best in small lakes and ponds, preferably private ponds and lakes since the jugs are clearly visible and anyone passing by might help themselves to your catch.

The nice thing about this method (and the next two) is that you have multiple lines out so you greatly increase your chances of catching fish, and you can set everything up and then go do something else. Be sure to check the legality of these methods.

Limb lines are done in a similar way except instead of tying the line and baited hooks to plastic jugs, you tie the line to tree limbs that hang out over the water. Set the length of the line so that the bait dangles at the best depth for the fish you're seeking. Again, check the lines daily.

A caution here: please be sure to retrieve these after you're done fishing. I was floating down a river in a canoe once when the hook from an old limb line caught my life jacket and nearly pulled me out of the canoe (almost capsizing the canoe in the process). I had a knife handy and cut the line to avert disaster, but even today I shudder to think what would have happened if the hook had caught me in the eye or another part of my body instead of the life jacket. The lines had evidently been set when the water was higher and when it receded they were dangling about two feet above the surface. This was not a matter of someone not locating this one line. There were dozens of these abandoned on this stretch of river.

Trotlines are another way to catch more fish. These are used mostly for catfish, although they will work on other fish as well. Trotlines are made by using one long, heavy line approximately the diameter of paracord, with baited hooks tied to the main line. The hooks are tied with regular fishing line so that they dangle about a foot or so below the main line. The trotline is usually anchored to shore on one or both ends. In lakes or ponds they are often anchored to shore on one end and to the bottom with a heavy weight on the other end.

Usually large hooks are used with limb lines and trotlines to catch large fish. I've seen many 25- to 40-pound catfish caught with these rigs.

If it's legal, fish traps and nets work for catching large amounts of fish. I have no experience with either of these methods, so I'll take Mark Twain's advice when he cautioned that "it is better to be thought a fool than to speak and remove all doubt."

Another way to get fish is to capitalize on the efforts of others. I have a son who participates in a semiannual fishing tournament in a large lake in northwestern Montana. The purpose is to thin out the population of a particular species of fish, and the contestants are encouraged to donate their fish to the local food banks or find other uses for them. It doesn't take him long to fill a freezer, so he's more than happy to give the extra fish away. These are not trash fish. Most tend to be in the 5- to 10-pound category and are very good eating. If there are any fishing tournaments in your area, find out what they do with the fish that are caught. Spend a little time at the weigh station and ask contestants if you can keep any extra fish they don't want.

Our state wildlife agency also traps salmon to obtain eggs (or at least they did a few years ago). The fish are given away to food banks and to volunteers who participate in the program. We had a man in our church who provided salmon by the bucketful to anyone who wanted them. Check with your local game wardens to see if anything like this is available in your area. They are usually ecstatic to have volunteers on these types of projects.

Finally, check your neighborhood for avid fishermen. Lots of people love to fish but catch more than they can eat. They'll usually be quite happy to share their catch with you and your family.

A quick note on hunting and fishing: Every survivalist should have a copy of Ragnar Benson's book *Survival Poaching* (available from Paladin Press) in their library. As he notes, the techniques he describes are seldom legal, but they are effective. If it ever comes to the point where society has broken down and you must be able to harvest fish and/or game for food or clothing, the knowledge he provides might make the difference between living and dying. Just remember, this is not an endorsement to violate game laws; it's simply good information to know . . . just in case!

FORAGING

There's a lot of great food available free for the picking if you do a little searching. On our property we have wild strawberries, gooseberries, serviceberries (aka saskatoon), rose hips, grapes, and a bunch of different spices and wild edibles that are often considered weeds by the unknowing. True, wild foods tend to be smaller than domestic varieties, but the taste is usually on par or better than anything grown on a factory farm, so take advantage of them.

Our wild strawberries are typically producing fruit weeks before our domestic plants, so we get a

head start by picking them and using them in cereal, pancakes, and pastries. Our wild grapes make excellent jams, jellies, and juice and in some years are very abundant. Every year in late summer, we spend a few days picking huckleberries in the mountains. We dehydrate most of them for later use in pies, jams, jellies, syrup, ice-cream, and pancakes, but we eat quite a few fresh also. We'll normally pick several gallons to get us through the year.

In spring and fall, mushrooms are plentiful. Our preferences are for morels and the various types of boletes that grow in the area. It isn't difficult to gather 20 pounds of boletes in one fall afternoon of walking old logging roads. Morels grow by the hundreds in any place that a fire burned through the previous year, although they can be found in lesser numbers in other areas as well.

Serviceberries grow in abundance in our yard and along nearby lakes and rivers. Some people don't like the seeds they contain, but we don't mind them. They're great in pies and pancakes.

We also have wild raspberries and thimbleberries. Thimbleberries look like raspberries and have a mild raspberry taste. They're good fresh or in pies, pastries, ice cream, or any other way you'd use raspberries.

Foraging opportunities are endless. Be aware of your local choices. In Kansas we foraged for walnuts, pecans, pears, and apples at abandoned farmsteads (with the owner's permission, of course). City parks often have opportunities for foraging. Be sure they haven't been sprayed with pesticides or other poisons, though. (It's a good bet, for example, that cattails beside water in a public park or golf course will be saturated with chemicals from the fertilizer runoff.) Take some courses in edible wild plants. You'll be surprised at the number of edible plants growing in your neighborhood. Again, be sure you have permission from the proper authorities before harvesting on land that you don't own.

GLEANING

Gleaning is mentioned in the Bible where landowners were encouraged to set aside parts of their fields so that the poor would be able to eat too. Gleaning is still an option today, although few take the opportunity to do it. The main difference between gleaning and foraging is that foraging is collecting *wild* plants, berries, etc., while gleaning is

Huckleberries are a favorite in our house. We pick them on national forest land about 20 miles from home.

Bears like huckleberries too. Since this is grizzly country, we always carry handguns with us when picking huckleberries.

Huckleberries picked, cleaned, and in the food dehydrator.

This is what dried huckleberries look like. If you look closely, there's another full stack of trays behind Susan. We have three electric dehydrators, but we also dry food outside on racks when it's not raining.

the harvesting of *domestic* fruits, grains, vegetables, and other edibles that are left in fields or orchards after the harvest.

If you aren't familiar with modern agriculture, it might surprise you to know that harvesting machinery leaves a lot of corn, wheat, beans, and other crops in the fields. These are often in corners where the large equipment couldn't turn sharply enough or in wet places where they'd get mired in the mud.

Sometimes, primarily when harvesting soybeans, the cutting heads simply can't reach low

enough to harvest all the beans so some are left at the bottoms of the stalks. It's hard on your back, but you can glean a lot of soybeans off that bottom eight inches of stalk.

In other cases, such as in wheat fields, I've seen bushels of wheat left when the harvesters didn't cut low enough and missed the shorter stalks. In almost every field, you'll find uncut wheat in the corners where the combines turned to go the other direction. It usually works best to just cut the heads off and put them in a bag for transport. When you get them home, you can feed them to livestock as they

Gleaning is an excellent way to get food. Prices for cherries were so low that the orchard owners were giving them to anyone who'd come pick them. Always take advantage of opportunities like this.

are or separate the grain and chaff and use it for human consumption.

In addition, many farmers burn the wheat fields instead of plowing the stubble under as in past times. If the combine didn't have a "chopper," you can take a pickup, rake, and pitchfork and get straw by forking it out of the windrows into the back of your truck. If you have access to a hay baler, they may let you bale the leftover straw for your own use and for sale. I did this for a couple of years until the farmer learned how much I was making selling the straw and began baling it himself.

Corn stalks are often knocked over when combines make their turns at the ends of the fields, and the ears of corn can be easily harvested by hand. I've gleaned a pickup load of corn this way in an afternoon of work.

The point is that if you live in farm country, you may be able to get enough grains to feed your family and livestock by asking farmers for permission to glean the leftovers from their harvested fields. Most farmers I've dealt with are happy to give permission if you'll just ask. Be sure to inquire about leaving gates open or shut, and get permission to drive your vehicle onto the field. See if they've got any livestock in the field as well. Be very careful to avoid areas where you might get stuck, and treat their property with the utmost respect.

But grains aren't the only thing to seek. Go for a walk in your neighborhood and you'll probably see many yards with fruit trees where the fruit is never picked. Sometimes the residents are elderly and can no longer harvest the fruit themselves. In most cases, though, they just don't want to mess with it. I've seldom been turned down when asking permission to harvest abandoned fruit. Most property owners are glad to have someone clean up the mess the rotting food leaves in the yard. It always helps to offer them a share of what you pick, but in my experience they're usually just wanting someone to clean up the fallen fruit.

Get to know your local neighbors who garden. We've had elderly neighbors who were excellent gardeners and usually grew far more than they could eat. Later in the season, they'd gladly share what was left in the garden to whoever needed it. We've done that ourselves. The most distressing thing about this is that many people will be glad to take the extra produce off your hands—if you'll pick it, package it, and deliver it to their door. So, if you get an offer to share the excess from a neighbor's garden, don't be a slug and expect them to bring it to you. Get over there quickly and harvest it yourself.

FOOD PRESERVATION AND STORAGE

Some people have the luxury of long growing seasons. If you're one of them you have our envy, and some (most?) of this section won't apply to you. For us, it's a major consideration.

I grew up in Kansas, where growing seasons are long and the land is fertile. I planted short- and long-season corn and we ate it fresh out of the garden from Memorial Day to Labor Day. I planted spring crops and fall crops and cover crops. The garden furnished fresh food all summer and deep into fall. We now live in the mountains of northwestern Montana. We have no early- or late-season crops. We get one crop per year. What's harvested in the fall needs to sustain us until the crops mature the next year.

Our preferred methods of storage are the root cellar, dehydrating, and canning in that order. We adore root cellar crops like potatoes, rutabagas, turnips, and carrots because they take little preparation for storage. Pumpkins and squash are stored in an unheated room in the cabin. We've kept spaghetti squash for over a year this way. If you've ever canned enough food for a family of six to live on for a year, you'll appreciate the ease of storing crops in a root cellar.

It doesn't take a NASA engineer to build a root cellar. Ours is a hand-dug hole in the ground topped with scrap boards, a layer of plastic, a layer of dirt, another layer of plastic, and more dirt. We have approximately two feet of soil covering it. It stays about 45 degrees (plus or minus five degrees, depending on the season) all year long. We should have put a vent in it to help dissipate condensation, but it stores potatoes and carrots very well even without a vent. We just can't store metal cans in it because they rust. If you have an unheated basement, you can partition off a section of the wall, insulate it heavily, and store veggies there instead of digging a separate cellar.

Mini root cellars can be made in the garden by burying a plastic food-grade barrel in the ground, storing your produce inside, and insulating it with bags of leaves or straw. The best book you can get on building and using a root cellar is *Root Cellaring: Natural Cold Storage of Fruits and Vegetables* by Mike and Nancy Bubel. This is another book every homesteader should own.

Dehydrating is our second preference. This is the only way we can store onions long term, but we also dehydrate peas, tomatoes, squash, peppers, herbs and spices, strawberries, huckleberries, mushrooms, and almost everything else we grow or forage. Dried food takes only one fourth of the storage space that canned food needs. We also dehydrate our own food for backpacking and bicycle trips, giving us a lightweight alternative to store-bought trail foods.

We have a passive solar dehydrator and three electric dehydrators. In a sense they are also solar powered since we live off-grid. On long, sunny days, our solar panels generate plenty of electricity to run the dehydrators.

We store dried food in glass jars that aren't suitable for canning and reuse the lids that came off the canning jars. Another advantage of dehydrating is that we can store the food in outbuildings where freezing is a problem for canned goods.

Canning is the third method. We use it mostly for meat and homemade jam, jelly, syrup, cheese, butter, and prepared food like chili, soup, and stew. When considering long-term self-sufficiency, you'll need to remember that canning lids must be replaced after use. Stocking up on lids is an option, but it's only temporary at best. Eventually the rubber seals get brittle and won't work. We've seen reusable lids advertised, but they're expensive and we are not familiar with them. This is one of the main reasons canning is third on our list.

Freezing is an option for those who have grid or solar power or use propane- or oil-powered freezers. We have an electric refrigerator and may get an electric freezer in the future. Solar panels normally last 20 years or more, but even the best batteries have only a 10-year lifespan. Freezers don't last forever either, so if things ever get really bad, freezing will eventually be impractical just as canning will. Kerosene-powered freezers could possibly be adapted to other fuels, but again, they'll eventually quit.

We plan to use canning and refrigeration while they're available, but we'll be relying on our root cellar and dehydrating for long-term sustainable ways of storing food.

Our hand-dug root cellar is perfect for keeping things from freezing. This photo was taken during our first winter on the homestead, so the food inside was store-bought rather than home canned or produced.

Some of the food we dehydrated in 2003 and 2004.

FOOD PREPARATION

We have a propane cookstove, yet we still do most of our cooking by other methods. When we first moved to our homestead, all cooking was done on an open fire in the front yard or occasionally on a small, single-burner propane camp stove. We used a Coleman Camp Oven for baking.

Now that we're all settled in, we use our wood-burning heating stove for most of our cooking except in the summer when it heats the cabin too much. We have a wood-burning cookstove on our screened-in porch we use as a summer kitchen. We also purchased a solar cooker a couple of years ago that we use when the sun's rays are strong.

We still use our propane stove. It's handy for quick jobs like boiling a pan of water or baking, and it gets heavy use when we're canning. We've

canned using the woodstove, but it's much easier to maintain the steady heat needed for canning on the propane stove. We use less than 200 pounds of propane a year, and most of that is during canning sessions.

Cooking on the same wood-burning stove you use to heat your home is relatively easy. We just set the pan, griddle, or skillet directly on top of the stove. It takes a little longer than the propane stove, but that's rarely a problem. If the firebox of your stove has an outer shell around it, you may not be able to use it for cooking. In that case you'll need to get a different woodstove for cooking.

We bake on our woodstove with a Coleman Camp Oven. These were originally designed for use on Coleman camping stoves, but they work on top of our wood heating stove too. Again, they take longer than the oven in our propane stove, but that's not a

We use a solar cooker in the summer. It works well, but it's slow. Be sure to allow plenty of time.

problem for us. We sometimes cover the vents on top with aluminum foil to make the oven hotter, but usually we just bide our time cooking. Our only real complaint with the camp oven is its small size; we can't use pans over nine-inches wide in it.

We've cooked outdoors over an open fire, but in our climate that's a summer option only. Be forewarned: it will blacken your pots, pans, and skillets. We often put a large steel plate over the fire and put the cookware on that when cooking. It keeps the pans cleaner and diffuses the heat somewhat. We also set the camp oven on the steel plate when baking.

If we lived in coal country, we'd seriously look into using it in our stoves. While it may not be a renewable resource, it's not something you're going to run low on for the next couple of centuries. What we don't want in our homestead is to be dependent on fuels that take a lot of technology to mine, transport, or refine. Fuel must be low tech and available locally.

• • • • •

This is one of the longest chapters of the book not so much because it's important (although it is) but because in the modern world of factory farms, supermarkets, refrigerators, freezers, fast food, and microwave ovens, the knowledge of how things were done in the past has been nearly lost. Food growing, gathering, preserving, and preparing is a large part of homestead life. It helps to have plenty of options available.

9 Sanitation

ew people see any desirable options for replacing the bathroom throne. Outhouses have the reputation of being cold, dark, and smelly; composting toilets are practically unheard of in the United States; and to even suggest chamber pots or bedpans is to elicit an upturned nose and change of subjects. But as we all know, "what goes in must also come out." So now what do you do with "it"?

THE TRADITIONAL WATER CLOSET

Lavatory lovers take heart! Under the right conditions, you can keep the commode operational for many years and may never even be faced with its replacement options.

Commodes need only water, sewer pipe, and a septic or lagoon system to function. You don't even need running water. Helen and Scott Nearing (well-known homesteaders from the 1970s and '80s) used a bucket of water each time they flushed. So, as long as you have a plentiful supply of water and keep your septic system in good repair, you can keep your flush toilet. If you need to conserve water, flush only when the need dictates. Remember the saying, "If it's yellow, let it mellow; if it's brown, flush it down."

Now, about septic systems . . . regardless of which waste-disposal system you end up with, you will need to know the zoning regulations for your area. While the flush toilet is acceptable in every state I'm aware of, regulations vary regarding septic systems. The county next to ours requires that septic systems with a drain field must have a "uniform pressure distribution system."

Most septic systems use gravity to move the overflow from the septic tank to the leach lines. With the pressurized distribution system, the overflow is pumped through the leach lines. That won't be a problem as long as your electrical system holds up, but if you're planning on living off-grid, you'll need enough generating ability to power the pump whenever it's needed. If you're interested in a completely self-sufficient survival homestead, you'll need to ensure you have that generating capacity forever if you want to keep using your flush toilet. Otherwise, have a backup plan available.

I've known of instances where flush toilets and holding tanks were used. The tank was pumped out when full and the contents taken to a treatment plant. This might be an option for a vacation cabin or retreat, but it isn't a good long-term solution. It's too dependent on outside assistance and, at $200 or more each time you have the tank pumped, it can get expensive (especially with a large group of people present).

Lagoons are sometimes used where soil conditions make drain fields impractical. Instead of the effluent going from the septic tank to the drain field, it flows into a lagoon, where bacteria finish the process of decomposition. In order to prevent ground or surface water pollution, lagoons must be located where the soil is impermeable. You do not want it percolating down and contaminating

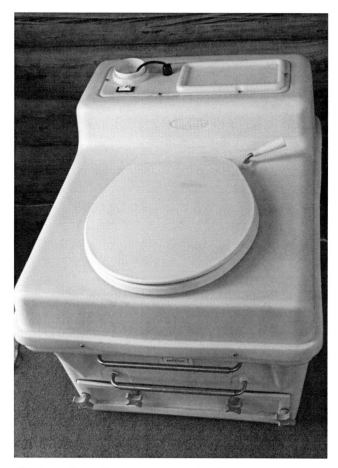

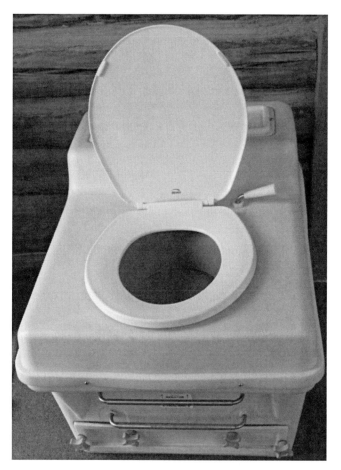

This is an Envirolet composting toilet that we purchased to install in our home. These units are a bit pricey at around $1,500 and up, but we got this one used for much less. The previous owners had never installed it. So far we haven't either! These use no water and are rated for four people at full-time use or six people if installed in a vacation home. They do require electricity to run a small vent fan when needed. Plus you'll need to vent it outside the building. These units are waterless and chemical free.

the groundwater. If you live on a floodplain the lagoon system is not a good idea, as floodwaters will carry the contents to anyone downstream. That being said, if a lagoon system is properly designed and maintained, it is usually trouble free for 30 years or more.

COMPOSTING TOILETS

Composting toilets are popular where septic systems are impractical, where water is scarce, or for composting human excrement for use as fertilizer. They're seen far more often in European countries than in the United States.

The insides resemble a porta-pot like those sold in sporting goods stores, but these only need to be emptied occasionally. A porta-pot does not compost its contents, whereas these do.

The aerator and rake bar help stir things up inside for more complete composting, while the door at the base provides access to empty the (now composted) contents. How often it will need to be emptied depends on several factors.

Composting toilets are waterless and, when functioning properly, odor free. They come in different styles, from store-bought units intended for in-home use only to homebuilt facsimiles for indoor and outdoor applications. Sizes vary as well. Some manufactured units have large reservoirs with intake tubes reaching to the toilet in the room above. Other smaller, manufactured composting toilets are fully self-contained and take little more space than a recreational vehicle's porta-pot. The advantage of the larger units is that the reservoir doesn't need to be emptied as often.

Many types use a small fan for odor control. These toilets are sealed like an RV toilet, so there is no odor when the unit is not in use. While it's being used, the chamber is open and the fan pulls air from the room and forces it through the outside vent, very similar to the ventilation fan located in the ceiling in most bathrooms. It's a much more efficient way of dealing with odors than a ceiling fan. During times when the power is out, doing without the fan will not affect the operation of the toilet.

Homemade compost toilets also range in size from diminutive sawdust toilets constructed with plastic buckets to large outdoor designs with two separate chambers. Just like the commercial models, the only real advantage to the large toilets is they need to be emptied less frequently.

The sawdust toilet is one of the simplest compost toilets you can make. You just do your "chores" in a plastic bucket and cover the waste with sawdust. As you deposit more excrement to the pile, you add more sawdust to cover it. When the bucket is as full as you want to contend with, take it outside and dump it in a compost bin to continue composting. Clean the empty bucket and put it back with a new layer of sawdust on the bottom and repeat the process. Most people build wooden boxes to put the bucket in and then install a regular toilet seat. Sawdust toilets are virtually odorless and, with careful construction, look like nice additions to the home.

There are lots of variations in outdoor composting toilets, but the process is the same for them as for the sawdust toilet. Outdoor units look like outhouses, except provisions are made to shovel out the composted excrement when the storage area is full. There are a couple of variations, though. In some instances, people use a removable tub to hold the waste. When it's full, you remove it and dump it in the compost pile or replace it with an empty tub and let the first one decompose further.

One of the fanciest designs I've seen was a double-chamber composting toilet. It looked like two joined outhouses made out of stone. Only one was used at a time. When its chamber was full, the door was locked and the other side put to use. By the time the second chamber was full, the first chamber was finished composting. It was shoveled out and put back into use and the other side locked. The only real advantage was that by the time you shoveled out the first chamber, its contents were finished with the composting process so there were no fresh feces to deal with.

Sawdust is not the only material you can use to cover the "evidence." Any dry materials you'd put in your compost pile is acceptable: chipped wood, chopped straw, cereal hulls, shredded paper, or any other carbon-rich organic material is quite sufficient.

The advantages of composting toilets on the low-budget homestead or retreat are that they're cheap to construct, they are low tech, and they bridge the gap between the traditional pit toilet and the water closet. Composting toilets don't need electricity or water, and instead of a potential source of groundwater pollution like septic systems, the end result is a rich soil enhancer.

OUTHOUSES

Now on to the next option: the infamous outhouse. In this case, "outhouse" isn't a fair term to use because outside composting toilets are also a form of outhouse. Outhouses are merely toilet facilities located outside the house. In this case, though, we're talking about the traditional outhouse.

Traditional outhouses take one of two forms: the pit privy or the shovel-out backhouse. A pit privy is built over a pit. The waste fills the pit over time and when it's about full, you cover it with dirt, dig another pit somewhere else, move the building to the new location, and start over. If you put your used toilet paper in a bag or diaper pail instead of dumping it down the hole, your pit will take about twice as long to fill up. (You can dispose of the used TP by burning, composting, or disposing of it in the local landfill.) Be very sure to situate the privy well away from any water sources it could pollute.

A shovel-out backhouse is built with a ground-level reservoir you can periodically empty. You'll

Using an outhouse when the temperature is 20 below zero can be a chilling experience! Some people have Styrofoam seats stored in the house and take them out with them when the temperature drops this far.

need to leave a door in the back to make removing the contents easier. You'll also need a place to compost the "night soil." Be sure to cover the deposits with sawdust or other organic material to reduce the smell and keep away flies. I'd advise putting a good fence around it to keep dogs out. We once had the unique experience of our dog discovering a latrine in the woods made by a group of campers and joyously rolling in it. She was immediately walked to the nearest lake, and we played "fetch the stick we throw in the water" until the evidence of her indiscretion was eliminated. Then it was back to the house for her bubble bath.

The only difference between a shovel-out backhouse and a composting toilet is that, with a composting toilet, the waste is covered with sawdust after use. With a shovel-out backhouse, the excrement is moved in its original condition and composted later. (Okay, there's also a considerable difference in smell when shoveling out the backhouse!)

The advantages of an outhouse in its various forms are that it is low tech and sustainable. You don't even need to gather sawdust or other organic materials as with a composting toilet.

The disadvantages are obvious and all are related to our vanity. Yes, they do smell bad at times, although if properly ventilated the smell is reduced considerably. They are cold in the winter, but then, how long do you expect to be out there anyway? When it's really cold, use a bedpan and dump it in

the outhouse later! It's a pain to dig a new pit, but again, even with a family, a pit measuring three feet square and five feet deep will last three years or more if you don't fill it with toilet paper. A shovel-out backhouse will need emptying more often, and it is indeed a smelly, disgusting job. If that's the option you've chosen, just smear a little Vicks VapoRub (or a generic equivalent) under your nose and get it done as quickly as possible!

BEDPANS

I mention bedpans last because even with a bedpan, you're going to need a way to dispose of the waste. It wasn't that long ago that bedpans (also known as chamber pots) were common for a couple of good reasons. First, when it's cold out, especially during the night, getting bundled up and making that trip outside is something few will embrace. Second, if you've ever made a nighttime trip to outdoor facilities in the country where wild animals prowl and trees cast scary shadows in the moonlight, it

This is the porta-pot we use in our camper. These need to be emptied when they are full, so you'll need somewhere to dump the contents. There are deodorants and other chemicals you can use to make their use more pleasant. There should be no odor when everything is closed up properly. The contents will freeze, so keep them in a heated room unless they're empty. Again, the time interval for dumping them depends on how often they're used.

can be a frightening experience to those not used to that environment (especially for kids). We've had skunks, bears, moose, mountain lions, coyotes, and wolves near the cabin. The occasional grizzly and Bigfoot have made neighborhood rounds as well. (Okay, there's no solid proof on the Bigfoot!) Little critters like mice and pack rats rustle leaves, as does the wind. Add in shifting shadows or dark, moonless nights and even a mild imagination can make a trip to the outhouse a frightening ordeal. We've had guests that wouldn't go alone during the day! In cases like these, bedpans are a viable alternative to dying of fright (or constipation).

After rearing seven children, we've changed enough diapers in our lifetime that an outhouse or bedpan is not a big deal. Look at the bright side: you'll never have to worry about the toilet backing up!

GRAY WATER DISPOSAL

Don't you just love the old Westerns where the cook steps outside the door and empties the wash pan with a fling? Like many things depicted by Hollyweird, it just doesn't work that well in real life. In summer, you'll end up with a smelly, muddy mess infested with flies, bugs, and other vermin. In the winter you'll have an ugly area of gray, soggy snow covered with little pieces of leftover food and whatever other garbage was on the plates when you washed them.

In chapter 7 we looked at options for recovering gray water and using it around the homestead. If recycling gray water is not an option, you'll need to find another way to dispose of it. If you have a

septic system, the problem is solved; just plumb your sinks, bathtubs, etc., into the system and be done with it. If you don't have a septic system, it gets a little more complicated.

If you're building your house and plan on a gray water recovery system, it's best to construct it when you build your home. In that case, perhaps a holding tank with a sump and filtering system in the inlet and pump in the tank would be a good idea. Install an electric pump for the good times, but have a manual pump just in case.

I've also seen old homesteads that employed a modified Dutch drain system. They buried a barrel that had holes drilled in it (in one case, they used a rifle and shot the holes in it), then ran the drainpipe to the barrel. If you're worried about the barrel's sides collapsing, fill it with large rocks. If the soil is permeable, the barrel will drain okay for awhile. For long-term use, you'll want to filter the water going into the barrel or the holes will eventually become plugged. At the very least, be sure to put a fence around it to keep people away. A better idea is a concrete slab. If (or when!) the top of the barrel rusts through, someone could fall in and get hurt (which is another good reason to fill the barrel with large rocks).

In another instance, the gray water was just drained through a pipe onto the ground about 50 yards from the house. It was a long time ago at a rural residence. I wouldn't normally recommend that system, but it worked for them.

When it comes to waste disposal, be aware of the legalities involved. If you violate the law, you might be visited by county or state authorities.

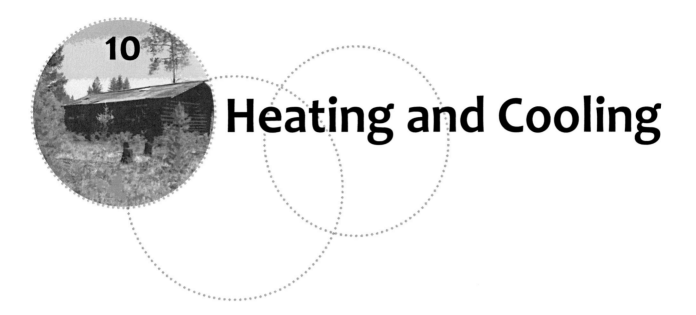

Heating and Cooling

There are very few places on this earth where it's neither too hot nor too cold at least part of the year. So, you're going to need some low-buck, low-tech, sustainable options for dealing with it.

When it comes to heating and cooling, contemporary housing is 100 percent electricity dependent. Normally that isn't a problem, but if you're planning on living off-grid and don't have a pile of money for solar panels, wind turbines, and massive battery banks, or you don't live near a vibrant, rushing stream for a hydroelectric generating system, you'll be better off with passive heating and cooling systems.

Modern houses are tightly sealed and well insulated. That's a good thing, and you'll want to keep that in any low-budget alternative you design. I've lived in my share of poorly insulated, drafty houses, and even with the best heating system you always feel cold in those places.

The bad thing about new houses is that they have long hallways and multiple rooms (and most bedrooms have their own bathroom), with low ceilings and small doors and windows. The reason these are bad is that if you're using a woodstove or other low-tech heating source, the only room that'll be warm is the one with the stove. Unless you use a fan to circulate the air, heat will stay in that one room and venture no farther. Bathrooms in particular get pretty cold in the winter.

Forced-air systems overcome that problem by blowing the air (whether hot or cold) directly into the rooms through heating/air conditioning ducts. The motors used to power the fan are large and use approximately 1,200 watts of power every hour (and require about three times that amount to start them each time). Winter poses special problems for the off-grid, solar-powered homesteader. There is less sunlight to generate electricity, and long, cold nights mean the blower on your furnace runs more often and for prolonged time periods (which requires a hefty battery bank to keep the furnace going during the night). So even if you have a wood- or coal-fired furnace, you're still going to need a steady source of electricity to heat your house.

If you want a home that's warm in the winter and cool in the summer, the best place to begin is with your home's design. While we'll go over that in more detail in chapter 12, the basic concepts you'll want to keep in mind are that to keep warm in cold weather, you'll want lots of insulation, open rooms with few (if any) hallways, windbreaks on the north side, and windows on the south side. The keys to keeping cool in hot weather are insulation, shade, and ventilation. Those are the things to think about if you're designing your home. If you're moving into an existing structure, you'll have to make the best of what you have.

COOLING YOUR HOME

Aside from earth-sheltered housing, your options are limited when it comes to good, low-budget ways to cool your home. Air conditioners

Wood heat is the most self-sufficient way to heat your home in winter. Wood is a renewable resource, and since the best trees for the stove are trees that have already died, you're making a healthier forest by cutting them up and hauling them off.

are energy hogs. Even where the sun shines brightly, it will cost a bundle to set up an off-grid power system that can keep an air conditioner running all day long. Inverters will also have to be large. Their continuous duty rating must be adequate to power the blower fan for hours on end. For most heating and AC systems, that means your inverter will need to be rated around 10,000 watts or higher. (There's more about inverter duty cycles in the next chapter.) Likewise, it'll take a huge battery bank to keep the system going at night. If you have that kind of money, you won't need this book. However, there are some things you can do within a limited budget.

Even a small solar power system is capable of running low-watt fans in the summer. We have several small fans and a couple of ceiling fans. We each have a small fan for use at our desks when writing. These take 10 watts. We also have a 12-inch fan

that uses 27 watts on the "high" setting. It oscillates, so it's usually found in the kitchen/dining room. We have a couple of 20-inch box fans that we put in windows for whole house cooling. These can be set to blow inward to cool a room or outward to draw air through the cabin. These take from 24 to 96 watts, depending upon fan speed. Our low-watt ceiling fan uses less than 50 watts at maximum speed. We can run every fan in the house on less than 200 watts of power.

Just for comparison, most houses use three or more 60-watt lightbulbs to illuminate each room, so it doesn't take a lot of energy to run a fan a few hours each day. In contrast, a room air conditioner requires between 600 to 3,000 watts, depending on its size. Central air conditioners need anywhere from 2,000 to 5,000 watts. A 100-watt solar panel costs approximately $400 at this time. You'd need six of them to power a small room air conditioner.

(Actually, you'll need more than that, but those details are found in the next chapter.) A large central air unit would need more than fifty 100-watt panels at a total cost of over $20,000. And that's for the solar panels only!

Evaporative coolers (swamp coolers) use considerably less power than an air conditioner since you aren't running a compressor. They do need a constant supply of power, though, for the fan and a small water pump. Although water use is relatively low (around 15 gallons a day), it needs to be consistent throughout the day. They work best in dry climates. The lower the humidity, the better they work. Power consumption will vary according to the size of the fan but is typically about 1,000 to 1,200 watts. You'll still be stretching the limits of most low-budget, off-grid power capabilities, especially if you run an electric refrigerator or freezer in addition to the swamp cooler.

We'll look at passive home cooling ideas in chapter 12, but large shade trees are helpful, as are lots of windows for ventilation, awnings over windows, and covered decks that shade the walls of your home during the day.

Cooling Yourself

Historically, an afternoon siesta was the norm for outside laborers in the southwestern desert of the United States. Temperatures over 100 degrees are normal in that region, and it was just common sense to rest during the hottest part of the day and work in the cooler morning and evening hours. Nights are generally cool in the low humidity of the desert, so sleeping wasn't usually a problem.

In the Midwest and southeastern United States, people often slept outdoors on hot summer nights. The high humidity retains heat so even though the sun was down, the nights were still hot and sleep could be elusive.

Always drink lots of water when the temperature is high, especially if you're not used to working in the heat. You lose a lot more to perspiration than most people realize. Know the symptoms of heat exhaustion and heat stroke. Know the signs of dehydration.

A good trick to use in hot climates is to wet a bandana and drape it over your head so that it hangs over your shoulders and back. Put your hat on over it to hold it in place. It acts like a portable swamp cooler to keep your head and neck cool and shaded from the sun.

Schedule your work so that the more labor-intensive tasks are done in the mornings or evenings when the temperature is lower. One advantage of the self-sufficient lifestyle is that you set your own schedule, so make your health and productivity a high priority.

HEATING YOUR HOME

When it comes to heating, you'll have some choices to make. Liquid and gas fuels are easier to use, but you'll have to buy them from outside suppliers. If you're aiming for self-sufficiency or even trying to depend only on locally available resources, these are a short-term solution.

There are options to make your own fuels, such as diesel (a close relative to fuel oil) from soybeans and other crops, but to grow the quantities needed for fuel will take some work, and I'm not sure how complicated the "soybean to fuel" process is. However, if you can make your own fuel to power your vehicles and equipment, then you'll probably have the machinery needed to grow enough soybeans for home-heating fuel as well. If you go that route, you're probably not looking at the low-budget angle.

It's possible to make fuel from alcohol and methane as well. These have been used for powering motors, but I've never read much about using them to heat homes or buildings. If you can produce an adequate supply, maybe you could use them to power a generator. Again, if you go that route, you probably aren't working from a low-budget angle.

Waste Oil

Another option includes recycling waste oil (automotive oil, transmission fluid, used vegetable oil from restaurants, etc.). Waste oil heaters can be purchased or made with a few commonly found items. They come in both electric (using a fan to circulate the heat) and radiant (nonelectric) heat designs. Plans are available on the Internet, so I'm not going into a lot of detail on how to build one.

If your tank is large enough to run the heater for a couple of days, it will give you a chance to get away in winter without worrying about your canned goods or small pets like birds, hamsters, gerbils, or fish freezing while you're gone. These do have ash pans that must be cleaned periodically, so don't expect to be gone weeks at a time without maintaining them.

Waste oil is often available for free at auto repair shops. Years ago, vendors bought the used oil for recycling, but since the Environmental Protection Agency (EPA) has tightened up regulations, the vendors now charge repair shops disposal fees. For that reason, many business owners are enthusiastic to have you take it off their hands. They'll probably need you to sign for it to leave a paper trail in case the EPA starts asking what happened to it. There's nothing nefarious in their request; it's just a way to keep them from facing fines and penalties for improperly disposing of the oil. You're going to need a pump to draw the oil from their tanks and a vessel of your own to pump it into. Admittedly, waste oil will still keep you dependent upon outside suppliers so it's not a long-term, self-sufficient solution, but it is a low-budget solution to heating your home or shop.

Coal

Coal is a great long-term heating option if it's locally available. It isn't renewable, but in many places it's found in large enough quantities to keep you and future generations supplied in fuel for several lifetimes. Be very careful mining it, though. I know of one instance when some property owners worked diligently at mining their own coal until the day they went out to work and found that the mine had collapsed. The only thing that saved their lives was the timing. If it had happened during the previous day's work, they would have become a statistic cited in the local paper.

You can safely burn wood in a coal stove, but it's inefficient. Coal-burning stoves have grates that allow air to freely circulate under the burning coal and they have no baffles in front of the chimney opening. The fireboxes on coal stoves are usually smaller, so it may be difficult to get enough wood in the firebox to generate much heat. You'll probably have to split the wood into small pieces, which increases its burn rate so you'll need to feed the stove more often. The end result is that you'll use a lot more wood.

Be very careful about burning coal in a wood stove. Coal burns hotter than wood, and there's a real danger of warping or cracking the metal of a stove designed for burning wood. If you want dual-fuel capability, the safest bet is to purchase a stove intended for burning coal. You'll lose efficiency when burning wood, but at least you won't have to be as concerned about melting your stove.

Wood Pellets and Corn

I've lumped stoves that burn wood pellets and corn together because they both operate in similar ways. Wood pellets and corn are a similar size, and both are poured into reservoirs and fed into the firebox by small augers. If the hopper is large enough, you may only have to fill it once each day. Both wood pellets and corn are cleaner than wood to transport, store, and handle.

Wood pellets are wood by-products that are compressed into small pellets about the size of corn. They're bought in plastic bags, usually around 40 lbs. per bag, and can be transported in your car or truck and stored in your garage or an outside building. They burn clean and hot, with very little ash residue. Be aware that they come in different grades, so know what you're buying.

Corn is combustible and may be an option if you live where winters are short and the growing season is long. The major advantage of corn in a long-term self-sufficient homestead or retreat is that it can be grown and harvested on your property under primitive conditions. Even if you're buying corn for fuel, it's one of the lowest cost heating options available. If you grow your own, you'll have the corncobs left after shelling the corn. If you're doing it yourself, I'd recommend getting a hand-cranked machine to shell the corn. They're reasonably priced (under $50) and work without electricity. In the past, the cobs were often burned in cookstoves. They put out a lot of heat for a short amount of time, so they were perfect for cooking or baking. Corncobs were also put to use in the outhouse as a toilet paper substitute.

The biggest weakness of corn and pellet stoves on the self-sufficient side is their requirement for electricity to run the auger (which is minimal) and the blower (takes a lot more juice). Wood pellets and corn can be burned in a regular wood-burning stove, but they are inefficient. It's kind of like burning a pile of leaves, in that they pack so tightly that air can't circulate for good combustion. They'll work best if you add them to the fire in small doses.

I need to stress again that if you're depending upon off-grid power, you need to be careful of any essential need (such as heat) being powered by solar or wind energy. Most of us who live off-grid know that there are times—especially in the winter—when the sun doesn't put out much energy for weeks at a stretch and the wind can stop blowing as well. If you use heating systems that need electricity to function, be sure to have nonelectric backup systems set up and ready to go with an adequate supply of fuel in storage.

Wood pellets require special processing so in a long-term survival or self-sufficient situation, wood pellets are classed the same as propane or other fossil fuels. You may be able to store a bunch of them, but eventually you're going to run out.

WOOD

Aside from passive solar energy (covered in chapter 12), the best self-sufficient option for heat is burning wood.

Wood is a renewable resource that's available almost everywhere. Ideally, you'll be able to cut the wood you'll need on your own land. Years ago, fast-growing trees were advertised for just this purpose. You can also gather wood by cutting up limbs that have been broken off by storms. Scrap wood from construction sites, wood pallets, and other sources can be used as well. If you live near a lake, river, or ocean, driftwood is an option. Even if you can't get enough wood from your own land, it will be available locally. In a survival situation, there will be people selling or trading firewood for the things they need. Ideally you won't have to buy wood, but if you do, it will probably be locally available in a long-term survival situation—unlike natural gas, propane, or heating oil. Just be sure you have barterable skills or merchandise.

If your home isn't too large or poorly designed and you've insulated it well, you may only need two or three cords per year. Of course, living where the winters are short will help too!

Wood-Burning Stoves
The market is flooded with wood-burning stoves. These can be categorized as internal, external, airtight, not airtight, forced air, fireplace inserts, fireplaces, or a campfire in the middle of your teepee.

Wood-burning stoves of any kind are either airtight or not airtight. An airtight stove is built so that all seams are sealed. Rope-type gaskets are used around the stove's door to stop air from entering there. The only place air can enter the combustion chamber is through the air intake vent. If you close the vent, the fire will die from lack of oxygen.

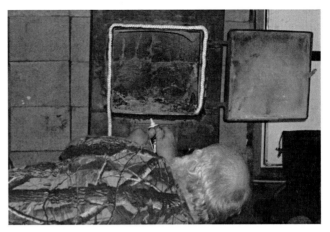

Wood-burning stoves need periodic service. Firebrick linings need to be replaced every few years, while replacing door gaskets is best done every year.

If you have one of the old cast-iron stoves going at night, you can often see firelight through the seams where the cast-iron panels meet. They have so many air leaks that even if you close the damper or vent completely, the fire will keep burning.

The advantage of an airtight stove is that you have much more control over burning rates, which means the temperature stays more consistent in the house and you use less wood. They're also safer in the event of a chimney fire, since you can close off the air supply to (hopefully!) suffocate the fire. However, once a chimney fire begins, you'll need to do more to put it out than just close the vent on the stove. (More on that later.)

When you use an airtight stove, the tendency is to stuff the wood box full, close the vent most of the way, and let the fire smolder all day and/or night. While this is easier on you since you don't have to add wood as often, it's hard on the environment and your chimney. Cold, smoldering fires produce more creosote (corrosive and highly flammable tar buildup) in your chimney. Even with an airtight stove, you're better off putting less wood in the combustion chamber and opening the vent more to make a small, hot fire than to stuff the stove full of wood and let it smolder.

Many modern stoves have catalytic converters built into them to burn pollutants before they reach the atmosphere. In congested areas or places where air inversion is a problem, these may be mandatory.

Some stoves use fans to circulate the hot air. They usually have hollow pipes running through the stove's combustion chamber or a metal shield around the stove or fireplace insert. The idea with the pipe method is that the heat in the firebox will heat up the pipes; then fans can blow air through the pipes and into the room. The stoves with outside shielding blow air between the stove wall and the shield. These will function without the fans, but they won't be as efficient. Most of the time you can put a fan over a regular woodstove and circulate the heat just as well. Additionally, the outer shield makes it difficult to cook on the top of your wood-burning stove. The outside shell just doesn't get hot enough.

Fireplace inserts are just that—they are wood-burning stoves that fit into a fireplace opening. The original Franklin stove (named after its inventor, Benjamin Franklin) was a fireplace insert. Fireplaces are notoriously inefficient. The only methods of control are a damper (a metal gate that can be opened or closed) in the chimney and the amount and kind of wood you use. Fireplaces also send most of the heat up the chimney in a futile attempt to increase the temperature outside.

Modern fireplace inserts are typically airtight stoves that fit in or in front of the fireplace opening. You get the fuel-saving advantages of an airtight stove with the aesthetics of an open fire (most of them have clear fronts to view the fire as it burns). They usually have fans to circulate the hot air. When you confine a stove in a small area as happens with a fireplace insert, it loses much of its ability to heat through convection, so the heat needs to be forced or blown out into the room.

Wood-burning stoves heat like a campfire by radiating heat in all directions and work best when standing away from walls. The potbelly stoves you see in old-time movies were always situated in the open parts of the room with chairs sitting around them. Very seldom did you see one in a corner because there wasn't much point in heating up the wall. Leave plenty of space around them for air to circulate. Another potential problem when crowding them in tight spaces (other than catching the house on fire!) is that it's easy to overheat the sides of the stove that are next to the wall. Even stoves with thick steel walls will warp and crack if they overheat. If you install your stove in a basement corner, be sure to leave plenty of air space around the stove.

The primary advantages of external, or outdoor, wood-fired furnaces are that they keep the mess outside (you'll always be sweeping up wood chips,

sawdust, ash, and pieces of bark around the woodstove) and you can load them up with huge amounts of wood so you won't have to make a lot of trips outside to refill the stove.

The disadvantage is that they need electricity. Most of these heat your home by either blowing hot air into the house through ductwork just like a forced-air furnace, or they heat water in a boiler and pump it into the house for radiant heat in the floor or through baseboard heaters. These distribute heat to individual rooms, which is more comfortable than radiant heat that mostly heats the room the stove is in. As I've already mentioned, electricity can be a problem in the winter. With outside furnaces, you'll need electric thermostats for heat control in the stove and the house; plus you'll be powering either a fan for forcing air through ductwork or a pump for pumping hot water through pipes. They have some good points if your power supply can handle them.

Heat Values of Wood

Not all wood is created equal. When firewood cutters get together and discuss which wood is the "best," they're usually referring to the heat value of the wood itself. Heat value is commonly measured by BTUs (British thermal units). One BTU is the amount of energy needed to increase the temperature of one pound of water one degree Fahrenheit at a constant pressure of one atmosphere (the air pressure at sea level).

In the spreadsheet, you'll see the heat value of one cord of wood expressed in million BTUs. There are often discrepancies between lab findings due to such factors as moisture content, the actual cubic feet of wood per cord, and different testing methods. Still, the numbers are generally reliable.

BTU ratings are based on a full cord of wood. That's a stack of wood measuring four feet high, four feet wide, and eight feet long. That comes to 128 cubic feet of space. However, the actual volume of the wood in a cord will vary depending upon how large each piece is and how tightly they are packed. Since there will always be airspace between the chunks, you're probably only getting about 85 cubic feet of wood in that 128 cubic foot "box."

The BTU numbers on the spreadsheet should be multiplied by one million (M-BTU). To compare the heat output of different types of firewood to fuel oil, propane, and wood pellets, use the follow-

FIREWOOD RATINGS

	Heat Value	Million BTUs Per Cord	Easy to Split	Rating
Alder	Med.	14.8	Yes	Poor
Apple	High	26.5	No	Medium
Ash, Black	Med.	19.1	Yes	Excellent
Ash, White, Green	High	23.6	Yes	Excellent
Aspen	Low	14.7	Yes	Fair
Basswood	Low	13.5	Yes	Fair
Beech	High	24	Yes	Excellent
Birch, Black	High	26.8	Yes	Excellent
Birch, White, Gray, Paper	Med.	20.3	Yes	Excellent
Birch, Yellow	High	23.6	Yes	Excellent
Boxelder	Low	17.9	No	Fair
Butternut	Low	14.5	Yes	Poor
Catalpa	Low	16.4	No	Poor
Cedar, White, Red	Med.	17.5	Yes	Good
Cherry	Med.	20	Yes	Good
Chestnut	Low	12.9	Yes	Poor
Cottonwood	Low	13.5	Yes	Fair
Cypress	Med.		Yes	Fair
Dogwood	High	30.4	Yes	Excellent
Douglas Fir	High	21.4	Yes	Good
Eastern Hornbeam	High	27.3	No	Excellent
Elm, White, American	Med.	19.5	No	Fair
Eucalyptus	High	33.5	No	Fair
Fir, Balsam	Low	14.3	Yes	Poor
Gum	Med.	18.5	No	Fair
Hackberry	Med.	20.8	Yes	Excellent
Hawthorn	High		Medium	Good
Hemlock	Low	15.9		Fair
Hickory	High	27.7	Medium	Excellent
Locust, Black	High	26.8	No	Excellent
Locust, Honey	High	25.8	Medium	Excellent
Maple, Hard	High	29.7	Yes	Excellent
Maple, Soft, Red	Med.	18.7	Yes	Excellent
Maple, Sugar	High	24	No	Good
Oak, Red	High	21.7	No	Excellent
Oak, White	High	25.7	No	Excellent
Pecan	High		Yes	Excellent
Pine, Norway, Jack, Pitch	Low	17.1	Yes	Fair
Pine, Ponderosa	Low	15.2	Yes	Fair
Pine, Sugar	Low	15.8	Yes	Fair
Pine, White	Low	14.3	Yes	Fair
Pine, Yellow	Low	15.8	Yes	Good
Poplar, Yellow	Low	16	Yes	Poor
Redwood	Med.	18.8	Yes	Fair
Spruce	Low	14.5	Yes	Poor
Sycamore	Med.	18.5	No	Fair
Tamarack/Larch	Med.	20.8	Yes	Fair
Walnut	Med.	20	Yes	Good
Willow	Low	14.5	Yes	Poor

ing numbers. The heat output of heating oil is rated at 138,700 BTU/gallon; for propane it's 92,000 BTU/gallon; for wood pellets it's approximately 8,000 BTU/lb.

For example, one cord of tamarack/larch produces approximately 20,800,000 BTUs of energy. Divide that by 138,700 BTUs (energy rating of one gallon of fuel oil) and you will need almost 150 gallons of fuel oil to equal the heat output of one cord of tamarack.

Remember, this is a guideline for comparison purposes only. Actual energy output may vary depending on factors like the moisture content of the wood and the actual volume of wood in the cord. Even wood pellets, propane, and fuel oil vary on their actual energy content.

Seasoning

Firewood needs to be seasoned before use. Seasoning is just another term for drying wood. When a live tree is cut down, 60 percent or more of its weight may be water. This is called "green" wood, and the moisture in it may cause several problems when you burn it. First, a large percentage of the heat must be used to evaporate all of that water before the wood fibers can burn. As this water evaporates, it's trying to put out your fire just as if you were sprinkling water on it. You end up with a cold fire, which produces excess creosote, which clogs chimneys and is the number one cause of chimney fires.

When a tree dries, very little moisture escapes through the sides, traveling instead through the cut ends. The best way to dry firewood is to cut it into stove length and stack it where air can circulate through it. The shorter the sections of wood and the better the air circulation, the faster it will dry. It's seldom necessary to season stove-length wood longer than six months, although longer wood may need a year or more. Unless you live in a climate where rain and high humidity are the norm, covering wood doesn't speed things up much. Likewise, splitting the wood helps a little, but again, the improvement is minimal.

Wood is considered properly seasoned when the moisture content is reduced below 20 percent.

Splitting

Splitting "problem" wood is simple if you have a motorized splitter. However, if you're splitting it by hand, you'll want wood that's easier to split. The spreadsheet has a column rating the different types of wood by how easy or difficult they are to split. Again, use this as a general guide. I know from personal experience that some trees that should be easy to split aren't due to anomalies like twisted grain or multiple and/or large knots. It's also easier to split dry wood than green wood.

There are some good reasons to split firewood. First, large-diameter logs that won't fit through the door of your stove must be split. Similarly, if the pieces are too heavy it's best to split them. Finally, split wood is easier to ignite. When you split wood, you leave at least one sharp edge. Because the mass at the edge is smaller, it heats faster and reaches the ignition point sooner than wood that's in the "round." Split wood often has splinters protruding from the wood. These splinters also ignite easily and provide more heat to get the log burning sooner.

Firewood needs to be split if it's too big for the stove. I like it small enough that I can pick it up with one hand.

Purchasing Firewood

If you ever buy firewood, be sure that you and the seller are talking about the same amounts. We've already discussed the measurements of a full cord of wood (four feet wide, four feet high, and eight feet long). Sometimes merchants sell what's called a "face" cord (aka "rank," "rick," "stove," or "fireplace" cord). A face cord is a stack of wood that is four feet high and eight feet long but is only as deep as the pieces of firewood. For example, when the wood is sold in stove length (usually 16 inches long), a face cord will measure four feet by eight feet by 16 inches deep, which is one-third of a full cord of wood.

You'll also get less wood in a cord if the wood is split. If you don't believe me, get a box and fill it with unsplit wood. Now split the wood and try to get it all back in the box. So if you don't mind splitting your own wood, buy it "in the round." You'll get more wood for the same amount of money.

Whether you buy your firewood or cut it yourself, it pays to know which types of wood will get you the most heat for the least amount of work. Review the "Heat Value of Wood" section above.

A quick note on storing wood: keep your woodshed at least 100 feet from your house. In most locations, wild-land firefighters will not try to save outbuildings. If a wildfire rolls through, you don't want it catching your woodshed on fire and then having fire from the woodshed burning your house down as well. Additionally, you may bring home uninvited guests when you cut wood. You don't want things like termites, ants, and other insects taking up residence in your house or cabin.

Do cover your wood. Wet wood is hard to ignite, and an ice storm can leave the whole stack frozen solid just when you need it the most.

Chimney Cleaning

How often your chimney needs cleaning will depend on how much wood you burn, the quality of the wood you burn, how hot you keep the fire in your stove, and the design of your chimney. Wet or green wood, cold fires, and cold chimneys make a lot of creosote. Efficient chimneys, seasoned wood, and hot fires (whether small or large) keep your chimney clean longer. To simplify this, think hot equals clean and cold equals creosote.

Chimneys need to heat up quickly for best efficiency. If you've ever tried to start a fire in a fire-place on a damp, cold morning, you'll know what I mean. Fireplaces with large brick or stone chimneys are cold. When you try to start a fire, the smoke just rolls out into the room instead of drafting up the chimney as it should. The problem is that you have a big slug of heavy, cold air inside the chimney and until you can get enough heat from below to push the cold air out, you're going to have a lot of smoke in the room.

The remedy is to take a big wad of crumpled newspaper, stuff it up in the chimney, and light the paper. The quick-burning paper creates a lot of heat fast, which pushes the cold air up and out of the chimney. Even then, the chimney won't draw well until the heat from the fire has warmed the brick or stone. Remember this when you think about building that beautiful stone or brick chimney. They draw well as long as they are warm. Let the fire go out for a few hours and when the chimney cools down, you'll be starting all over again.

When you install your stove and chimney, try to keep the chimney as straight and open as you can. Any bends, curves, or restrictions cool down the smoke entering the chimney. Remember, cool equals creosote. I once hooked a stove with a 6-inch flue to a 10-inch-diameter chimney. The large portion was always sooting up because when the hot gasses went from the 6-inch pipe to the 10-inch pipe, they expanded much like air passing through a venturi. This expansion cooled down the gasses and no matter how hot the fire or how dry the wood, we were always cleaning that chimney. Our present chimney is straight and the same 6-inch diameter from start to finish. We have very few problems with creosote now.

Aside from chimney design, the next best things are to keep your fires hot and no larger than necessary and to use only seasoned wood. Green wood and cold, smoldering fires are ideal recipes for making creosote. Airtight stoves are more prone to creosote buildup because you can dampen them down enough to make your fire smolder. Older, non-airtight stoves usually have enough air leaks that you can't shut down the oxygen supply completely. Don't let that lull you into complacency, though. It still pays to use only seasoned wood and keep the fire small and hot.

Another tip is to burn the fire good and hot when you first build it up in the morning. This warms the chimney quicker and may burn off thin layers of creosote before they build up and cause a chimney fire. Do not try this if you've let the creosote build up to dangerous levels. The resulting fire might be more intense than you bargained for. If you have too much creosote, get the chimney cleaned; then keep it clean forever after.

There are chemicals you can add to your fire to help rid creosote from your chimney. I've never used them, but that doesn't mean they don't work or are not a good idea.

Chimney cleaning tools are widely available and cheap. Equipment needs are minimal in most cases. Brushes can be purchased in the size and shape of your chimney. Steel brushes are the way to go. Creosote may look powdery or it may appear as a shiny, paint-type residue in the inside of the flue. Soft brushes just smear it around. The cheapest method is to tie a weight to one end of a chimney brush and a long rope to the other. Let the weight pull the brush to the bottom and use the rope to haul it back up. Keep it up until the chimney is clean. We have a brush clamped to a long section of electrical conduit. We just run it up and down the chimney from the top. If you have any bends, you'll have to remove the pipe elbows and do each straight section individually. Watch out for overhead power lines. If you get too close to one, the chimney won't be the only thing on fire!

I've heard of people using burlap sacks filled with rocks drawn up and down the chimney or using tire chains to rattle around inside the flue. These work somewhat, but brushes are cheap, last for years, and do a much better job. This is one place where making a small investment will pay a huge dividend in fire prevention and peace of mind.

Be advised that you're going to make a big mess doing this, so wear eye protection and a surgeon's or painter's mask to keep the dust out of your lungs. Leather gloves and old coveralls help too. We keep the door and vent tightly closed on the stove and work from outside. That way the creosote falls into the stove, where we shovel it out afterward. If for some reason you need to work from the inside and can't keep the door to your stove closed, cover your furniture and the floor around the stove or fireplace for easier cleanup. This stuff is dusty or flaky with an oily base, and it's very difficult to clean up if you get it on the floor or furniture.

Clean chimneys draw better and reduce the chances of chimney fires. Cleaning isn't difficult with the proper equipment. Regular chimney brushes are inexpensive and do a much better job than flailing the inside of the chimney with tire chains or gunny sacks filled with rocks.

Chimney Fires

Take my word for this: you do not want to experience a chimney fire. I've never had one (yet), and hope I never do. Those I know who have had them become very religious about cleaning their chimney. Chimney fires start when creosote deposits in the chimney ignite. Once they begin, they quickly become self-sustaining, reaching incredible temperatures within minutes. They can burn through steel chimneys and crack tile chimney liners with their intense heat. Once they've ignited flammable materials near the chimney, you also have a house fire to extinguish. The best way to deal with them is to prevent them by regular chimney inspections and cleaning.

However, if you have a chimney fire, here are some do's and don'ts.

- *Do:* Evacuate the house and call the fire department immediately. You may get the fire out or you may not, but if you don't get it out, you're going to need their help. If you do get it out before they arrive, have them check for residual fires hidden in walls or the attic before they leave. They will not get mad at you for calling if you extinguish the fire before their arrival.
- *Do:* Throw in any chimney fire suppressant you have on hand. These are available most places where wood-burning stoves, chimneys, or chimney cleaning equipment are sold. Familiarize yourself with the manufacturer's recommendations for use *before* you need one of these in a crisis. If you have a chemical fire extinguisher, use it to put out the fire in the stove; then shut all vents, doors, etc. to deprive the chimney of oxygen.

  Some recommend having plastic sandwich bags on hand filled with the same fire suppressant found in dry chemical fire extinguishers. They drop one in the top of the chimney. The heat melts the bag and coats the chimney, (hopefully) putting out the fire. Take some extras just in case you need more than the first one! Baking soda might work too. However, *be very cautious about getting on the roof near a chimney that's on fire.* If the fire is burning inside the attic, the roof could collapse. It's best to use a long stick and drop the bags in from a safe distance.
- *Do:* Shut down draft controls to restrict as much air as you can from entering the stove or chimney.

- *Do:* Very carefully inspect the chimney after any fire to check for cracked pipe or liners, loose mortar in brick or stone chimneys, or any other damage the chimney may have sustained.
- *Do:* Install a chimney thermometer to monitor flue temperatures.
- *Do not:* Throw, spray, or pour water in or on the stove or in or on the chimney. It could turn to steam and react very violently (blowing stove pipes loose or burning you or others nearby), and/or the rapid cooling may crack steel stoves, shatter glass stove fronts, and crack chimney liners. It may also wash smoldering coals out and into the room, setting more fires inside the house. If you must use water, dampen a paper towel, newspaper, or small cloth towel or washrag and toss it in the stove. Repeat as needed.

One final note on chimneys: If you purchase, rent, or commandeer an old house or cabin with a brick or stone chimney, do not use the existing chimney until it passes a thorough inspection. Many of these relics have loose mortar, bricks, or stones that allow flames and poisonous gasses to leak through. My father had a house catch on fire due to loose mortar in an old brick chimney. It got put out before it caused excessive damage, but the whole family was busier than a one-legged man dancing the Charleston. Don't take chances.

There're few things as satisfying as the heat from a hot stove on a cold morning, but always be safe. In the case of wood-burning stoves, you really are playing with fire. Don't let it get out of control.

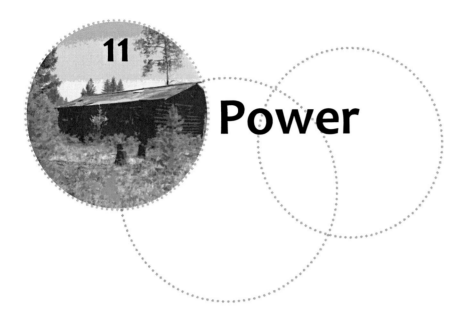

11 Power

My first exposure to a home power system came when I visited the remote homestead of a retired electrical engineer. What a setup! Housed in its own building was a diesel generator, shelves lined with batteries, and a control panel that looked like something designed by NASA. Outside stood a three-legged tower with an elevated platform crowded with solar panels that automatically tracked the sun. When he told me the price tag of his investment, I came to two conclusions. First, he had more money than sense. Second, there was no way I'd ever be able to live off-grid without reverting to a nineteenth-century lifestyle. Well, I was wrong on both counts!

That was more than 15 years ago. I have a lot of respect for those who have the knowledge and cash to set up a classy solar energy system. Our problem is that we are not electrical engineers, nor are we financially able to build a system that can compete with the power company. We needed something simpler and cheaper. What we've learned is that, with careful planning and self-discipline, it is possible to have your electrical needs met without investing a fortune in a home power system. Here's how we did it.

STEP ONE: REDUCE DEMAND

When you think of electrical demand on a home power system, visualize a 50-gallon barrel of water. Water is running into the barrel at the rate of five gallons per minute. The barrel also has a hose attached to the bottom in which the water is running out at the rate of 10 gallons per minute. It doesn't take a rocket scientist to see that the water is running out twice as fast as it's going in. Obviously you're going to run out of water. To avoid that you need to (a) reduce the rate the water flows out, or (b) increase the rate the water flows in, or (c) put in a larger reservoir, or (d) some combination of the above.

To apply this to powering your home, think of the water flowing in as your charging system (solar, wind, or hydro power). Think of the barrel as the storage system, which would be your batteries. The outflow is the amount of electricity you are using.

Obviously, wind and solar energy outputs fluctuate according to the amount of sunlight or wind you have available, so you're going to need batteries to store the electricity they produce. The more batteries you have, the more electricity you can store. The more or larger solar panels or wind generators you have, the more power you can produce. The problem is that batteries, solar panels, and wind generators are expensive. In addition, you're going to need an inverter to convert the electricity stored in the batteries from direct current (DC) to alternating current (AC). Good inverters are (like everything else!) expensive, and the larger the inverter the more it's going to cost.

Cutting back on your electrical needs is the most economical way to save money when setting up your home power system. By cutting back on your needs, you can get by with a smaller inverter (which saves

ELECTRICAL APPLIANCE WORKSHEET

(Note: Multiply volts times amps to get the watts needed to run the tool or appliance.)

Electrical appliance	Watts start/run	Need rating	Frequency used	Home-power friendly?	Available alternatives	Notes or comments

you money), fewer batteries (which saves you money), and fewer or smaller solar panels or wind generators (which also saves you money).

Using the spreadsheet provided, you should first take an inventory of everything on your property that uses electricity. Include all electrical appliances and tools, from the big electricity hogs like the water heater and electric range all the way down to the bulb in the porch light.

Second, list the number of watts the item uses. (This figure can be found somewhere on the tool or appliance.) Some appliances use an amp rating instead of watts. Multiply the amps by the voltage to get the number of watts needed to run the appliance.

For example, our vacuum cleaner uses 12 amps, so 12 amps x 120 volts = 1,440 watts. The reason you'll need to know how many watts are required is because solar panels, wind, and gas generators and inverters are rated in watts rather than amps.

Some things may have two listings. One is the number of watts needed to start the tool or appliance; the other is the number of watts needed to run it once you get it going. Be sure to figure in the higher number! Your power supply must be adequate for the highest figure.

Third, decide if this is an essential or nonessential item. This is entirely subjective. If Mom can't do without her hair dryer or curling iron, then list it as

While floor sweepers won't replace vacuum cleaners, they make sense for those quick jobs between major cleanings. Plus, they don't require a single watt of electricity.

batteries never go completely dead, or (b) you have an automatic backup system such as a generator that will kick in if your batteries get low. There is a third option, if you don't mind the clock flashing the wrong time or waiting a bit longer for the television to come on: you can put in a separate switch to completely shut off the power to the unit and end the drain on your batteries. We use multiple-outlet power strips for this purpose.

Overall electrical draw may or may not be a red flag in this category. A microwave may draw a lot of power but only run for a few minutes, whereas a toaster oven with the same watt rating may be in use 30 minutes or more. Obviously the toaster oven will use a lot more power in the long run. The same might be true of a circular saw when compared to a vacuum cleaner. They may both use the same amount of power per minute, but the vacuum cleaner will be in use for longer time periods than the saw.

Sixth, are there practical, nonelectric alternatives to the appliance? For example, a refrigerator or freezer may not use much electricity per hour, but you'll need to have power to it 24 hours per day, seven days a week. That's no big deal if you're on the grid, but when you're generating your own power it can be a problem. That doesn't mean you must go without a refrigerator. There are propane- and kerosene-powered models that work just as well, so under this column you'd write "propane." The same could be done for electric lights. There are multiple alternatives, such as lights powered by propane, kerosene, or gasoline. There are also low-wattage, fluorescent, and LED lights that work quite well.

An example from our household is the toaster. We like toast but due to the high electrical draw, the toaster didn't make the move with us. However, we still have toast. We just make it on top of the woodstove. So under this column we wrote "use woodstove." If the woodstove isn't in use, we make it in a skillet.

Seventh, under this section write in your thoughts on the appliance in question. For example, you might want to write in "purchase propane refrigerator" or "purchase gas dryer." One thing to be aware of is that some gas appliances must have electricity to operate. We once owned a gas stove that had electrically powered oven controls. No electricity? No cake or cookies!

essential. The same goes for Dad. If he can't imagine life without his table saw (or hair dryer?), then it too must be listed as essential.

Some things might be considered essential even if they are seldom used. We kept our waffle iron even though we use it only occasionally. You decide what you want to keep.

Fourth, estimate how often and how long it's used. If it's daily, then put daily (or weekly, etc.). For example, if you have a laptop computer that you use five hours every day for work, put "5h/5days" in this column.

Fifth, is it home-power friendly? For example, some televisions, VCRs, and DVD players draw power even when the unit's power switch is turned off in order to maintain memory, run clocks, or energize "instant on" circuits. If you have appliances like these, you'll want to be sure that (a) the

STEP TWO: CONSERVE ENERGY

This should be a basic part of everyone's routine whether on or off the grid. I can guarantee that if you go to someone's off-grid home, you will not see lights left on in unoccupied rooms, nor will you see a television left on with no one watching it. People tend to be wasteful when there's an abundance. Use only what you need. You don't need lots of overhead lighting if you're just lounging on the couch reading. Use an LED reading lamp drawing less than three watts.

Other ways to conserve include using energy-efficient appliances whenever possible. Laptop and notebook computers need far less power than desk models, and a 15-watt fluorescent bulb or 5-watt LED light puts out the same amount of illumination as a 60-watt incandescent bulb. Replace high-draw items with energy-efficient models.

When you live off-grid, you gain a new appreciation for the electrical power you use. Conservation becomes a way of life.

STEP THREE: BE SHREWD

Don't run things like the vacuum cleaner, iron, clothes washer, and computer at the same time. This saves you money in several ways.

First, your inverter must be able to handle the maximum load placed upon it. If you use the vacuum cleaner *and* the toaster *and* the microwave at the same time, you'll need a 3,300-watt or larger inverter. If you run them one at a time, you can get by with a 1,500-watt inverter. Quality inverters are expensive and as the output of the inverter increases, so does the price. By spreading out the demand, you can use a smaller inverter. A smaller inverter is a cheaper inverter. A cheaper inverter means more money left in your pocket, or extra money that can be used for other projects.

Second, spread the power usage out over the week.

Remember the water into the barrel vs. the water out of the barrel? If the bottom spigot is closed, the 50-gallon barrel will fill completely in 10 minutes. Then if the spigot is opened all the way (10 gallons per minute), it will take 10 minutes to empty it. (Remember, you are also putting in five gallons per minute while the spigot is open.) If you open it only three-fourths (7.5 gallons per minute),

One easy way to reduce demand is to use reading lamps instead of overhead lighting when curled up with a book. Use LED or low-watt fluorescent bulbs to reduce demand even more.

it will be 20 minutes before it runs dry. *That's twice as much "run time" by reducing your draw by only 25 percent.* Your home power system works the same way.

When you produce more electricity than you are using, the batteries store it. The batteries allow you to use that excess power during times your system is not charging or when you're using power at a faster rate than the system is replenishing itself. Anytime you draw power out faster than you put it in, you're going to run your batteries down. By spreading out the work, you'll get by with fewer batteries and a smaller generating system.

So, instead of doing the wash, vacuuming, and all the other housework in one day, spread it out. Do the wash on Tuesday and Thursday and vacuum on Monday and Friday. Spend the other time reading, working in the garden, walking, or doing something that doesn't require electricity.

STEP FOUR: USE A GENERATOR FOR BIG-DRAW ITEMS

A 5,000-watt generator is much cheaper to purchase than a 5,000-watt inverter. When we fire up the generator, we forget about step three. We may use the fast charger to charge batteries and use the electric grain mill (much faster than the hand mill!) to grind enough flour and corn to last a month or more. We might also run the vacuum cleaner and/or use any high-draw power tools like my shop equipment or the cement mixer.

If you have the resources to build a first-class system, then more power to you! For us that wasn't an option. Rather than live totally without electricity, we designed a sustainable system that would meet our needs at a price we could afford.

At this point we wouldn't hook up to the grid if they ran the power lines under the front porch. We've pared down to the point that we need very little electricity, and we sure don't need monthly electric bills staring us in the face. If you're looking into producing your own electricity, you have four options: solar, wind, hydroelectric, and fuel-powered generators. Each have their strengths and weaknesses, and to have your bases covered, you'll probably need a combination of two or more.

ELECTRICAL TERMS AND OPTIONS

In the rest of this chapter we'll be looking at ways electricity is measured, so before we get into more detail on your four power options, it's appropriate here to define some terms and look at formulas for converting volts to amps to watts. We'll also take a quick look at your options for wiring hookups and voltage systems.

Basic Terminology

A volt is a "unit of electric potential difference: the unit of electromotive force and electric potential difference equal to the difference between two points in a circuit carrying one ampere of current and dissipating one watt of power. Symbol V."

An ampere (or amp) is an "SI unit of electric current: the basic unit of electric current in the SI system, equal to a current that produces a force of

2x10-7 newtons per meter between two parallel conductors in a vacuum. Symbol A."

A watt is a "unit of electrical power: the international SI unit of power equal to the power produced by a current of one ampere acting across a potential difference of one volt. Symbol W."

An ohm is a "unit of electrical resistance: the SI unit of electrical resistance, equal to the resistance between two points on a conductor when a potential difference of 1 volt produces a current of one ampere. Symbol Ω."

Now that we know what we're talking about, we'll continue . . . right?

Wrong! Unless you're an electrical engineer, the definitions above don't make a lot of sense, so we'll try to understand them on layman's terms.

Now, please don't take the following analogies to extremes. I've oversimplified some complex interactions in order to grasp some fundamental concepts.

Volts are a measurement of electrical force or pressure. The higher the number, the greater the power.

Amps are the instant "volume of flow rate" of electricity. It's kind of like a "gallons per second" measurement.

Watts are the measurement of the total volume of electricity used in a specified time period of one hour. Kind of like "gallons used in one hour."

Ohms refer to resistance in electrical terms, i.e., the restraining force electricity must overcome to flow. We're not going to compute resistance values but, as we'll see later, it is important to understand how resistance affects our power system.

Volts, amps, and watts are all measurements of electrical energy, and all three are present whenever electricity is being used. The problem we have is that devices that generate electricity and the devices that use electricity don't always list all three on the data plate. Generators of all types (a solar panel is a generator that's powered by the sun) are rated in watts. Appliances are rated in volts and sometimes amps and sometimes watts.

So, we need some formulas for determining watts, amps, and volts in order to properly size our home-power system. As long as you know two of the numbers, you can determine what the third number is.

To determine the number of watts produced or used, multiply the volts times the amps. V (volts) x

A (amps) = W (watts). People who do this for a living have different letters for their formulas, using E for volts, I for amps, and P for watts (and they have their reasons for doing so), but I'm trying to keep this as simple as possible, so let's just stick to V, A, and W. Otherwise I'll get confused, and I have enough problems with that already.

So, here are the formulas in the easiest format I can think of:

Volts are computed by dividing watts by amps (W / A = V)

Amps are computed by dividing watts by volts (W / V = A)

Watts are computed by multiplying volts and amps (V x A = W)

We'll be using these equations throughout the rest of the chapter, so you might want to mark this page or write them on a piece of paper and keep it close by.

Series vs. Parallel

You have different options for connecting the wiring of batteries and solar panels. The first is called a parallel circuit. Batteries and solar panels have one positive and one negative post or wire. In a parallel circuit, you connect the positive outlets together and negative outlets together. Your voltage remains the same but the amperage increases. For example, if you connect two 12-volt batteries together in parallel, positive to positive and negative to negative, your voltage remains at 12 volts but your amperage doubles.

If you connect the batteries in series, connecting the negative terminal to the positive terminal, you double the voltage but the amperage stays the same. This is how you can use two 6-volt batteries in a 12-volt system, or two 12-volt or four 6-volt batteries in a 24-volt system.

It works the same way with solar panels. Connect the panels in parallel circuits and the voltage stays the same but the amperage increases. By connecting them in series, you can increase the voltage but the amperage stays the same.

Voltage Options

In a low-budget, off-grid power system, you'll most likely be working with either a 12- or 24-volt battery/panel/inverter system. In deciding what's best for you, remember that voltage is electrical pressure. A 24-volt system is more efficient (meaning less power is lost in transmission) than a 12-volt system. Some manufacturers recommend a 24-volt system anytime the panels are 50 feet or more from the charge controllers and batteries.

Another reason for a 24-volt system is that while your voltage doubles, the amps remain the same. Charge controllers are rated in amps, so you can run twice as many panels (producing twice as many watts of power) through your charge controller if you go to a 24-volt system instead of a 12-volt system. If you're opting for a large inverter (over 2,400 watts), you'll probably have to go to a 24-volt system to handle the power demands.

The drawbacks to a 24-volt system? Everything will have to be purchased in pairs (or foursomes). It takes two 12-volt batteries connected in series to power a 24-volt system. If one battery goes bad, you'll have to replace both batteries. (You should never mix old and new batteries because the old batteries will draw the new batteries down.) If you are running four 6-volt batteries and one goes bad, you'll have to replace all four of them. If you buy 12-volt panels and wire them in series, you'll have to buy them in pairs. On a low-budget homestead (or any low budget for that matter), it can be a challenge to come up with that much money. You'll need a 24-volt battery charger to run off your generator. And finally, if you switch to a 24-volt system after beginning with a 12-volt system, you'll have to buy a new inverter (and possibly a charge controller) because they are not interchangeable between voltages.

Our system is 12 volts for several reasons. We began with one 12-volt panel and a used 12-volt, 800-watt Trace inverter. After that we added another panel, then three more, and then four more. To change to a 24-volt system, we'd have to buy a new inverter ($1,000 and up!) and at least one more panel. That's not going to happen anytime soon!

My recommendation is to stick with 12 volts unless your panels are over 50 feet from the battery bank and charge controller or you need an inverter rated over 2,400 watts.

SOLAR POWER BASICS

Off-grid solar power systems are fairly simple and consist of solar panels, charge controller, batteries, inverter, and wiring. If your power needs are miniscule, you can get set up with just a solar panel and a battery.

It's important to note here that the system I'm describing is for off-grid applications only. Setting up a grid-tie system is more complicated, so if that's your plan, consult a professional.

Solar Panels

Solar panels are the primary component of most off-grid systems. Solar panels are nothing more than electrical generators powered by the sun. Like any other generator, they're rated by their output in watts, volts, and amps.

Shopping for solar panels can be confusing. When you talk to a salesman, you're going to hear terms like "single-crystal silicon," "polycrystalline silicon," and "thin film." These are the three most common types of solar panel construction. Single-crystal silicon and polycrystalline silicon are the old standbys of solar modules. I could bore you with more details about how they're made and how they work, but I won't. There is lots of information on the Internet going into more detail, so if you want to know more, check out some of those websites.

The most important information for the low-budget homestead or retreat is that the original single-crystal silicon panels manufactured in the 1950s are still working today, as are panels using poly-crystalline technology from the 1980s. Their major strength is durability.

Thin-film panels are a more recent development and use various technologies to produce electricity. All tend to be less efficient than single-crystal silicon and polycrystalline silicon panels, and their durability factor is not yet known. However, manufacturing costs for these panels are lower than traditional methods, and installation can be much more creative. Some are even transparent enough for use over windows and tough enough to be walked over. (Okay, you have to be really careful walking on them, but it can be done.) When applied to a roof, they are not as susceptible to wind lift as traditional solar panels. This technology bears watching.

You'll hear a lot about efficiency and performance of different materials and manufacturing

These are the first five solar panels we purchased. I made the tower out of salvaged pipe and bed rails. We manually turn it to face the sun several times during the day. If we're going to be gone, we just lock it facing south.

techniques. The differences are minimal. Generally, a more efficient panel has smaller external dimensions. In other words, a 100-watt panel with a higher efficiency rating isn't as large physically as a 100-watt panel that's less efficient. You'll also hear about some materials charging sooner and later than other materials. Again, the difference is slight. Compare prices and see if more "efficient" panels are worth the cost. Remember, a 100-watt panel still produces 100 watts of power no matter what it's made of.

Another issue regarding photovoltaic (PV) panels is watt ratings. Watt ratings are the maximum power a solar panel can produce at its maximum voltage. It's very important that you understand this. Suppose you're considering a panel rated at 10 amps, 20 volts, and 200 watts. However, your charge controller will limit charging voltage to 15 volts to protect the batteries from being overcharged (note: voltage will vary according to battery type). To compute watts, you multiply volts times amps. At 20 volts output, the solar panel will produce 200 watts of power (20 volts x 10 amps = 200 watts total output). However, the charge controller will limit voltage to 15 volts, so now the output is 150 watts (15 volts x 10 amps = 150 watts). You just lost 25 percent of the solar panel's maximum output when you installed it in your system.

Now don't get mad at the manufacturer or salesman. It's just the way things work. Solar panel manufacturers make many models for different needs. You'll need a solar panel with at least 15 volts to have enough power to adequately recharge your batteries in a 12-volt system. (Actually, due to other losses in the system, you'll want a panel with an 18-volt or higher rating.) If you needed to produce 1,000 watts of power and thought your five 200-watt panels would do the job, you're going to be disappointed. In reality, the most they can produce at 15 volts is 750 watts. To ensure you can produce 1,000 watts, you'll need two more panels. Just remember to do the math when you're sizing your system and purchasing panels.

There is an exception to this, however. I'll cover that in more detail in the section on charge controllers.

Tracking the Sun

When a panel is "tracking the sun," it moves so that it faces the sun directly through its entire arc across the sky. Solar panels produce most efficiently with direct sunlight. In the northern hemisphere, solar panels are usually pointed south. They begin charging as soon as the sun rises but only hit peak output when the sun is shining more or less directly

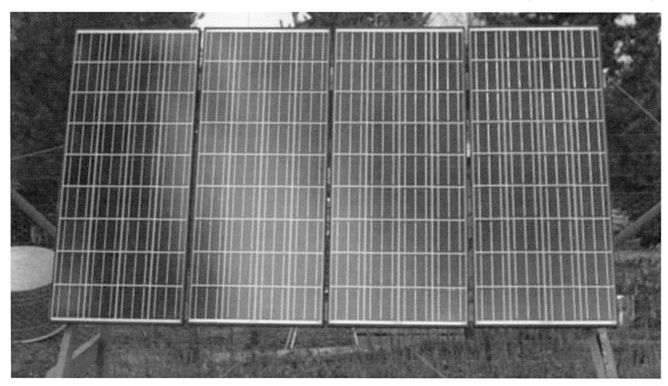

These are the last four panels we purchased. We have them temporarily mounted to a south-facing wooden frame.

on them. Tracking devices increase the length of this peak output by turning the panels to keep them facing the sun. In some cases you can gain 40 percent more output with a solar tracking system. Depending upon price and local conditions, it might be cheaper to increase your charging output with a sun tracker than to acquire more solar panels.

Plans are available over the Internet for making your own tracking system, or you can purchase one that's factory made.

We have our panels set up on a pivoting mount. I change the angle depending upon the season; then we pivot the panels by hand during the day so that they continually face the sun. If we aren't going to be home during the day, we lock the panels in the south-facing position.

Batteries

Batteries store the excess power from your solar panels for use after the sun goes down or at times when your electrical loads are drawing out more than the panels are putting in.

You'll have to choose between deep-cycle batteries, golf cart batteries, sealed (or not) batteries, lead-acid batteries, absorbed glass mat sealed lead acid (AGM) batteries, gelled electrolyte sealed lead acid (GEL) batteries, and a few others that aren't so well known. Each one has strengths and weaknesses. For the most part you'll get what you pay for, so make your choice wisely.

The two most common types for the low-budget homesteader are the deep-cycle batteries

This is a deep-cycle battery purchased at Wal-Mart. It's rated at 125 amp-hours and comes with an 18-month free replacement warranty.

sold to boat and RV owners, and similar (but larger and more durable) golf cart batteries. Golf cart batteries are usually 6 volts, so you'll need multiples of two for a 12-volt off-grid system and multiples of four if your system is 24 volts. The big complaint about regular deep-cycle batteries is their short lifespan in off-grid applications. The big drawback to other types is the price. This is another area in which you'll need to do your own research before you make a purchase.

You'll hear different arguments about the lifespan of different types of batteries, and while these may be good for comparative purposes, there's no way anyone can tell how long your batteries will last. The most important factors in battery life are how many charge/discharge cycles they go through, how deep these cycles are, and how well you maintain them.

When a battery is discharged and then recharged, it's called one "cycle." The problem is that not all cycles are equal. The deeper your battery is discharged, the more wear the battery sustains. Additionally, not bringing the battery up to full power before discharging it increases wear further. For this reason, it's recommended that you have enough battery capacity to power your needs for five days without having to charge them. It may sound like a lot, but if your storage capacity is too low you'll be discharging the batteries to a deeper level in each cycle, which shortens battery life considerably.

Battery life is extended significantly if you discharge them no more than 50 percent of their capacity before recharging. Batteries are rated by how much energy is available from the full charge level down to the level where the battery is completely discharged. In order to ensure that the batteries are never discharged below 50 percent, some manufacturers recommend that you determine how much storage capacity you need and then double that. For example, if you need 100 amp-hours (Ah) of storage capacity, it's recommended that you purchase the number or size of batteries required to achieve 200 Ah of storage capacity.

If you get in the habit of running your batteries in a continually discharged condition, it will shorten their life. This often happens in the winter, when daylight hours are short and nights are long. In these circumstances, batteries may never reach full charge during the day, so you're constantly using them in a partially discharged state.

Batteries function best in temperatures between 60°F and 80°F. Temperatures over 100°F shorten battery life significantly. Colder temperatures require higher charging rates to bring the battery to full charge. If you store your batteries outside, it's best to get a charge controller that compensates for battery temperature.

Batteries Are Rated by Voltage and Storage Capacity

Voltage is the number of volts the battery is rated at. This might be 2, 6, 12, or 24, depending upon battery type. Most batteries used for home power systems will be either 6 or 12 volt. Most charge controllers come in 12-, 24-, and 48-volt configuration. In order to get the correct voltage, you put together different combinations. Two 6-volt batteries connected in series will equal 12 volts. Four 6-volt batteries connected in series will get 24 volts, as will two 12-volt batteries. Unless you really know what you're doing, I wouldn't recommend anything larger than a 24-volt system. (More on that later!)

There are two ratings you'll want to take a look at. The first is the ampere-hour (Ah) rating. The amp-hour rating is the maximum sustained amperage that can be drawn from a fully charged battery over a specified time period (usually 20 hours) until the battery is dead. For example, our deep-cycle batteries have a 125 Ah rating. That means

they can be discharged at a constant rate of 6.25 amps for 20 hours.

The second measurement is reserve capacity. Reserve capacity is the amount of minutes a battery *can maintain a useful voltage* under a constant 25-amp discharge. Our batteries have a 205 (minute) reserve capacity, meaning that they can power a 25-amp load for 205 minutes without falling below 10.5 volts.

It's important to note that these figures are for comparison purposes only. A battery's performance is impacted by its age, number of discharge/recharge cycles, depths of discharge/charge, and temperature. Even the condition and size of the wiring and connectors affect the amount of power that's available. Wiring that's too small or connections that are loose (a fire hazard!) or corroded may significantly reduce storage capacity and output.

Remember the formula for converting volts and amps to watts? Multiply your volts by the amps to get the number of watts produced. A 12-volt battery with a 125 Ah rating will produce 1,500 watts over a 20-hour time period. If you take the 1,500 and divide it by 20 (total number of hours), you'll see that this battery, under ideal conditions, will power one 75-watt lightbulb for 20 hours. In theory, it will power a laptop computer (50 watts) for approximately 30 hours. In reality, it won't last that long!

If you figure the watts of power available by the amp-hour rating compared to the reserve capacity

The Wal-Mart deep-cycle battery viewed from the top. It has a reserve capacity rating of 205 amps. We purchased four of these at $80 each. We've since replaced them with six golf cart batteries.

rating, you'll get different numbers of watts available for use. The reason is that the rate of discharge impacts the amount of energy the battery can release. You'll get more power from a battery if you discharge it at a lower rate. The higher the discharge rate, the quicker the battery runs out of power.

Charge Controllers

The charge controller keeps the voltage at levels that will bring your batteries to a full charge without harming them.

In normal operating mode, the charge controller varies the voltage output of the solar panels according to the charge level of your batteries. If your batteries are low, the controller increases the allowed voltage to bring the batteries up to full charge quickly (bulk charge setting), then maintains that voltage (absorption phase) for a specific time period to ensure that the batteries are fully charged. Once that occurs, it reduces the voltage (float or maintenance phase) to prevent overcharging the batteries.

Controllers also put your batteries through an equalization cycle every three to four weeks. In the equalization cycle, the inverter steps up the charge level in order to ensure that the battery is deeply charged. As a battery is discharged, the outside of the plates discharge faster than the inside does. Because the charge level on the surface is less than at the center, the center of the plates slowly transfer power to the outer surface so that the voltage is equal throughout the plate. When the battery is recharged, the opposite occurs and the surface of the plates charge faster than the center. If the battery is discharged again before the inside of the plates are fully recharged, you can end up with a situation where the inside is constantly undercharged and begins to deteriorate. The solution is to periodically overcharge the battery in order to "force" the electricity deeper into the battery's plates. This is called equalization. When done properly, it will extend the life of your batteries significantly.

Charge controllers are rated in amps and your solar panels are rated in watts. So once again, you'll have to do a little math to choose the right one.

Most charge controllers require that you wire your solar panels in parallel circuits. In other words, you may have six panels with a maximum output of 20 volts each hooked into a 12-volt system. That means the maximum voltage pushing the

This is one of our charge controllers (we have three) that limits the voltage from the solar panels to prevent the batteries from overcharging.

electricity to the charge controller is limited to 20 volts. Remember, voltage is electrical pressure. I said earlier that some solar panel manufacturers recommend that you go to a 24-volt system if the panels are over 50 feet from your batteries and inverter because you need the extra voltage to overcome the resistance in the wiring. You could go to larger wire, but you may end up spending more for the wire than you did for the panels!

There is a charge controller manufactured for off-grid use that alleviates the problem. It's manufactured by Outback and allows you to wire your panels in series, which increases the voltage going to your charge controller. The increased voltage from your panels to the inverter means you lose less power in transmission and you can get by with smaller size wire. It's a much more efficient system than conventional charge controllers, sometimes increasing output by 30 percent, which means you may need fewer solar panels. The downside (there's always a downside!) is that they cost considerably more than other charge controllers. My advice? Do the math to decide if the increased cost is worth it.

Inverters

The charge controller takes the power from the solar panels and charges the batteries with it. The inverter changes the 12 volts of direct current (DC) from the batteries to 120 or 240 volts of alternating current (AC). (If your system is 24 or 48 volts, the inverter converts that to 120 or 240 volts AC.)

If you're not familiar with AC/DC current, AC (alternating current) is what you get through your power lines. It's electricity that changes direction from positive to negative. The number of times it changes direction every second is called a cycle or, more commonly, "hertz." In the United States, our electric grid functions at 60 hertz (the electricity changes direction 60 times each second). It's sometimes different in other countries. DC, or direct current, is electricity that travels in one direction only. Your vehicle operates on DC, while your household appliances operate on AC. You can purchase DC appliances, but it makes more sense to just buy an inverter and use the things you've always used.

Inverters have outputs of 120 and/or 240 volts. The 240 volt will give you a little more versatility. It is better, for example, if you're going to run your well pump off your inverter.

Sine Waves

When looking at inverters, the first thing you'll probably hear about are "sine waves."

Remember that in a 60-hertz (Hz) system, the direction of flow changes 60 times every second. The best way to visualize this is to draw a horizontal line, then put a "plus" above the line and a "minus" below the line. Now draw a bunch of waves through the line so the peaks and valleys are an equal distance above and below the line. If you could see electricity as it enters your house from

This is our 800-watt Trace inverter. It's currently dedicated to the refrigerator because our other inverter can't handle the constant load. It has a built-in battery charger that automatically recharges the batteries when we run the generator.

the power line, it would look like this as it changed direction from positive to negative. These are called sine waves. The problem with inverters is that they are digital. They can only turn electricity on or off. To represent this, you draw the horizontal line again but instead of drawing waves intersecting the line, you make a vertical line above the horizontal line, then a short line parallel to the horizontal line, then another vertical line that goes an equal distance to the negative side, another horizontal line, then another vertical line up . . . repeating this process over and over again. This is what an inverter would do to change DC into AC current.

The problem is that many electrical appliances cannot function with such abrupt changes of direction, so inverter manufacturers have what they call modified sine wave inverters. Instead of switching the current from positive to negative so abruptly, they do it in stages. Instead of having lines going straight up and down with horizontal "ledges" between them, the inverter does it more like a staircase. The smaller the steps on the staircase, the more "pure" the sine wave. Thus the difference between a pure sine wave inverter and a modified sine wave inverter is the size of the steps. A pure sine wave is like riding on the waves with a gentle rise and fall with the swells. A modified sine wave is more like riding on top of a piston in your vehicle's engine. You go straight up, hang for a split second, then go straight down again, hang for a split second, then get slammed upward again (and again and again and again). Now, which would be the gentlest on your body? It's the same with electrical gadgetry. Pure sine wave inverters lengthen the life expectancy of your electrical appliances.

Duty Cycles or Continuous Watt Ratings

Inverters have what are called "duty cycles." Duty cycles are the amount of time a device can work at a specific percentage of maximum output before it needs to rest. It's the difference between running and sprinting. A person running a marathon goes at a slower pace than a person running a hundred yard sprint. Inverters are the same. If you put a huge load on them, it won't be long before they must take a break. However, if you use a smaller load, they'll continue working for hours without stopping.

Our Trace inverter is rated at 800 watts output for 30 minutes before it overheats and shuts down.

This is our 1,000-watt Xantrex inverter. We purchased this unit at Costco for $49.99 a few years ago. It replaced a similar model that was fried by lightning.

If the load is 600 watts, it can go for 60 minutes, but if the load is 575 watts, it can go forever without needing a break.

This is one of the first places where you can tell a difference between a high- or low-quality inverter. Low-quality inverters have a much lower 100 percent duty cycle than better quality (more expensive) inverters.

Surge Watts

Many appliances need an extra boost to get started. Since these surges are short-lived, most inverters and generators have enough power available (called "surge watts") for a few seconds to get things started. As soon as the appliance or tool is running, its power needs diminish substantially. Here's another place you can tell the difference between a low- vs. high-quality inverter. Our 800-watt Trace inverter's surge watt capacity is 2,400 watts, while our cheaper 1,000-watt inverter's surge rating is . . . 1,000 watts.

A word to the wise on surge ratings and duty cycles. I can't say that every cheap inverter is over-rated, but I can say that the four different brands of cheap inverters we've used have all performed significantly under their manufacturer's assertions.

So, should you avoid cheap inverters? Not necessarily. Just be aware that a cheap inverter will probably not do all that the manufacturer claims. Again, this is my experience in using them. You may have different results.

Battery Charging

Inverters can be purchased with or without built-in battery chargers. There is conflicting information from different manufacturers on the good and bad points of the built-in charger. Naturally, the people who don't build chargers into their inverters say that an external charger is the best way to go, while the people who do build chargers into their inverters say that their way is best.

I prefer inverters with built-in chargers, primarily because they are tailored to the specific needs of off-grid power. Your solar panels' charge controllers have different charge levels, depending upon the stage of charge your batteries are in. When the batteries are low, they increase the charge voltage to around 14.9 volts to bring the batteries to full charge quickly, then maintain that higher voltage (called the "absorption" phase) for a time period to ensure that the battery's plates get a full charge. After that, they reduce the voltage to approximately 13.0 to 13.5 volts for what's called the "float" or "maintenance" setting to keep from overcharging the battery. The charger built into the inverter changes voltage to accommodate each stage. Automotive-type battery chargers are limited to a compromise setting of approximately 13.8 volts maximum. If you have a 24-volt or larger system, an automotive charger probably won't be an option for you.

That being said, we used an automotive charger for a couple of years with no apparent ill effects on our batteries.

Inverters with built-in chargers usually have transfer switches so that when you start your generator or plug it into the grid (with grid-tie systems), the inverters automatically transfer the load from your batteries to the outside power source and also activate the charger to recharge your battery bank. In some cases, the switch is done so quickly that your computer won't even know it happened.

In my opinion, the nicest thing about built-in chargers is that they're less work. When we used an automotive charger, I had to start the generator and manually connect the charger to the battery bank. Now I just start the generator and the inverter makes the connections.

Sizing the System

Okay, we've looked at reducing your power demands and using your power wisely. We've looked at solar panels, batteries and inverters, and charge controllers. So what's next? Now we put it all together.

Remember at the start of the chapter how we looked at the electrical appliance worksheet? Now it's time to put it to work. Begin going across the rows and adding things up. Suppose in line one you have a laptop computer that takes 50 watts of power and you use it five hours a day for five days a week. That gives a daily total of 250 watt/hours per day.

A small, energy-efficient refrigerator draws about 200 watts of power. A refrigerator only runs about a third of the time on average, so the per-hour watt rating is approximately 67 watts. It's on 24 hours a day, though, so the daily total will be 1,608 watts.

We could continue with examples, but I think you understand what we're doing here, so go on down the list estimating your daily electrical consumption. If an item (such as a vacuum cleaner) is used only sporadically (like four hours a week), don't worry

When we're low on power, you see us working by kerosene lamp and running our computers on their internal batteries.

about it yet. What we're looking for is a starting point to estimate how large your battery bank and solar generating capabilities need to be. Once you've finished the daily tally, add them all up. For example, we'll assume 250 for the computer, 1,600 for the fridge, another 500 for the television, and maybe 400 for lights. The total per-day usage is 2,750 watts.

Now look at the occasional-use items. The vacuum cleaner used four hours a week at 450 watts per hour totals 1,800 watts per week. The washer at four hours per week using 400 watts per hour totals 1,600 watts per week. Go on down the list and total these up, then take that number and divide it by seven. This is the average use per day. It's important to include these items; otherwise your system will not be large enough.

So we have 2,750 watts per day plus an average of 486 watts per day for occasional-use items, which means that our total daily energy use estimate is 3,236 watts. We'll round it off at 3,250 watts. *Write that number down!*

Resistance

Remember when I said that we'd look at resistance later? It's now "later." Resistance in any form is the force that impedes motion. In electrical jargon, it's called "ohms." Think of it as the difference between bicycling on the level with no wind to bicycling uphill against the wind. There is no such thing as a perpetual motion machine because resistance makes that impossible. For example, if you draw

100 watts of power from a battery, it takes 125 watts of power to recharge it to its previous level because of internal resistance in the battery. When electricity flows through the wiring from your panel to the batteries, some of the energy is used up to overcome the resistance in the wiring.

If you used 3,250 watts of electricity, you will have to generate approximately 30 percent more than that to compensate for the resistance in the system. That means you'll have to be able to generate 4,210 (rounded up from 4,207) watts to replace the energy you've used.

If you're using solar panels, they only charge when the sun is up, and they only charge at their maximum under direct sunlight. There are charts available online showing how many hours of direct sunlight you'll receive in the part of the country you live in. What you'll want to know is how many hours of direct sunlight you can expect on the shortest day of the year. Why? Because if you size your system for the most hours of sunlight you can get, you won't be able to generate enough electricity on the short days. If you size the system to be adequate on the short days, you'll (almost) always have adequate power all year long. If you don't want to look up the charts, use five hours as a default figure. This means that your solar panels need to generate 4,210 watts in five hours, or 842 watts per hour (round up to 850). You'll need enough panels in the right combination to meet that number.

So far we have:

- 4,210 watts daily use
- 850 watts in solar panel output

Your charge controller must be adequate for the solar panel's maximum output. You can use two or more charge controllers if necessary. (That's what we did when we added four more panels to our system.) Another thing you can do is go to a 24-volt system rather than a 12-volt system. With a 12-volt system you'll need one charge controller rated at about 75 amps or two rated at approximately 40 amps.

Now we have:

- 4,210 watts daily use
- 850 watts in solar panels
- 75-amp charge controller (or an equal combination of smaller controllers)

Batteries should be able to power all your needs for a minimum of three days, with five days being preferred. So take 4,210 multiplied by three for a total of 12,630 watts. Batteries are rated in amp-hours, so we divide 12,630 watts by 12 volts to get 1,052.5 Ah for three days. Round it up to 1,055 Ah. If your batteries are rated at 125 Ah each, you'll need nine batteries to get you through three days. For five days storage capacity, you'll need 21,050 watts divided by 12 volts for 1,755 Ah storage capacity. Again, using the 125 Ah number, you'll need 15 batteries.

Now, batteries are rated under ideal conditions. By the time you add the inverter, wiring, connections, and temperature variations, you're going to lose 25 to 30 percent of your power to that bad guy known as resistance (and some other factors), so increase your battery estimates by 25 percent. That means you'll need 11 batteries for three days reserve, or 18 batteries for five days reserve.

Now we have:

- 4,210 watts daily use.
- 850 watts in solar panels
- 75-amp charge controller (or an equal combination of smaller controllers)
- 11 batteries for three days, or 18 batteries for five days

The inverter must be large enough to handle the highest load expected of it, including surge watts. When it comes to inverters, the price will vary significantly. It is especially true that you get what you pay for when purchasing an inverter. Lower-priced units are lower priced for a lot of reasons. That doesn't mean they won't be functional. Just be aware of their limitations.

In our case here, we've got the vacuum cleaner and washing machine listed as the highest draw items. Assuming that neither are used at the same time, we can figure the run watts at 450 and the surge watts at double that, or 900 watts. The fridge may be on at any time, as will the computer. So on a day when the computer is on (50 watts) and the television (100 watts), vacuum cleaner (450 watts), and fridge kick on (200 watts), you'll be drawing 800 watts of power. You might have a few lights on as well, which, with LED lighting, may only be another 30 watts, but it all adds up! So we have a continual load at 830 watts (50 + 100 + 450 + 200 + 30 = 830 watts). Plus, you'll have the surge loads when the vacuum and refrigerator kick in. These may add another 650 watts to the total for a few second's time, so your inverter must be capable of at least 830 watts continual load and 1,480 watts surge load. The cost of a 1,500-watt, heavy-duty inverter with a built-in battery charger will run approximately $750.

Now we have:

- 4,210 watts daily use
- 850 watts in solar panels
- 75-amp charge controller (or an equal combination of smaller controllers)
- 11 batteries for three days, or 18 batteries for five days
- 1,500-watt inverter

The estimated cost of these items will be approximately:

$1,913	850 watts in solar panels	
	(a good price will be around $2.25 per watt)	
250	75-amp charge controller	
	(or an equal combination of smaller controllers)	
990	11 (12-volt) batteries for three days, or . . .	
1,620	18 (12-volt) batteries for five days	
	($90 each)	
750	1 inverter	
$3,903	Total cost for a three-day battery bank, or . . .	
$4,533	Total cost for a five-day battery bank	

These prices do not include wiring and hardware for mounting panels.

There are a couple of things to keep in mind here.

First, this is a very minimal system for the majority of people.

Second, it would have cost us over $27,000 to get hooked up to the grid. That's *twenty-seven thousand dollars!* And then we'd have been stuck with monthly utility payments and the periodic power outages. *If* you can cut down on your electrical needs, you can literally save thousands of dollars and still enjoy the benefits of electricity.

A quick note regarding the solar power systems sold in various sporting goods and other outlets. We've had a lot of questions about how good these are. The answer is that you get what you pay for.

These tend to be very low watts—generally around 60—with a cheap inverter and charge controller. If all you want to do is power up a small television to watch a video now and then, and run a notebook computer or maybe a few lights at night, they'll do fine. Don't expect much more than that. They aren't a bad deal as long as you remember their limitations.

The key to a low-budget system is to pare down to the bare essentials. We began without any electricity and even though we have a decent system now, we've made a commitment that we will never become dependent on electricity again. It's nice to have, but it's not essential for our lifestyle.

WIND POWER

Wind power can be a good thing under the right circumstances. The wind is not limited to daylight hours and often blows during cloudy or stormy weather, when solar panels are useless. We have a small, 400-watt wind turbine to supplement our solar panels. In my opinion, this is the best option if you have steady wind available. At this time, these range in price from $500 to $750. You'll either need to build a tower or purchase one (about $500 and up). They need to be mounted 30 feet above any obstructions (trees, tall buildings, etc.) within 300 feet. Otherwise the turbulence will keep changing the wind's direction. Every time the wind changes direction, even slightly, the turbine blades slow down while the body realigns itself to the new direction. Those I have experience with have a slight vibration when working. You get used to it and even like it when you think of the power it's creating. Many of these small turbines have charge-controllers built in. Some are convertible from 12 to 24 volts.

If you have good, dependable wind, these are great as stand-alone systems with a battery backup. You can get up to 24 hours per day of charging out of these if the wind blows steadily. So if your daily use is 6,000 watts, you'll need enough solar panels to produce 1,200 watts per hour on five hours of-direct sunlight. A 600-watt wind turbine at maximum power, running 24 hours, will produce 14,400 watts in that same 24-hour period. That takes a lot of wind, but even at 50 percent of maximum output, it will produce over 7,000 watts of power. If the wind is sporadic, they're still good for supplemental power in addition to your solar panels.

WATER POWER

Hydropower is the Cadillac of electricity generation if you have access to the power source (flowing water). We don't have it but would love to. The best thing about it is that it's available 24 hours a day, seven days a week. If you have a good volume of water available, it's a steady output as well. Even if you don't have a large volume, it's still a good deal. If you can count on generating electricity 24/7, you can use a smaller power plant to accomplish your goals.

Remember, when you sized a solar panel generating system, you had to size it to produce all the power you needed on the shortest days of the year. That may have only been five hours of actual power generation. The panels had to do a full day's work in five hours. A hydroelectric generator has 24 hours to do its work. It's like the race between the hare and the tortoise. Slow and steady can get you a long way with less wear and tear on your generating system.

GENERATORS

While generators are not a solution to long-term self-sufficiency (as in a total collapse of the world forever), they do have a place on the off-grid homestead. At least they do until you've figured out how to do without them. I've seen a few people try to set up an off-grid home without a generator, and they've usually regretted it. Even with the reliability of hydropower, there'll be times when the system needs to be shut down for maintenance. Therefore, it's wise to make a good choice when purchasing a generator.

If you go the opposite extreme and are planning on running a generator all day long, think about this: a generator that will survive continuous duty is very expensive to purchase and run. If you thought your previous electric bills were pricey, wait until you purchase gasoline, diesel, or propane to run a generator 4,380 hours a year (12 hours per day for 365 days). We've known people who've tried it. Not only is it expensive, but the noise will not be appreciated by neighbors who moved out to the woods seeking peace and quiet. In addition, if your goal was to conserve our natural resources, running a generator for hours at a stretch will definitely defeat that purpose.

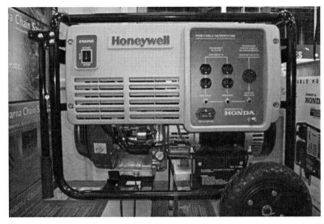

This is a 7,000-watt portable generator. These are good for occasional use to charge a battery bank or run tools and equipment, but they are not the best option for continuous duty.

Generators come in all sizes, and prices ranging from $100 for new 1,000-watt portable units to thousands of dollars for large generators mounted permanently with automatic transfer switches. With these you don't even have to be home when the power goes out. Everything is automatic, from turning the unit on when the grid goes down to turning it off when things are back to normal. But before you rush out to purchase a standby generator, there are some things to consider.

Size

Begin by reviewing your power demands. Any generator you purchase needs to be large enough to run essential appliances or tools.

Generators, like inverters, have two watt ratings. The lower number is "running watts." This is what the generator can be expected to produce as long as it's running. The higher number will be the "surge watts." This is what the generator can produce for a short length of time (a few seconds) without overheating or damaging the unit. Be absolutely sure that your generator can handle the highest surge load you have listed.

In my experience, it's better to have a generator that's larger than you think you'll need rather than one that's barely adequate. You may need extra power to overcome resistance in any extension cords you're using. Also, older appliances or tools may use more power than they did in their prime. Likewise, as a generator ages it may not be as powerful as it was in its youth. Other factors such as altitude, temperature, humidity, and fuel quality may keep your unit from reaching its maximum potential. I'd recommend a generator rated 25 percent or more above your estimated power needs.

Why not just buy a big generator and not worry about watt ratings? Big generators produce more power but use more fuel. (A serious consideration if you're going to run it more than a few hours!) Larger generators usually cost more than similarly equipped smaller units. Finally, smaller (portable) generators are easier to transport.

Outlets

If you're using a portable unit, you'll need to know if it has an adequate number of outlets with amp ratings that will meet your needs. Of course, you can use power strips and other devices to connect multiple cords to a single outlet, but be sure these devices are rated to handle the current those loads will demand from them. Generally, the smaller the watt rating, the fewer outlets you'll have. Outlets should be convenient to use where they won't be subjected to fuel spills or oil leakage and where you won't get burned by the exhaust.

Noise

Noise is rated in decibels. Anything over 90 decibels (db) can damage hearing. Some typical sound levels include residential area without traffic (40 db), normal conversation (60 db), normal street noise/average radio (70 db), truck without a muffler (90 db), lawn mower (100 db), trains (110 db), and jet aircraft (140 db).

If you plan on using a generator at a secluded retreat, noise is definitely a concern. The only thing that will advertise to the world that you have power and they don't faster than a loud generator is a brightly lit house at night. Even with temporary power outages in the suburbs, you're going to have neighbors calling to use your generator.

Stealth reasons aside, there are other reasons you should be concerned about noise. It's difficult to concentrate on tasks when being bombarded with noise, and in already stressful situations it's even worse. Plus, hearing can be permanently impaired by high noise levels.

Fuel

Most portable generators use gasoline. Other fuel options include propane, natural gas, and diesel fuel. Each has good and bad points. Whatever fuel you need, be sure to have an adequate supply on hand for emergency use.

Gasoline is the most common fuel choice for portable units. It is easily obtained now and can be stored in large or small containers. You'll have to take some precautions to store it long term, including finding a suitably safe location and using fuel stabilizer.

Propane has a long shelf life and can be easily stored in small or large tanks. It's not as convenient to purchase as gasoline but is still easy to get. If you use a bulk tank, you'll have to have a propane company fill the tank, but you won't need to buy any for a while either. Most propane generators are permanently mounted.

Natural gas is clean burning and, as long as the gas lines are functioning, you have an unlimited supply of fuel piped to your home. It's usually available in times of crisis. Earthquakes are the most dangerous threat to natural gas lines. These units are permanently mounted.

Note: some natural gas-powered generators require higher gas pressure than that used by your home's supplier. If this is the case, find out if your gas supplier can install a meter with the higher line pressure. If they can, you'll need a separate gas regulator to reduce the pressure for the other appliances that use natural gas for fuel.

Diesel fuel is easily obtained and the least flammable of the four (making it safer to store). Bulk delivery is available if you have a large enough tank (talk to the nearest supplier). Diesel generators are usually large and may be either portable (usually mounted on a trailer) or stationary. You can use what's known as "red dye" fuel for off-road use and avoid some of the taxes levied on automotive fuels.

A note on fuel consumption: most generator manufacturers list a fuel consumption rate at 50 percent load. Just remember that the higher the load, the more fuel it will consume. Plan your fuel reserves accordingly.

Portable or Stationary

Stationary generators are usually mounted on cement pads. Permanent installations are easy to use and can often be wired so that you can start and run them from the house. Also, most stationary units have bulk tanks so you don't have to refuel every few hours. The disadvantages include expense (they're usually large and pricey), and you can't take it with you if you need to bug out.

Portable units are, well, portable. You can take them with you if you leave or take them where the power is needed. If the weather's extremely cold, you can bring them in the house to warm them up prior to trying to start them. (Something to think about when it's 25 below outside!) Portable units are also cheaper. Some disadvantages include small fuel tanks that will need frequent refueling, and extension cords must be run from the generator to the appliance(s) or your inverter/charger. Make sure extension cords are properly sized to carry the electric load, as overloaded cords can overheat and cause fires.

Small units (under 50 pounds) can be moved by carrying. Mid-size generators usually have wheel kits available to roll them to new locations by hand. Large generators can be mounted on trailers to pull behind a vehicle.

Any generator used in an enclosed area may cause a buildup of carbon monoxide or other harmful gases. Set them up outdoors in a well-ventilated area away from living quarters.

Liquid or Air Cooled

Liquid-cooled generator engines run at a more consistent temperature for longer engine life and better performance. These are usually large, stationary (sometimes trailer mounted) generators designed to run nonstop for days, weeks, or months at a time. Almost all portable gasoline generators are air cooled. They function quite well for emergency or occasional use.

Design Features

Now that you have the basics down, it's time to look at some optional features.

- Overhead valve engines start easier and last longer than side valve engines.
- Cast-iron cylinder sleeves in aluminum engines reduce cylinder wear and extend engine life.
- Low oil shutdown switches shut down the engine if the oil level drops below a safe operating level. Don't rely on them; I've seen them fail. Keep a close watch on oil levels.
- Electric start enables easy starting without having to pull a starter rope. If you want this, be sure your unit comes with a battery! (Some don't!)

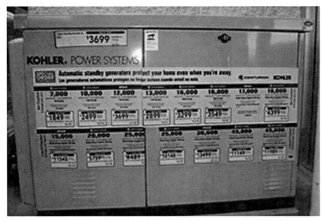

This is a Kohler permanently mounted generator available from Lowes. These are continuous duty units powered by propane or natural gas. Some are large enough to power your entire house. The problem with these and similar generators is that they depend on fossil fuels, which means they are not good long-term options for the self-sufficient homestead or retreat.

- Idle control switches let the engine throttle down when no load is present. They save fuel and wear on the generator and cut down on noise levels while idling.
- Hour meters keep track of how long the motor's been running. (Helpful for maintenance purposes.)
- External/replaceable oil filters extend engine life.
- Full power switches allow you to switch off the 240-volt output to get more power to your 120-volt outlets. This is especially useful when powering air compressors and water pumps with a minimally sized generator.
- Brushless alternators require less maintenance and produce power that's more suitable for sensitive electronic equipment.

There are other options available (mainly on high-end, permanently mounted units). Most of these add to the cost and aren't necessary unless you're powering a hospital or office with a lot of electronic equipment. Use your own judgment when talking to a salesman.

• • • • •

If you're looking at long-term survival, no power option mentioned is foolproof. In our case, we can continue to generate electricity for quite some time, but we ask ourselves why? Eventually, components will fail and, depending upon the event that brought us to that point, such as a massive solar flare or electromagnetic pulse, there may not be any functioning electrical devices left. The way we've dealt with this possibility is to find ways to live comfortably without electrical power. Aside from food preservation, the most important thing to consider is housing. That's the subject of the next chapter.

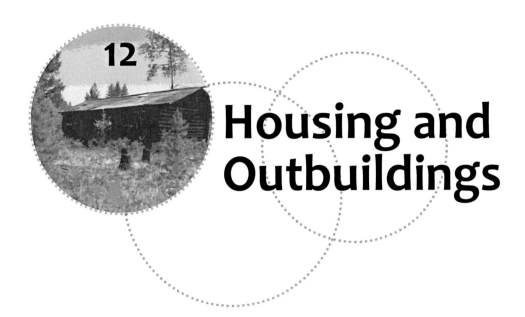

12 Housing and Outbuildings

I f you have lots of money, you can purchase your property with a home and all the outbuildings you'll ever want, or you can hire them built as needed. However, that isn't going to be an option for many people reading this book. You'll be building some or all of your structures, just like I did. Most of what I know about construction was learned through reading and assisting real carpenters. Some of it was learned by the things I did wrong. Hopefully, the information below will help you avoid some of the mistakes I made.

BASIC CONSTRUCTION METHODS

One of the things that's vitally important on the low-budget self-sufficient homestead or retreat are construction skills. You can never know enough. At a minimum, you should be aware of such different construction methods as conventional frame construction, timber frame, pole buildings, log cabin building, slip form, stone work, adobe, cement block, straw bale, cordwood, earth shelter, the fundamentals of using cement, and a basic understanding of foundations in their various forms (post, cement, stone, wood, etc.).

You don't have to be proficient in all of these, but you should have a general understanding of each in order to cover all your bases. By having multiple options in mind, you can take advantage of local windfalls. In our location there is lots of timber and rocks. That means we can harvest building materials suitable for stone, log, or cordwood construc-

tion methods and possibly save ourselves a lot of money. We can also cut timber on our own land and have it milled into dimension lumber for conventional frame construction. We can also cut trees for timber frame construction if that works best for us.

For the same reason, if you can gain some knowledge of unconventional designs—such as using tires or sandbags, tree house construction, and other less-known methods—you'll also be ahead of the game.

Remember, the reason most people are going the low-budget route is because they don't have a lot of money. Housing and building projects get expensive in a hurry, so you want to keep those costs down everywhere possible.

If you really want to expand your options, get some knowledge of permanent ancient shelters such as hogans in their various forms, cliff dwellings, and adobe structures. It's especially beneficial to learn what kind of primitive housing was used in climates like yours.

Have some temporary shelter ideas in mind. Wall tents with wood floors used to be a common sight in frontier towns. On backwoods properties today, you'll still see teepees built on wooden platforms and lived in year-round.

Get in the habit of exploring ghost towns, historical villages, museums, theme parks, old farmsteads, or other links to our past. Don't forget modern-day historical reenactments such as mountain man rendezvous, American Indian festivals, and other living history events. Learn how people lived in the days when they used local materials to construct their homes and outbuildings.

Watch the news, paying special attention to living conditions in developing countries. If you get a chance, go on a short-term mission trip to a third world country with your church or some other sponsoring agency. If that's not an option, find a group that is going and send along a camera. Tell them to take lots of pictures of the houses and outbuildings. Evaluate the positives and negatives of their homes and shelters.

As always, read, read, read! Peruse the Internet, especially YouTube, but don't forget websites focused on primitive living and skills. Talk to your elderly neighbors and relatives. Ask questions about their life and housing when they were kids.

As you do your research, you'll want to be looking at some specific areas. First, foundations. What's the purpose of a foundation? Why do banks and mortgage lenders usually require permanent foundations? Is there anything wrong with just laying logs, rocks, or cement blocks on the ground and building on top of them? How much technology do you need for each method? What kind of tools or equipment are required?

Second, building construction materials. What was used and why? I've seen buildings constructed of boards, rocks/stone, cordwood, straw bales, tires, and sandbags. How well does each type of material hold up over time? What skill level is required to use the material? What kind of equipment or technology is needed? I know of African tribes that used dried cow dung for covering outside walls. Some primitive peoples lived in grass houses, some in sod houses, and others in earth-sheltered lodges. Holes dug into hillsides were often used as permanent shelters in pioneer times. (In modern times we do the same thing, only we line the walls with cement and add more windows!) Natives and pioneers generally used whatever materials were available locally. Remember, we aren't just looking at walls but also the roof and foundation materials. Can you name three roofing materials other than asphalt or fiberglass shingles or metal roofing? (Be creative! I've seen roofing materials made from tire sidewalls, old newspaper plates, and hand-split wood shingles, just to name three.)

Third, how do you obtain structural integrity? By this I mean how do you hold the structure together? Let's face it: gravity and wind are not a

This shows the south and west sides of the cabin when we first took possession of the land.

One of the first things we did was cut out large openings for windows. With an off-grid home, large windows are needed to let in lots of light. A couple of years earlier, we had purchased the windows from Habitat for Humanity for $10 each. We put tarps over the roof until we could afford roofing materials.

building's friends. How do you put everything together so it doesn't fall down around your head? Be familiar with things like "top-plate," "sill-plate," and "headers" as they apply to frame building construction. What's a "load-bearing wall"? Where do you start the walls when using masonry or stone construction and why there? What are the different ways of notching logs for log building construction, and what're the advantages/disadvantages of each? Why do you see so many triangles in post-and-beam construction? Under primitive conditions, how do you set a ridge beam in place so that it's strong enough to bear an earthen covering? (North American Natives used forked posts set in the ground.)

Fourth, how are the structures insulated, heated, or cooled? Many primitive cultures had chronic lung problems due to smoke inhalation. Others had chronic death problems due to being burned when their homes caught on fire. What –materials have the most insulating value for your climate? What terrain features help with heating and cooling? Rows of evergreen trees planted on the north side offer shelter from cold north winds, while large shade trees offer cooling shade in hot climates. Study so that you don't have to reinvent the wheel every time you build.

Fifth, what's the lifespan of your building method? Let's face it: "permanent" means different things to different people or cultures. Suppose you can build a structure in two months for nothing except the labor involved that will be useable for 10 years. Now suppose you can build a structure with an estimated 30-year lifespan, but it'll cost you $40,000. Which is the better deal? That may well depend on your future plans and your financial situation.

What the low-budget homesteader or survivalist needs to know is the principles of construction rather than be an expert in one type of building method. (Although if you're an expert, that can help too!) The reason is versatility. If you have a good grasp of the five basics above, you can experiment or freelance as well. The cost of conventional building methods is often considerable, while unconventional or primitive structures can be built for nothing other than the labor involved. There's also the time factor. Suppose you've just moved onto some undeveloped land and you must have shelter built within a very short time frame? In homestead or survival situations, it might be handy to have some unconventional ideas up your sleeve. If it's an EOTWAWKI situation, your options might be severely limited. You'll need to be able to adapt your building method to the materials on hand.

The best thing about knowing construction fundamentals is that you don't need to fabricate a bunch of structures to have some basic understanding of how these things work. This is one area where you can read, study, and put that information away in your mind for future reference. But the time to do it is now. Shut off the television and go to YouTube, or head for your local library and hit the books. Buy copies of the best books to keep as reference manuals for the time when you have to put your knowledge into practice. (Used books can often be purchased for far less than new and will serve you just as well.)

The more knowledge you have, the more options you'll have. Be as versatile as possible to take advantage of the natural resources around you. One of our neighbors looked over the mountains and remarked that it wasn't that long ago when the settlers provided almost everything for themselves and needed very little money for anything. And she was right! You don't need piles of money to live a self-sufficient life, but you do need creativity, knowledge, skill, and determination.

DESIGNING THE NONELECTRIC OR OFF-GRID HOME

My wife and I purchased our property with some clear goals in mind and years of experience living off the grid. Our goals were to simplify our lives, cut expenses to a bare minimum, and be as self-sufficient as possible. Most of us have experienced power outages and their results. We wanted to be set up so that if the power went out for a day, week, month, year, or forever, we'd still live in comfort. That doesn't mean we don't have anything electrical in our house, but we resolved to keep our electrical usage to a minimum and 100 percent optional. Here are some of the things we did.

Evaluate your space needs carefully. Our original home was a 16 x 32-foot log cabin nestled in the woods of northwestern Montana. We added a 12 x 16-foot, 1½ story addition to the south end. The main living area (kitchen, dining, and living room) is completely open. At the time we made our move we still had four children at home, so the six of us lived in 512 square feet of space that first winter. Even after the addition, we had only 896 square feet of living area. Was it cramped at times? Absolutely, but we made it and so can others.

Large homes are difficult to heat and cool, increase tax and insurance expenses, and are more costly (and more work) to maintain. If you have piles of money, these aren't important issues. However, if you're living on a tight budget, you can save a lot of money over the years by building small and using that space wisely. If it comes down to a long-term survival situation and you have to cut and haul wood by hand or purchase coal or oil out of home-generated income or trade goods, you'll be thankful for the small house.

Modern houses are designed for forced-air heat. That means you've got to have a fan to blow (force) the warm air through metal ducts and into the individual rooms. As long as the electricity is working that's not a problem, but in a disaster or long-term survival situation, you're going to be mighty cold in the winter. Even in normal times you'll be married to the utility company, with sky-high heating bills all winter long. If you're living off-grid, you'll be looking at huge solar arrays and battery banks to handle the power needed by furnace fans.

When heating with wood or any type of space heater, there are some things to think about. First, the heat kind of emanates from the stove, so it'll always be warmer near the stove and colder farther away. Also, it's easier to get warm air to flow up than it is to get it to flow through doorways or around corners. If you're designing your home for passive heat circulation (not forced air), keep everything open. We once viewed a cabin that had upstairs bedroom lofts on each end, with an open ceiling between them. The upstairs lofts stayed very warm in winter . . . and summer! (More on cooling the house later.)

Position your stove in a central location and locate bedrooms upstairs over the main living area. What you don't want is a single-level home with long hallways going to rooms far from the stove. Mobile homes are extremely difficult to heat evenly without forced-air furnaces. The long, narrow hallways do not allow the heat to reach back bedrooms and living quarters.

Another thing you don't want is high, cathedral-type ceilings. Remember, warm air rises, so you'll be heating a huge volume of empty space above your living area. By the time it's warm at floor level, it will be over 100 degrees near the ceiling. Ceiling fans will help some in that situation, but then you're depending on electricity. If you're on grid, this means one more monthly bill to pay; if you're off-grid, it means you'll have to generate electricity to power the fan(s). As mentioned, winter can be a bad time for solar power. The days are shorter and the nights are longer, which will tax your panels and battery bank.

This is what the inside looked like when we took possession. There had been a room partitioned off in the back (south end) of the cabin, but vandals had broken the drywall, and a leaking roof and pack rats had destroyed the insulation in the ceiling.

The first thing we did was a major cleanup of the interior. It took hours of scrubbing to get the plywood floor clean. We set up tents inside for the kids, and my wife and I slept in a double bed with mosquito netting over it. The original builders had stuffed fiberglass insulation between the logs, and a lot of it had fallen out. The mosquitoes came and went at their leisure.

Shielding from cold north winds is always a good idea. Many older homes had lots of south-facing windows but no windows at all on the north side of the house. It's common in prairie country to see wind breaks planted on the north side of the homestead. These are usually east/west rows with two or three rows of evergreen trees and a couple rows of large shade trees. Their only purpose is to protect the home and it residents from harsh winter winds.

Where we live, cooling a house in summer isn't much of a problem, mainly because we live in mountains near the Canadian border and have very little summer! For many people, though, summers are long, hot, and humid, and the heat must be dealt with.

When you look at houses built before forced-air heating and air-conditioning, you notice some design features that modern houses, with their artificial climate controls, don't possess. Before the forced-air era, houses had large, covered porches and lots of outside windows and doors for ventilation. To cool a nonelectric home in summer, two things were needed: shade and ventilation.

Houses built in the southeastern United States often had large verandas. These were great places to relax in the shade after a hard day's work. Many had summer kitchens built outside so that the heat from the wood-burning cookstove didn't heat the house excessively during meal preparation.

Windows were numerous, as were French doors. These let in lots of cool air to take full advantage of evening summer breezes. Windows had awnings to shade room interiors from direct summer sunlight. Shade trees were prized for their beauty and practicality on hot summer days. When I was a child, we often slept outside on hot summer nights. Not only was it cooler, it was an adventure!

In the southwestern United States, homes were built with adobe bricks. The thick walls moderated heat during the day and helped warm the house on cool desert nights. These often had outside porches as well as many windows and doors for good air circulation.

Obviously, these features won't cool a home as well as modern air-conditioning, but if you're serious about low-budget homesteading, you're going to have to put up with some inconvenience.

WINDOWS ARE YOUR FRIEND!

Home designs have changed over the years to take full advantage of forced-air heating and cooling. Electric lights replaced kerosene lamps, so less external light and fewer windows were needed. Windows also have less insulating value than walls, and since windows were no longer necessary to provide light and ventilation, they became smaller and fewer were installed. Modern houses and apartments with their artificial climate controls are designed more like a refrigerator than a home. All of that is okay if you live on the grid and like sending money to the utility companies, but if you're going to live a low-budget and/or off-grid life, windows are your friend.

We got some criticism from neighbors when we remodeled our cabin for full-time off-grid life because one of the first things we did was cut huge holes in the walls and install lots of double-pane windows. We were warned that we'd never be able to keep the place warm in winter. They were wrong. The first really cold spell (-25°F) found us toasty warm while others struggled to keep their homes at 60 degrees and wore sweaters inside. Did we lose some heat through the windows? Probably, but other factors in our home design made up for the heat loss, and the windows provided many other tangible benefits.

There are some very practical reasons to have lots of windows in your low-budget homestead. First, there's the economic standpoint. It costs money to generate electricity to run lights. We have people express awe at all of the "free" electricity we have. We remind them that it isn't free. We bought our solar panels, wind generator, inverters, charge controllers, and batteries. While most of those components have a 20-year or longer life expectancy, the batteries still need periodic replacement. Do we spend less on electricity than most people? Yes. Is our electricity free? No! As you saw in the previous chapter, the best way to save money on electricity is to not need much of it. Windows let in lots of natural light, which means we need less energy to power lights. They also help heat the house on sunny winter days. If you don't believe me, just ask the cat who likes to bask in the warm sunlight streaming through the windows.

The second reason has to do with long-term

survivability. If, at some point in our future, for some unknown reason, the power would ever be switched off permanently, our need to make our own light is greatly reduced. We have plans to make our own lamp oil if we must, but it will take extra work that could be used more beneficially doing other things. Because of the number and size of our windows, every room in the house is usable from sunrise to sunset. Others we know are not so fortunate and must have artificial light all day long.

The third reason, even though we can't prove it scientifically, may be most important of all. Having outside light streaming in, even on overcast days, helps fight against the cabin fever and depression that many get during winter.

We also have skylights. Visitors to our cabin are often surprised by how bright and cheerful our home is without a single artificial light burning.

LIGHTS AND LIGHTING

Despite the emphasis on natural lighting, there'll still be times you'll need artificial illumination. We used kerosene lamps the first couple of years living here. We also used propane lights and pressurized lanterns burning Coleman fuel. While propane- and gas-powered lights do put out a lot of light, we found the noise they make objectionable. The fuel also gets expensive if you use them a lot.

In our experience, candles were the worst option. They put out very little light and are more expensive than buying kerosene or Coleman fuel. The best to be said about candles is that they can be made from local materials using primitive technology. If we reach that point, the world will really be a dark place.

If you use kerosene, a couple of options are available. The first is the wick-type lamp. These are really nothing more than a high-output candle. When we used ours, we usually lit one lamp and set it on the kitchen table. We'd all gather round the table to read, play board games, knit, or whatever other activity we did in the evenings. The soft, yellow light was enjoyable, and having everyone gathered around the table brought us closer together as a family. Those were good times. Don't expect one lamp to illuminate an entire room, though. Despite what you see in movies, kerosene lamps are for close-in work only. Buy some extra wicking and chimneys. Wicks get used up and chimneys get broken.

I measured and chalk lined the window openings and began cutting the holes with the chainsaw. The tarp in the background kept the sawdust confined to the area where I was working. The board at the left was used as a vertical guide for cutting.

As a temporary fix, we shoved more fiberglass insulation between the logs to keep the mosquitoes and cold air out, which made the cabin insect and air tight. We put new flooring down and had new roofing installed. We installed another door on the south wall. Once the windows were all in and caulked, it began to feel more like a home. The cabin was almost ready for the first winter.

The second kind of kerosene lights are the mantle-type Aladdin lamps. We have some experience with these but found them to be too much hassle and returned to the wick-type lamps. They do put out a lot of white light, and one will illuminate a small room, but in our experience they need constant adjusting and readjusting to prevent carbon buildup on the mantle. I've been told it was because of our altitude and that may be correct, but we sold ours at a yard sale years ago and have never regretted it. If you go this route, be sure to keep extra mantles on hand. Few stores carry them, so if you break one, its replacement will have to be ordered through the mail.

If you use kerosene lighting of either variety, here are some things to watch for. First, buy the shortest lamps you can get. We cut a hole in the center of an aluminum pie plate and set it over the lamp's chimney for a shade. It keeps the light reflected down on the tabletop and out of your eyes. If the lamp is tall, the reflector will be above eye level and it'll be shining directly into your eyes. Second, yellow highlighting on books (e.g., Bibles) becomes invisible under kerosene lights. Use a dark color such as blue or pink if you highlight as you read. Third, we use number 1 fuel oil in our lamps. It's much cheaper than kerosene and works just as well. It's also dyed red, so it looks nice. Some people prefer scented lamp oil. It's nice if you can afford it, but it will set you back a bunch if you're stocking up on it for the long term.

Now that we have our solar power system, we've gone to electric lights. The first couple of years we used low-watt fluorescent bulbs; then we bought our first LED (light-emitting diode) light. We paid around $30 for it. Thankfully they've come down in price as their use has increased.

A 25-watt, compact fluorescent bulb puts out light equal to a 100-watt incandescent bulb. The savings may not sound like much to someone on the grid, but when you're off-grid the savings make sense. If you have a 100-watt solar panel getting five hours of direct sunlight on a winter day, it will produce about 500 watts of power. That's enough to run a 100-watt incandescent light for five hours. In comparison, it will power a 25-watt compact fluorescent light (CFL) for 20 hours. Or you can use the CFL for five hours and have enough power to run a laptop computer for eight hours.

LED lights use even less energy. The last pack of LED bulbs we bought used 1.5 watts to produce light equal to a 40-watt incandescent bulb. If we used three of them, we'd have output equal to a 120-watt incandescent bulb but use only 4.5 watts of electricity.

We also use reading or desk lamps instead of overhead lighting most of the time. These are portable LED lamps that plug into wall outlets and direct their light down onto your book, computer, or whatever activity you're doing. Why light an entire room if you're sitting in your easy chair reading or sewing?

Finally, paint the walls and ceilings white or some other light color and use light-colored curtains or venetian blinds to reflect light.

GO PASSIVE

It wasn't that long ago that passive heating and cooling were the buzzwords of the environmental movement. That was before being green became a race for new technology. Now, there's nothing wrong with using technological advances in solar heating and cooling, but a lot of it is pricey anddepends on electricity to power pumps, fans, and thermostats. If you have the money to set these systems up, go for it! However, there are ways to harness the sun that don't require huge amounts of money to build and use. Nor are they so complicated that you'll need a specialist to install or repair them.

Passive solar heat can be as simple as building your living room with a stone floor and a glass, south-facing wall. The sun warms the floor (and room) during the day; then the stone floor releases the stored heat through the night. The adobe homes built in the southwestern United States were examples of passive solar energy use. The massive walls absorbed heat during the day and released it at night. By morning they had cooled down enough that the interior stayed cool much of the day while the sun reheated the adobe walls. It wasn't as good as forced air or heat, but it was completely independent of outside power needs. In addition, it was built (often by the owner) very cheaply from locally available materials.

There are many variations of passive solar systems for heating rooms or water. Do some research. If you're building your home, incorporate as much passive solar energy into your design as you can. If you're moving into an existing home, there are ways to add solar heating to it to supplement your winter heating needs.

Passive solar hot water heaters can be used as stand-alone systems or with active systems. A stand-alone system supplies all the hot water used in your home. The advantage is obvious: no external energy sources are necessary. The drawback to these is that they are not always reliable. When the sun isn't available, their output diminishes severely.

If you're using them as an aid to preheat the water going into your hot water heater, you can save quite a bit in energy costs. Regular hot water heaters with the tanks and thermostats that maintain the water at a preset temperature are not energy efficient (especially on a low-budget, self-sufficient, off-grid homestead or retreat). Face it: you only need hot water sporadically during the day, so why keep 40 or more gallons hot all day and all night long? If you use an on-demand hot water system, then preheating the water through a solar collector makes a lot of sense. By raising the temperature of the water going into the water heater, you'll need less energy to heat it up as it passes through. You can have the best of both worlds. By installing a valve and a little extra plumbing, you can route the hot water from the solar collector around the hot water heater on those days you have lots of sun. That'll save even more money.

EARTH-SHELTERED HOMES

My wife and I agree that if we had to do this over from scratch, we'd go with an earth-sheltered home with a south-facing glass wall. We'd have sufficient roof overhang on the south to shade the wall in the summer, yet allow the sun to hit it full strength during the cold winter months.

Earth shelters have been used around the globe by indigenous people who needed a building material that was low maintenance and kept them cool in summer and warm in winter. The earth provides excellent protection from wind and extremes in the weather. Unless you live where drainage is a problem, it's difficult to imagine a locale where earth sheltering is not the best way to live.

The *$50 and Up Underground House Book* by Mike Oehler and Chris Royer is written for the budget-minded homesteader and shows what one can do with little money and a lot of grit. There are other books and websites dealing with earth-sheltered housing as well. Many earth-sheltered homes are as classy as any aboveground house you can imagine. Again, do some research. One thing you'll want to check is building codes. Some are written so stringently that it'll take some creativity to design an earth-sheltered home that meets all the requirements.

The following spring our materials arrived for the addition. (Some assembly required!) We purchased them at the Home Depot 65 miles away and had them delivered to our cabin. It was cheaper to pay them than to make multiple trips in our own vehicle.

The cabin with the 1 ½-story addition completed. Only basic construction skills were needed throughout the cabin restoration and construction of the addition. I'd already done some remodeling on previous houses we'd owned and had built smaller structures such as doghouses, storage buildings, and room additions. I'd taken every opportunity I could find to help professional carpenters, so I had some real-life experience to draw from there as well. This was my first time building a multistoried building, but after brushing up with some book study, I thought I could handle it. And we did. I learned from the mistakes I made building those small projects in previous years, so I was better prepared to handle the larger jobs when they came. It's not rocket science, but it's smart to gain experience in the little stuff before you tackle the big jobs.

TEMPORARY AND LOW-BUDGET HOUSING

These include campers, tents, teepees, yurts, dugouts, and other low-budget, temporary, or "replaceable" housing options. I'm going to include mobile homes in this section, for reasons I'll explain next.

Mobile Homes

First off, I have nothing against living in mobile homes. When it's wet outside, they are dry inside and when it's cold outside they are warm inside. That's pretty much the basic requirements of any shelter, so there's nothing wrong with living in one.

The reason I've put them here is that mobile homes are not designed for off-grid life. They are especially not designed for life without running water, if that's what you'll be doing. Their windows are small, so they are dependent on artificial light. They have long hallways and remote bedrooms, which make them difficult to heat without a forced-air furnace. The small windows and metal sides make them difficult to cool naturally during hot summer days. Many are woefully lacking in insulation. Water pipes are run alongside heating ducts to keep them from freezing in the winter. This means that if you are using radiant wood heat, the water in the pipes is more likely to freeze in cold weather.

However, if you have a mobile home, there are things you can do to make it more efficient for off-grid life. You'll need to open it up a bit for heat to circulate. You might also need to install more or larger windows for air circulation in summer. New windows are expensive, but we've purchased used windows from places like Habitat for Humanity and clearance sales at building supply stores, and by stopping where people are remodeling their homes and replacing their old windows. Sometimes they'll even give them to you just to have you haul them off. In most cases, you can retrofit these housing windows into a mobile home. If it's an older model with thinner walls, it may take extra work to accomplish, but it can be done.

You'll probably want to move the bathroom next to the kitchen to keep all your plumbing near your heat source and be sure that the kitchen is near the heating stove. In a homesteading, off-grid lifestyle, you're going to spend most of your time in the kitchen or living/family room, so you'll want to locate the stove in this area.

Railroad Cars

I've seen good things done with different types of railroad cars. If you begin with one designed for passenger use, you'll be ahead of the game because it takes less work to modify. Of course, you'll have to purchase it and arrange for transportation, which could jack up the price quite a bit, but if you can find creative solutions to these problems, a railroad car might be a good option. I've seen some nice (but small) homes made out of old rail cars. The caboose can be remodeled in a number of different ways to make it into a unique yet functional home. I've seen old coaches fixed up nicely as well. The best thing about rail cars is that they're constructed well and should last a lifetime.

Camp Trailers

You may be surprised that I'd rate mobile homes low on the list yet write favorably of camp trailers. The difference is that camp trailers are recreational vehicles and are designed for off-grid use. Of course, some models are more like mobile homes, so you'll have to be a little careful here, but if you can find one that's truly intended for camping rather than as a portable retirement home, you'll do okay. Many already have solar power installed and are equipped with both 12-volt DC and 110-volt AC power through an inverter. Their water systems are self-contained and have sinks, toilets, and holding tanks. Most also have three-way refrigerators powered by 12-volt DC, 110-volt AC, or propane. If you're going to use one in cold climates, you'll need to install an alternate heat source (preferably wood heat). Their furnaces go through a lot of propane trying to keep them warm.

Paladin Press has an excellent book written by M. D. Creedmore titled *Dirt Cheap Survival Retreat: One Man's Solution*. He uses a camp trailer for his survival retreat and has some great information. If you're contemplating this option, read his book.

Tents, Teepees, and Yurts

While I've read great reviews on how roomy, comfy, and easy to heat these are, I don't know anyone who uses them as permanent housing in cold climates. I know several people who've done it while they were building their house, but they all abandoned their tent dwellings as soon as the house was built. That's why I class them as temporary shelters. That plus the fact that their shells need to be replaced every few years.

If you live in a warm or moderate climate, one of these might be a viable long-term option. Historically, these home types have been the choice of nomadic people. Those living in the same place year after year usually opt for more permanent structures.

Indigenous or Native Shelters

Do some research on what indigenous people in your area lived in. They lived at a time when heating and cooling options were limited. Their housing reflected the qualities that were most important to them. Was it protection from wind? Heat? Cold? Rain? Learn from them before building your own home.

• • • • •

Remember, in hot climates you're going to need ventilation, shade, and insulation. In cold climates you're going to want insulation and protection from the wind. Any non-forced-air heating system needs open space to be efficient. Heat does not normally flow down long hallways and into distant rooms. Many old houses had multiple fireplaces or wood-stoves. Use heavy drapes or curtains to keep heat in at night.

If you're going off-grid, put in lots of windows to let in light. Keep interior colors bright to reflect light. Make use of passive solar energy wherever possible.

If you're aiming for self-reliance, use heat sources that do not rely on electricity and that use fuel that's local, low-tech, and plentiful.

If you're generating your own electricity, the best way to save money is to not need electricity. The second best way is to need very little electricity!

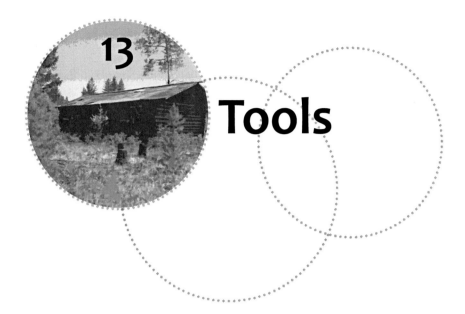

13 Tools

In the last year we've built a small, frame cabin on the property. It involved site leveling; cement work; constructing floors, walls, roof, and ceiling; installing windows and doors, shingles, siding, insulation, drywall, wiring, and a woodstove and chimney; and then giving everything a coat of paint. I replaced about 40 feet of drainpipe on a daughter's home and taught her some basic wiring for replacing worn electrical outlets and switches. I guess you could say that in the last year I've been a construction worker, electrician, plumber, roofer, drywall installer, and painter.

I've also welded up the solar panel mounting frame to add four more panels to the three already there, plus replaced all the attendant wiring from the panels to the charge controllers. We've replaced five 12-volt deep-cycle batteries with six 6-volt cart batteries for more electrical storage capacity.

I've soldered a neighbor's radiator after he hit a deer with his vehicle, repaired an aluminum canoe that had been hit by a car, tuned up the motor on our Cherokee, and replaced a leaking fuel line and changed the fuel filter, oil filter, and oil. I've welded up the exhaust on several vehicles, dismounted and remounted at least two dozen tires (including the rear tire on my motorcycle), repaired a couple of flat tires, replaced ball joints on two vehicles, replaced front axle universal joints on three vehicles, and replaced the thermostats on our home-built motor home.

I've tilled up the garden and built some new raised beds; gathered and composted old hay and

manure for the garden; built and repaired fencing; planted trees; cut down trees; removed stumps; cleared ground; cut and split firewood; sharpened and replaced the chains on our chainsaws; repaired the chainsaws, snow blower, lawn mower, string trimmers, and other small engines; cut hay with a scythe; and pumped and hauled water for the garden and livestock. I've cleaned the chimney several times in the past year.

I've dyed and waxed traps; ran a small trapline; skinned, stretched, dried, and sold furs; hunted and fished; and spent hours in the garden preparing ground and weeding.

I've trimmed and filed the hooves on horses, and ground the feed for all of our critters with a hand grain grinder. I've braided baling twine into collars and lead ropes for the dog and halters for the horse and goat.

My wife has canned and dried apples, oranges, bananas, herbs, potatoes, carrots, onions, squash, broccoli, celery, grains, wild grapes, huckleberries, serviceberries, rose hips, raspberries, rhubarb, blackberries, thimbleberries, mushrooms, butter, cheese, and the meat from the wild game we've harvested. That's in addition to the cooking, sewing, cleaning, laundry, and the countless hours it took to plant the garden, weed the garden, water the garden, harvest and preserve the garden crops, and put the garden to bed in the fall. She's painted our camper, chinked cabin walls, stained logs, and built storage buildings.

We've processed our own meat into steaks,

burgers, sausages, stew meat, and other cuts, and we've ground our grains to the consistency we desire, which might be flour in the cases of wheat and corn or in coarser textures such as corn meal. In addition to the grains we've grown, we've also bought grains in bulk and ground them in our hand-powered mill to feed to our chickens and other livestock.

And these are not exhaustive lists!

Now all of this is not to tell you what we do during the year but to help you see what skills, tools, and equipment are needed on the self-sufficient homestead.

In the first draft, I began this chapter with the question, "If you were a pioneer moving west, what would you have on your wagon?" I abandoned that line because I don't think it's a realistic way of looking at things. It might be a starting point for the absolute minimum in tools and equipment, but on your homestead you'll be able to have more than you'd carry on a covered wagon. So, if space and weight are not issues, what should you have in the way of tools and equipment on your self-sufficient homestead or retreat?

It's important to understand that your list will be different from ours and should reflect your personal skill levels and knowledge. I worked many years as a professional mechanic in every phase of automotive repair, including automatic transmissions, so I have some tools for that task that would mean nothing to most people. You most likely have professional skills or knowledge I don't possess and the equipment and tools that go along with that.

Your tool requirements may also be different depending upon the degree of independence you desire. We have hand tools to replace every power tool we own because we want to keep on, keeping on no matter what the future holds. We're also learning more primitive skills so that we can function at Stone Age levels should the need arise. That means we wouldn't need any tools except those provided by nature. But one result of learning primitive skills is that we recognize the value of "modern" innovations, especially steel tools, whether they're for digging, cutting, cooking, or sewing. If you've ever boiled water in a hollowed-out log, cut a tree down with a stone axe, or dug a hole using nothing but a stick or the shoulder blade of a deer, you'll know exactly what I mean. A few basic tools make the self-sufficient life a whole lot easier!

We have three reel mowers and one gasoline power mower. All were purchased used. The reel mowers don't need gasoline, but you'll have to keep up with the mowing. If the grass gets too tall, they won't cut it. Another advantage of a reel mower is that they don't throw out clouds of dust and pollen so they're more allergy friendly (which is very important in my case!).

In this chapter I've included a list of basic tools for the self-sufficient homestead or retreat. I remind you that this is what I'd consider the minimum requirements. You may be able to get by with less, but it's more likely that you'll add more things to the list. If you have special skills or business plans, be sure to include the equipment necessary for those as well.

Note: Do not enter into this lifestyle with an "el cheapo" attitude regarding homestead tools and equipment. The idea of self-sufficiency is that you have what you need to provide for yourself. You can't do that without the proper tools and equipment. So, if you need it, get it! Don't agonize over every purchase. If it's truly essential, buy two or more! For example, we have five chainsaws and four pressure canners because firewood acquisition and food preservation are very important on our homestead. Likewise, buying cheap junk defeats the purpose as well. What good is a tool if it lets you down when you need it most? You do not want to find out that the bargain canner you bought used has a warped lid when you have 50 pounds of venison to can and no refrigerator to preserve it.

So, here are the minimum tool requirements we'd recommend for the self-sufficient homestead or retreat.

Don't forget about the little things like tire pumps. We have one that runs off a cigarette lighter socket, one portable unit that uses 120 volts, one larger single-stage compressor, and several hand pumps. Hand pumps are slow, but they're cheap, portable, and don't need electricity. Be sure they have braided hoses; the slick plastic hoses crack and break after a year or two.

GENERAL TOOLS

These are general use tools and equipment that you'll find useful for multiple tasks and projects.

Generator

Even if you live on the grid, I recommend that you have a generator on hand and enough fuel to run it for at least 24 hours. Power outages are so common that they barely make the news unless they're widespread or long-lived. A few hours of no electricity might not be a big thing, but what happens if it's out for days? Will you be able to pump water, preserve food, or even heat your house? We had a lightning strike take out a transformer in our neighborhood one night. Thirty minutes later we received a request from a neighbor to use our generator because their basement was filling with water. Their sump pump needed electricity to run. The power was only off for about two hours, but in that time their basement would have collected about two feet of water without the sump pump.

We realize that being independent and self-reliant means you cannot depend on a generator for long-term viability, but many issues of life are short term. Even if it is long term, a generator can buy time while you can or otherwise preserve your frozen food for future use. (Umm, you do have a cookstove that's not dependent upon electricity don't you?)

I recommend a generator with at least 4,000 watts output. More is better.

Gas Cans

Buy some gas cans and fill them! You'll want at least one 5-gallon capacity can (preferably more) for straight gasoline and one small can for mixed fuel (chainsaw, string trimmer, etc.). We try to keep at least 20 gallons on hand at all times, and we live off-grid and are nearly self-sufficient. If TSHTF, the gasoline would be reserved for running the chainsaws. We have also used our stock of gasoline to fill up the car so that I could get to work (back when I had a "real" job). One time someone gained access to our debit card and cleaned out our bank account. The bank cleared it up and it didn't cost us anything, but while they were doing that, we couldn't use our debit card for anything. If we hadn't had some gasoline and cash laid back, I wouldn't have been able to get to work.

Keep some fuel stabilizer on hand and add it to any gasoline you've put away for long-term storage.

Wheelbarrows and Carts

Have at least one wheelbarrow or garden cart. We use wheelbarrows because they're more versatile on uneven ground. They get a lot of use, so purchase the best you can afford and the largest size you can handle. It takes a little practice to be comfortable using one, but they are the workhorses of the homestead or retreat. We use ours to haul hay, grain, garden produce, compost, manure, wood, rocks, gravel, cement, dirt, deer, and probably two dozen other things I can't think of at the moment. We consider them mandatory for the homestead or retreat. Get one for each adult present. We have two and often wish we had more.

We prefer the single-wheel type over those with two wheels in front. The two-wheel versions are less versatile and almost as difficult to balance on anything except level paths.

Garden carts are useful if you have wide paths. There are three advantages garden carts have over wheelbarrows. First is load balance: the weight is distributed over the wheels, which means you have less to lift when transporting your load. Second is stability. They aren't tippy like a wheelbarrow.

Third is size. Garden carts generally have larger cargo compartments than wheelbarrows. The main disadvantages are that garden carts are not as versatile as a wheelbarrow (e.g., they won't work for things like wet cement) and they need wide, level paths. You can take a wheelbarrow down a six-inch trail (or over a six-inch plank) as long as it's wide enough to get the handles and box through.

Hi-Lift Jack

I've had mine for over 30 years now and it's been used as a winch to unstick my truck, a jack for changing tires, and a bead breaker to break the bead loose from the rim to repair or replace the tire. I've used it for pulling posts and stumps, for stretching fence wire, and for spreading metal (to repair a canoe once and to repair body damage to vehicles at other times). Like the wheelbarrow, I'm sure there are dozens of other things I've done with it that I can't think of right now.

Come-along

A cable hoist is another item I consider essential. I've used ours for retrieving stuck vehicles, pulling logs out of the woods, hoisting animals for butchering, tying vehicles down on trailers, pulling engines from vehicles, pulling fence posts, stretching wire, and tying down loads on trailers or trucks.

WOOD-CUTTING TOOLS

I consider a chainsaw mandatory. We have a two-man crosscut saw for cutting firewood and, while it works, it is slow and labor intensive. Chainsaws are relatively inexpensive to purchase and use and are much faster.

Whatever chainsaw you choose, be sure to have maintenance equipment for it. That means tools to sharpen and change chains. You'll also need two-cycle oil to mix with gasoline and bar oil for chain lubrication.

Unless you're already an experienced sawyer, be sure to read the owner's manual. It will explain not only how to start and maintain your saw but will also tell you how to use it safely. Before you ever start the saw, you should be aware of common dangers like kickback and pinched chains. You should know how to properly fell a tree, then cut it into pieces small enough to fit in your stove. If possible, go with someone who knows what they're

A cable hoist (or come-along) and tow chain are versatile tools for the homestead. You can pull out a stuck vehicle, remove a stump, or hang a deer with one. We have two. One has a 4,000-lb. capacity and the other one is rated at 8,000 lbs.

Splitting mauls come in different sizes and types. The one on the right is my favorite. You should have at least two splitting wedges as well.

doing the first few times you use your saw. They can guide you and keep you out of trouble. Don't ever let your guard down when using a chainsaw. They are vicious, vindictive, and unforgiving.

Other wood-cutting tools include an axe (single bit first; get a double bit after you become proficient with the single bit type), splitting maul or axe, and at least two splitting wedges. It also helps to have a bow saw around. We have an 18-inch one we use for small trim jobs, and I keep a 30-inch one handy when using the chainsaw in case the chainsaw gets bound up and I need to free it.

DIRT-WORKING TOOLS

You'll need to include at least one spade-type shovel. Long handles are the most common and work well except when working in tight spaces, such as digging an outhouse hole or root cellar. In those instances, short-handled shovels are best. You'll also want a pick and a mattock in addition to a long steel bar (used for breaking up dirt in the bottom of a hole when there's no room to use a pick). If you're going to be digging postholes (and I can't imagine a homestead or survival retreat where you won't be digging postholes!), you'll want a posthole digger. I recommend the jabbing type over the auger style, unless you can guarantee there are no subsurface rocks on your homestead.

Even if you have a rototiller, you'll still need a garden rake and hoe. Get the best you can afford. The cheap ones bend and break, which requires a trip into town to replace them. Not a good thing if

We have an assortment of digging tools, and all were purchased at yard sales at a tenth of their new price.

the S has HTF. Also, if you're truly living the low-budget life, you aren't going to want to spend money on gasoline for a trip to town to replace tools that wouldn't have broken in the first place if you'd have made your initial purchases wisely.

CONSTRUCTION AND HOME MAINTENANCE TOOLS

The following list reflects the reality of low-budget, self-sufficient living. You're going to need some home construction and maintenance skills. Learn them now, before you make the move. You don't need to be a master builder, but you should be able to construct your own small outbuildings and do your own home repairs. Some of the tools (like the circular saw) require a large inverter or a generator to operate. You can get by with a handsaw in most cases (mankind did for thousands of years), but if you undertake any major projects, you'll benefit in both more speed and less sweat by using power tools.

- Circular saw (7 ¼-inch blade)
- Handsaws—Crosscut saw and rip saw (Again, there's a wide difference in quality, so get the best you can afford.)
- Framing square
- Speed square—Once you get used to one of these, they are almost indispensable!
- Levels—You'll want a line level, torpedo level, and a four-foot-long carpenter's level.
- Electric drill with wood, metal, and masonry cutting bits
- Hand-cranked drill and a "brace" (aka hand brace) and bits. The hand-cranked drill works with small bits, and the brace is designed for boring larger holes in wood.
- Claw hammer—Find one that fits you well. There are many different handle types and sizes. Also, be sure that the claw end is thin enough for pulling nails. This is a common problem on the cheaper hammers.
- Screwdrivers—Get #2 Phillips head and assorted flat heads
- Wood chisel set—1/4- through 1-inch cut
- Chalk line—Nonpermanent chalk, blue
- 25-foot tape measure
- Pry bar
- Jigsaw

- Hacksaw
- Slip-joint pliers
- Ladders—You should have an extension ladder long enough to reach your roof from the outside and a five- to seven-foot stepladder for inside work. Again, you'll find lots of uses for these.

HOUSEHOLD TOOLS AND EQUIPMENT

There are some things you'll need around the house if you want to be self-sufficient.

Kitchen tools

I'm not going into things like dishes, pots, and pans because if you cook your own food, you'll already have those. If you're newlyweds or newly single and just now getting these things together, be careful that you don't overspend on items you don't need. We've found cast-iron cookware to be the best bargain there is. The only drawback is that it's heavy. Learn how to season it and care for it properly and you'll find that it's easy to clean and use. It is truly the first nonstick cooking utensils made and will last through several lifetimes.

Grain Mills

We have a Kel-Tech electric grain mill and an old Corona hand-powered grain mill. The electric mill is fast and does a very fine grind, but it needs electricity and is noisy (as in loud enough that you need hearing protection). When we use it, we'll grind enough grains to last several months. The Corona hand mill was purchased relatively cheap at a pawn shop many years ago. It's cast iron and will last several lifetimes. It's slow (all hand-powered mills are slow), and if you want a fine grind to your grains, you'll probably need to run them through it twice. Some people like them, some don't.

The main advice I'd give on purchasing a grain mill is to get one with a large hopper (the part you put the grain in). I once owned a small aluminum mill that only held about a quarter cup of grain in the hopper. It was frustrating to say the least. You literally had to dribble large grains like corn into the hopper. I gave it to one of our kids, who just used it occasionally. We also use our Corona to grind feed for our livestock. The hopper holds four cups, and I've often ground 50 pounds of grain in one afternoon.

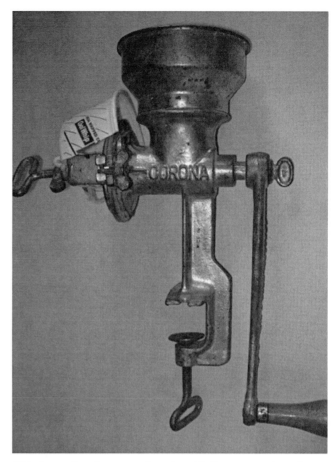

This is our hand-powered grain mill. It was purchased used at a pawnshop over 25 years ago. They're still available today for a relatively cheap price, and they last forever. The main drawback is that if you want a fine grind, you may have to run it through twice. More expensive mills will do the job on the first grind.

Meat Grinders

We have two manually operated meat grinders. Both are relatively small, but they do a great job. They're made out of cast iron and clamp to a table. I've used larger grinders and they work okay. With any hand grinder, you'll need a very substantial table to mount it on. We use a picnic table constructed of 2 x 6s. Electric grinders are easier to use, but they obviously require electricity. If you go the electric route, be aware that there are significant differences in quality. Get recommendations before making your purchase.

Meat grinders let you make hamburger and sausage from your homestead kitchen. Sausage is just ground meat with spices added. There are hundreds of sausage recipes, so it's easy to make it just the way you desire. We have two primary

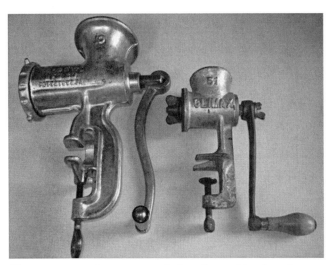

These are two of our meat grinders for making hamburger and sausage. Get one that has a cast-iron housing and a solid base. Stay away from the aluminum ones, and if they have a "suction cup" base, don't even touch it!

recipes: one for breakfast sausage and one for pizza sausage.

Pressure Canner(s)

Get a pressure canner with the weights instead of the gauge. Gauge-type canners need to be tested every year to be sure the gauge is accurate, and you'll need to stay in the room with them while they're in use in order to keep the pressure even. Weights never need testing, and because they make noise when in use, you can be in other rooms doing other things as long as you can still hear them. Don't lose the weight! They cost nearly as much as a new canner!

Like I said earlier, we have four pressure canners, and there have been times when all four were in use at once. We have room for two on our cookstove, and we use a large, two-burner "outfitter" stove when using all four. You can also can using a woodstove, but it takes some skill to keep the heat regulated through the canning process.

Water Bath Canner

Water bath canning is suitable for foods with high acid content and some fruits and berries. They work particularly well with jams and jellies, butter, and cheese. They used to be recommended for tomatoes, but some of the new hybrids are so acid-free that you should probably use a pressure canner to be safe. The advantage of a water bath canner is that it takes less heat and time, and some foods hold their texture better (pressure canning turns them to mush). Water bath canners are also much lower priced than pressure canners. Always use a pressure canner to can meats and vegetables.

Cutting Implements and Accessories

If you don't own a cutting board, get one. We like the plastic ones best. We also have several sizes on hand. Large boards are easier for cutting up meat; we use the smaller ones for fruits and veggies.

While you're getting the board, get some good knives and a sharpening steel as well. You should have a large butcher knife, a mid-size boning knife, and some paring knives in your kitchen.

A sharpening steel is hard to beat for keeping an edge on kitchen knives. The easiest way to use one is to hold the steel vertically with the point down on the counter and then run the knife down the steel as if you were trying to cut thin slices off the steel. Leave the choreographed swordplay you see in the movies to the professional chefs or meat cutters.

Dehydrators

We've gone more and more toward dehydrating our food and away from canning it. We still can meat, cheese, butter, jams, jellies, syrup, and other things that are either liquid or need refrigeration or freezing, but we dry most of our vegetables and fruit and berries. Dehydrating saves space, does not need special jars for storage, is impervious to freezing (a special consideration if you heat totally with wood or need to leave your home unoccupied during winter), and can be done without electricity. We have three electric dehydrators for those nice sunny days when we have lots of solar power, but we also have solar dehydrators. Dehydrating food is ridiculously easy, and the food keeps for years if stored in a cool, dark place. It can be stored in any type jar with a good lid or in plastic containers. We use jars (mayonnaise, peanut butter, jelly, etc.) not suitable for canning to store dehydrated food. We often take our home-dehydrated food on camping or backpacking excursions.

Jars, Jars, Jars: Lids, Lids, Lids

We have over a thousand canning jars and buy canning lids by the case. If those numbers shock you, think about this: If you open one jar of canned produce per day, that's 365 jars per year. If you have a family of four you'll probably need more than that.

Despite slowly weaning ourselves off pressure canning, we still do a lot of it. We can things like chili and stew for fast meals when we're tired or company arrives unexpectedly. We can fish, meat, chicken, jams, jellies, syrup, butter, cheese, and dozens of other things that don't dehydrate well.

Be sure to stock up on lids. We reuse lids for storing dehydrated food, but it's recommended that you use new lids for canning. We reuse lids when canning, but only with food we know will be eaten soon or when we make canned pet food. We keep a close watch on those jars.

LAUNDRY ESSENTIALS

We've seen movies where women wash their clothes in a stream using rocks for washboards. We've done it using buckets and still occasionally do small loads this way. But it's a lot of work. What we use most of the time is a pair of washtubs (one for soap and one for rinse), a Rapid Washer, and a hand-cranked wringer. If you don't want to be dependent on electricity, this is the best way that we know of to do laundry by hand.

We've used paddles, toilet plungers, sticks, and our hands to agitate the clothes in the tub, and none work as well as the Rapid Washer. We bought ours from Lehman's. We noticed that they now have plastic models, which may be better than our metal one with a wood handle. The wood handle shrinks when it dries out and the head comes loose. The metal head rusted through in about five years. Plastic shouldn't have that problem.

Forget scrub boards. They work better in movies than in real life and are very hard on clothes. We use one occasionally to scrub out ground-in dirt, but in the manner described in chapter 7 rather than the traditional way.

We used hand wringing and a mop wringer to squeeze the water out of our clothes prior to purchasing our crank-type clothes wringer. Hand wringing is a lot of work, and the mop wringer just didn't get enough water out. For us, the hand-cranked wringer is the way to go.

If you don't mind running a generator, you might look into a wringer washer. They use little water and do the agitating for you while you do other things. If you have a good well (lots of water!) and septic system and don't mind running your generator, then you can use a modern washer and even dryer to do laundry. Just keep in mind that you can't be dependent on outside resources and technology and live a self-sufficient life.

Hang your clothes on a line either inside (in winter) or outside when it's warm. We like plastic-coated steel cable for clothesline, but anything that's strong enough and won't stain your clothes will work. Clothespins for hanging clothes should have strong springs. A lot of the cheap ones are so weak they won't even hold socks on the line.

VEHICLE TOOLS

Even if you don't know how to use jumper cables, you should have a set in your vehicle at all times. If you have them on hand, there may be someone along who does know how to use them and can get your vehicle going if the battery is dead. The same is true of tow straps in case you get stuck.

Aside from a tow strap and jumper cables, you should always carry a jack, lug wrench, and spare tire for your vehicle. They came with the car when it was new, but things happen over time so be sure you have them now.

If you have to drive on snow or ice, get a set of tire chains and keep them with you in the winter. Learn how to install them in the comfort of your driveway in warm weather, not while standing on the side of an icy road on a winter night with your car in the ditch.

Keep a small tool kit consisting of a pair of slip-joint pliers, a combination screwdriver, and a couple of adjustable wrenches in the vehicle. Add to it as your automotive repair skills increase. Always keep a flashlight handy.

MISCELLANEOUS TOOLS

Have some traps on hand for pest control. Things like mousetraps and a small live trap for gophers, squirrels, pack rats, and chipmunks are good to have, as is a larger trap for raccoons, opossum, skunks, and similar size critters. You'll want live traps so you can set them around your home and garden without fear of harming your pets. Most pests are active at night, so we keep our cat indoors for the night when we have the traps out. When we're after daytime pests such as ground squirrels, we just make sure the trap isn't baited with any-

Get at least one live trap for such pests as pack rats, squirrels, skunks, and raccoons. They're safer to use when you have pets roaming your property. The dog got to this trap before I did and nearly destroyed it trying to get at the pack rat.

thing that would attract the cat or dog. Once you catch the critter, it's up to you to decide how to dispose of it.

If you're off-grid with solar panels, wind turbine, etc., and have batteries for storage, it's a good idea to have a battery charger and tester. If you have one bad battery in your battery bank, it will draw all the other batteries down with it. You'll need a way to test them so you can find the bad battery and remove it.

Power Tools vs. Hand Tools

We have both. Again, our goal was to be able to function well without electricity, so we have hand-powered alternatives for all of our electrical tools and appliances. It's important to note, however, that we kept our power tools. When electricity is available, your construction or processing time is greatly reduced by using power tools. If you're like me and can't cut a straight line with a handsaw, for example, you'll appreciate the precision cuts of a miter saw. We have a cement mixing tub for small batches, but if you're mixing a thousand pounds of the stuff, it's much easier and faster to use a gas- or electric-powered cement mixer. (If you're mixing more than that at one pour, I'd advise having it brought by truck!)

Again, there's nothing wrong with having power tools and equipment as long as you aren't completely dependent on them.

FIREARMS FOR THE HOMESTEAD

If you believe that a firearm isn't necessary on a homestead, you might want to consider a few things. Coyotes will come up to your home and try to entice your pets into chasing them. When they get them away from your house, they will kill and eat them. Wolves will do the same, but most people don't live in wolf country so they don't have to concern themselves with them. Mountain lions have been known to snatch dogs and cats off the front porch in areas where they roam. Everyone has heard about the proverbial "fox in the henhouse," but did you know that weasels, skunks, and raccoons will gladly visit as well? You'll know when it happens because they'll kill every chicken they can catch (which is usually every chicken in the chicken house).

Large animals such as deer, elk, moose, and bear love fresh garden produce. We have electric wire around our garden to keep the deer and bears out, but sometimes it takes a shotgun blast to run off a nuisance animal.

Pests are a real problem in homestead living. Mice, gophers, squirrels, rabbits, and dozens of other critters, small and large, are going to love having you around. They'll infest your home, outbuildings, root cellar, garden, machinery, and vehicles, and traps can't possibly get them all.

If your homestead is miles off the beaten path, you'll also want to be ready to defend your home from two-legged predators as well. Help is often a long way off when you live on a remote homestead. You need to be prepared.

A person could conceivably get by with just a shotgun if homesteading is your only goal. With slugs they're quite effective on big game, and with bird shot they're more than adequate for small game and birds. Add in some buckshot and you have an efficient short-range defensive firearm. Shotguns are relatively cheap. You can find good quality pump shotguns for under $300. Ammo is a bit on the expensive side, but no worse than ammo for high-powered rifles. Shotguns are relatively easy to become proficient with. The downside is that they can be cumbersome with their long barrels. If you purchase a pump shotgun manufactured by Remington, Winchester, or Mossberg, you can probably get different barrels designed for defense or hunting. Defensive barrels tend to be shorter (18 to 24 inches long) and are specifically designed for shooting slugs or buckshot. The general-purpose barrels are usually about 28 to 30 inches long and will also shoot slugs and buckshot.

There are two major drawbacks to a shotgun. First, it is a close-range weapon. Even with slugs, the range is limited to about 100 yards. Second, the ammo is heavy and bulky. It's not a problem unless you need to pack it as you would if you had to bug out or evacuate your location on foot. Stick with a 12 or 20 gauge, with preference going to the 12 gauge. Ammo is sometimes hard to find for 16 gauge shotguns, and a .410 isn't big enough for general purpose use.

Ideally, though, you'll have more weapons. A .22 rimfire semiauto rifle is a good investment. Both the rifles and ammo are cheap. The ammo is small, so a bunch can be carried with you if you have to bug out. A box of 500 takes up little more space than a box of 25 shot shells. It's a great cartridge for small game and has been used on larger game by expert marksmen.

A high-powered rifle would be my next recommendation if you live where you can see a long distance. Stick with a .30-06 or a .308 Winchester if you're not familiar with firearms. Put a good scope on it and practice enough to become proficient.

Disclaimer: I know that there are dozens of other fine cartridges I didn't list, but the fact that you know about them means you don't need the advice I just gave anyway. I do not mean to offend anyone by not listing their favorite cartridge. Even

though the .30-06 and .308 are not necessarily the best choices for all North American big game, with good shot placement they are adequate. In addition, the ammo is available virtually everywhere ammunition is sold.

A handgun can be an asset. The best thing about it is that you're more likely to have it when you need it because you can carry it on you while keeping both hands free for work. My recommendation would be to start with a .22 rimfire.

These are the only recommendations I'd make for those not familiar with firearms. Get some training in the use of whatever firearms you purchase. Be sure to buy a good quality firearm, meaning stick to familiar brands like Colt, Winchester, Marlin, Ruger, Remington, Mossberg, Glock, or Smith & Wesson. A gun that doesn't work makes a poor club.

Get lots of ammunition. You're far better off with one, good quality firearm and a thousand rounds of ammo than 20 firearms with 20 rounds each. This is where a .22 rimfire is great. You can purchase a good .22 semiauto and a thousand rounds of ammo for under $300, and usually for much less than that if you know where to look.

• • • • •

We have a lot more tools than those listed here, and you will too as your skill level increases. This is enough to get by on, though, so it's a good place to start.

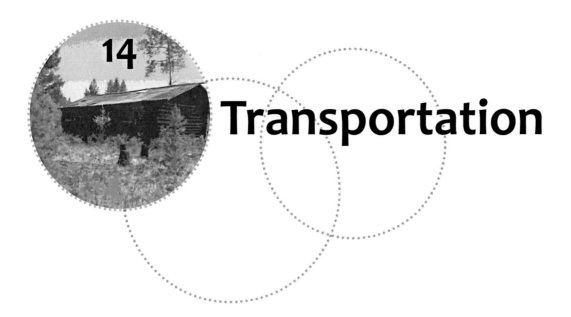

14 Transportation

I f I could figure out how to realistically live life without a motorized vehicle, I'd sell all of ours in a heartbeat! All motorized vehicles are energy hogs, expensive to purchase and maintain, need insurance, pollute the atmosphere with fumes and noise, and are just another way for the government to extort taxes from you. However, they're still needed on the homestead. Here's how to minimize your dependence on them.

THE HOMESTEAD PICKUP . . . OR TRAILER?

I'm going to make an absolute statement here, and if you can show me where I'm wrong, please do so. You're going to need something to haul things with. In most cases that means a pickup truck. We've known people who have opted for a trailer to pull behind their car or SUV, but in every case they've purchased a truck within a short time.

Trailers have some good points. They can be purchased and maintained for less than a truck. There's no engine, transmission, drive train, doors, windshield wipers, or other accessories to break or wear out. The taxes are usually cheaper, as is insurance. Another benefit of trailers is that the beds are closer to the ground, which makes them easier to load.

So, why don't we just use trailers and do without pickups? Because trailers are inconvenient. The biggest problem with them arises in close quarters. It takes more room to maneuver even a small vehicle/trailer combination than it does a pickup truck.

If you were only going to haul things occasionally that might not be a problem, but in most homesteads you'll be hauling things quite often. It gets to be a pain hooking up the trailer, backing it up, and unhooking it when you're finished. Plus, despite a trailer not having a drive train, it seems like the lights and wiring are always in need of maintenance.

With a pickup, you just start it and drive it where you need it. It's also easier to back a pickup into tight places. We cut firewood on national forest land (after purchasing the required permit), and there are many dead-end roads where it's almost impossible to get turned around with a trailer attached.

Using a trailer on icy roads takes some exemplary driving skills. With a pickup, you'll only have one vehicle to concern yourself with.

If you pull a trailer in areas with lots of snow or ice, they increase your chances of an accident and you'll need to "chain up" your vehicle more often. Trailers try to push your vehicle every time you stop. Larger units have brakes, but on icy roads these can be as much of a problem as a solution. If they apply too soon or too hard and lock the wheels up, the trailer may begin fishtailing. If they don't apply soon enough or hard enough, the trailer will try to push the tow vehicle. That gets real interesting on icy curves.

If you tow on icy roads, it's best to install tire chains on the tow vehicle. These will help you maintain control when stopping, and they'll help you get the vehicle moving after a stop. (Unfortunately, tire chains have problems too. They provide little control

A pickup truck is indispensable for those close spaces where it's difficult to get a trainer into.

A few years ago we were a thousand miles from home and made some purchases. We checked into renting a trailer, but we could buy one cheaper so we did. We've put thousands of miles on that little trailer since then. It's one of the best buys we ever made.

of sideways motion. I once watched a chained-up vehicle try to traverse a curve on an icy road when the rear of the vehicle slid down on the banked side and the front of the vehicle slowly made a 180-degree arc and began going back down the hill. They got up the hill by backing up it, but they didn't have a trailer to worry about in this instance.)

The disadvantages of a pickup are it's one more vehicle to keep running, poor fuel economy, higher taxes and licensing fees, and insurance. You can alleviate these somewhat by buying a truck that is small (better fuel economy) and old (lower taxes) and by paying cash (no need for full-coverage insurance).

We have two pickups. One is a Dodge one-ton four-wheel-drive that we use when loads are heavy and the roads are rough. We purchased a lifetime license plate and only insure it for about one month of the year, during which time I cut our year's supply of firewood and we haul any gravel, sand, etc., that we'll need for the homestead. The rest of the time it sits in its parking spot. It gets about 10 miles per gallon on a good day.

We have an old half-ton Chevrolet S-10 two-wheel-drive pickup that we've used for light hauling and regular transportation. It gets about 25 mpg but can only haul about a third of what the Dodge can carry. It gets better gas mileage but takes more trips to do the same amount of work. It isn't insured unless we need to drive it.

Our primary vehicle is an older Cherokee Sport. It's a small SUV that gets about 20 mpg. It's a station wagon with a roof rack and handles most of our hauling and transportation needs. It's insured (liability only) year round.

We also have four trailers. One is a small, 4 x 8-foot utility trailer we pull behind the Cherokee or S-10. It'll carry about a half ton of cargo. We use it quite often for hauling construction materials from town or other small jobs and can throw the boat on it when we go fishing. We use it much more than I ever thought we would. It's light enough that you can turn it around by hand in tight places.

Another trailer is made from an old pickup bed. We use it behind the Dodge when I'm cutting firewood. It nearly doubles our cargo capacity for about a 10 percent drop in fuel economy to tow it. I have to be careful where I take it. If I hit a dead end, I'll unhook the trailer, turn the truck around, turn the trailer around by hand, and then hitch it back up to the truck. If the trailer is loaded, I'll have to unload it to turn it by hand, then reload the trailer. Like I said, I'm careful where I take it!

The wood-hauling trailer is attached to the truck and ready to go. We can haul nearly twice as much wood in each trip using only about 10 percent more fuel by filling the trailer as well as the truck.

Our third trailer is for the snowmobiles, and the fourth is a horse trailer. These two are also homemade and definitely not fancy, but they are functional and get their respective jobs done when needed. All the trailers have lifetime license plates. We pay extra for lifetime plates so that we never have to renew the plates or pay taxes on them again.

So which is best, a pickup or trailer? In our case, it's both.

UTILITY VEHICLES

Four-wheelers, three-wheelers, and to a lesser extent motorcycles have their place on the low-budget homestead. They get good fuel economy and are perfect for those small jobs like checking on or feeding livestock, fixing fences, bringing in game you've shot, making a quick visit to a neighbor or a run to the store or post office, and dozens of other mundane tasks faced by the homesteader. They've taken the place of the horse on many ranches in the West, and they don't need feed when you aren't using them.

You can pull small trailers with them and purchase lawn mower attachments, manure spreaders, and lots of other farm-type equipment for them. Often you can use them to plow snow. However, don't expect them to perform like a full-size pickup or even a small tractor. If you work them hard, you'll spend a lot of money replacing clutches and other drive train parts. We don't have one (but it's on the list!) and don't necessarily advocate purchasing one, but they do make more sense than firing up a 6,000-pound SUV when a smaller vehicle can get the job done.

BICYCLES

Bicycles are a neglected resource in the United States. In third world countries, bicycles are more of a utility vehicle than a recreational toy. Those of us who grew up during the Vietnam War era saw news clips of Vietnamese villagers transporting everything from household goods to pigs and chickens by bicycle. Bamboo poles were lashed to the frames and the cargo was tied under the poles on each side, with more cargo resting across the top. They easily moved loads weighing 100 pounds or more on a daily basis.

Now, I'm not advocating a third world type of

Don't forget about bicycles when considering sustainable transportation. We purchased a couple of child carrier trailers for ours and modified them for hauling cargo. My wife is shown here heading into town (20 miles one way) for the farmer's market. She has her merchandise, a table, chair, umbrella, tablecloth, and everything else she needs loaded on the trailer. (There's a photo of her booth all set up in chapter 3.) Be sure to keep some extra tires and tubes on hand.

We ride our bicycles to town for the mail when the weather permits. It's seven miles from the cabin to the post office.

existence for modern homesteaders, but even if we don't adopt some of their methods, we should at least be aware of them. After all, the subject of this book is not only low-budget homesteading; it's also about building the low-budget homestead *survival* retreat. In a true SHTF or EOTWAWKI situation, we may all be reduced to third world status.

That being said, you don't need to wait for the end of the world to use your bicycle. We use ours for trips to the post office seven miles away and for trips to Eureka (a larger small town) 20 miles away. We have a rear rack, saddlebags, and trailers for both of our mountain bikes. The trailers can support over a hundred pounds of weight by themselves and are roomy enough for hauling jugs of water, gasoline, and sacks of feed.

With a bicycle comes all the gear you'll need to keep it rolling. This means a patch kit for flat tires, tire-changing tools, extra tubes, a hand pump, a small adjustable wrench, and assorted Allen wrenches. These items can all fit in a small stuff sack, which should stay with the bike at all times.

We take our bikes along as our "get home" vehicles when we travel. We pack our saddlebags for a trip home so that all we have to do if the need arises is throw them on the bikes and hit the road. My wife loves cross-country biking. On her last trip, she packed enough food and camping gear to travel 1,500 miles without restocking. It was all dried beans, rice, and dehydrated food, with the majority of it coming from our own pantry. Add in a .22 pistol or rifle, snare material, and some fishing gear

and she could have traveled even farther. The only thing she needed to resupply on the way was water. All of this was packed on her bicycle in a handlebar bag and front and rear panniers. If she'd have taken the trailer she'd have had even more cargo capacity.

ANIMAL POWER

Romance or reality? Draft animals are multifunctional, self-sustaining, and self-replacing. They can meet emotional needs as well as doing a lot of work around the homestead. They can also be your worst nightmare.

If we'd stayed away from horses and motorcycles, we'd have avoided some of the most serious accidents we've had to deal with. Animals need care. Horses need hooves trimmed regularly at the least, and if you work them hard they'll need shoes as well. If you can't do those things yourself, you'll have to hire someone to do them. Livestock gets sick just like any other animal. You need to be able to recognize symptoms and prescribe proper care, or at least know when to call for help! When a veterinarian is necessary, be prepared to shell out some dough. You need to know what kind of diet they'll need and how much. You'll need to know

Is horsepower practical on the self-sufficient homestead? Maybe! Horses can do tremendous amounts of work, but they're slow if you have to go far, and they need lots of care. We enjoyed riding ours when we had them, but for us the disadvantages of horse ownership outweighed the advantages. If you want to use horses, get some experience first.

how hard they can work without harming them. They aren't like a tractor—they get tired and sore just like we do when we overextend ourselves.

So the first prerequisite for using animals on the homestead is to know something about them. If you have no experience with them, get some *before* you acquire them. The good thing is that it's usually very easy to find people who'll teach you. Most animal owners are eager to teach others. 4-H organizations are a great place to start. They focus on children for the most part, but they're always looking for adults to assist. They'll teach you as well as the kids. Children's camps are always looking for adult volunteers and will teach you what you need to know in exchange for some of your time helping at camp.

Another thing about animals is that they require care all year long. When winter comes, you can't just store them in a garage until spring. You'll need hay and grain to get them through, as well as fresh water and shelter. If you live in cold country, you'll need a way to keep their water from freezing. Most farmers rely on electric heaters to keep the water in the stock tanks from freezing, but if you live off-grid you probably won't have adequate solar power to run a tank heater. There are other, nonelectric ways of dealing with this problem, but they take some research and work to implement. If you have a flowing stream, you've got it made, as these seldom freeze.

If you purchase hay, get it by late summer because the price escalates after that. If you grow your hay, you'll need a way to harvest and store it. If you use your horses to cut and transport your hay, you'll need at least a horse-drawn sickle mower, rake, and wagon. You'll also need to know how to cure it before storage. If you put it up green or wet, it turns into a giant compost pile. You'll know when this happens because you'll look out your window some cold morning and your haystack will be smoking like a chimney. By then the hay will be useless for animal feed but great for your garden, as the inside has now become a black, gooey mess of composting organic matter. In some cases it might even generate enough heat to catch on fire. I've been told that more than one barn burned to the ground due to improperly stored hay.

So far we've focused on horses as draft animals, but there are other options to consider. Oxen were used extensively in times past. If that's your desire,

you'll want to look at cattle breeds that are multipurpose. Charolais are good for draft work, milking, and beef. They aren't the best for any single use, but they'd be my choice for the homestead because of their versatility. There are other breeds that would also work well. These are primarily used as milk cows today, but they're larger, stronger, and faster than beef cattle when used as draft animals. However, don't get hung up on specialty breeds. The difference is like using horses. Some breeds function better than others at certain tasks, but they're still horses (or cattle), and even the small ones can outwork you.

Throughout history man has used what was available, and as a low-budget homesteader you'll do well to study history and other cultures. Here in the United States we tend toward specialization. Money is (even during the current recession) relatively abundant compared to third world countries, and with our push for maximum efficiency we discount what others have used or are using.

Before (and even after) the introduction of the horse, American Indians used dogs as draft animals. Natives in northern climates used dogs to pull sleds loaded with cargo and covered more miles per day than even a horse could traverse. Since the advent of snow machines, dogs have lost favor in many northern locales. In South America, llamas are still used as pack animals. In other cultures you'll find goats, sheep, caribou, donkeys, water buffalo, elephants, camels, and who knows what else being used for working animals! In short, people use what is available.

As a low-budget homesteader, you'll want to shrug off some of the specialization mentality and begin focusing on what you have that will get the job done. By knowing history and studying other cultures, you can avoid reinventing the wheel. One of my favorite countries for low-budget ideas is the Soviet Union. Our climate in northwestern Montana isn't a lot different from Siberia. Those living there also face economic challenges similar to the low-budget homesteader and have adapted well to using what's available and doing it with limited financial resources.

• • • • •

The key to a low-budget homestead or retreat is working with what you have available. If you have lots of money, you can buy and maintain tractors and other motorized equipment to do the work for you. Just remember, the higher the technology required to produce your equipment, the higher the costs will be to purchase and maintain it. Low-budget living doesn't allow for large monthly payments or even a bunch of small monthly payments. Keep life simple!

15 Entertainment

We're assuming that those who live the homestead lifestyle will be giving up certain things that used to keep them entertained for hours. If you live off-grid and don't have a monstrous bank of solar panels or plan on running your generator every day, you aren't going to be spending hours and hours playing video games on your big screen television. That doesn't mean life has to be boring. This section is about low-budget alternatives to a culture saturated and dependent upon television, Internet, and video games.

It has surprised us how many people ask what we do for entertainment. It's as if the advent of television, recorded movies, video games, and the Internet has sucked the creativity out of the last two generations of Americans. We often remind ourselves and others that mankind has thrived for hundreds of thousands of years without electricity, let alone telephone, Internet, radio, and movies.

That being said, we have a phone and Internet access. Our phone company will provide new service anywhere in their territory for a flat fee of $60. It doesn't matter if they have to run wires for 20 miles; it's still only $60. You'll find buried telephone cables to remote properties that don't even have homes on them. We decided it was worth the money to be able to communicate easily with family and friends, and since we use the Internet to make money, it made sense to bite the bullet and pay the monthly fee.

If conventional phone service is not an option, you may be able to get Internet service through your cell phone or subscribe to systems that use satellites. It costs a little more, but it's available. The thing you need to remember is that it's another monthly bill to pay. Last I checked, the phone company wasn't interested in taking chickens or eggs in trade for their services.

If you like network television, you can get satellite service almost anywhere in the United States. Again, you'll need to decide if it's worth the price. One of the keys to the low-budget life is avoiding monthly bills. If you move out to your homestead and quickly subscribe to the services you had in town, you're probably going to need to make as much money as you did when living in town. The problem now is that you have to commute farther to work over rougher roads, plus you'll have little time left for homestead and/or self-sufficient activities. All you've done is add to your workload and stress level. You'll be worse off than before your move. Modern "conveniences" come with a price tag attached. Be sure you can afford it!

We also have a television, DVD player, and VCR along with over a thousand videos and DVDs. We watch them mostly during the long winter evenings, but even from December through February we watch less than 10 hours of television a week. We live over an hour's drive from the nearest Redbox site, so renting is not really an option. We've thought about subscribing to Internet movies, but that's just another bill to pay and we don't think it's worth it. We do occasionally watch free movies over the Internet.

Now, on to nonelectric entertainment.

Snowmobiling may not sound like low-budget recreation, but if you have the money on hand when someone is wanting to sell, you can often get one at a good price. The one I ride was purchased for $125 at an estate auction. My wife's snowmobile (pictured) was bought for half of its book value from a friend.

Sledding is fun at any age and it's very cheap. You can even make the sled yourself!

Libraries! We can check out books for three weeks and then renew them for three more weeks over the Internet. Sometime during that six-week period, someone, either in our home or the neighborhood, will be going to town. We'll send books back with them (or return theirs if we're going in). We can also place holds on books and have books brought in from other libraries. They'll be waiting at the library for pickup. We just send our library card with whoever is going to town so they can check out the new books and bring them back. We can also check out movies, but they have to be back in a week so it's not often practical.

Our library has a new option of downloading library books to our computers. We can access their resources and never burn a gallon of gasoline! You can read for entertainment or to acquire new skills, and even though it requires Internet access, it's all free after that!

Outdoor sports and recreation are available year

And then there's backpacking in the early summer . . .

And ice skating . . .

And winter camping . . .

And piano playing . . .

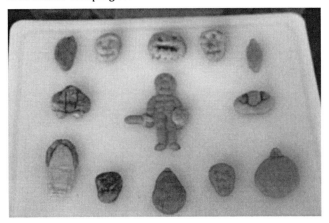

And creative cookie making . . .

And cross-country skiing and snowshoeing . . .

And renting backcountry U.S. Forest Service cabins . . .

And backpacking in mid-summer . . .

*And fishing and kayaking high
mountain streams and rivers . . .*

And playing in the wading pool . . .

And picking on the banjo . . .

And bouncing on the trampoline . . .

And playing Uno by the light of kerosene lamps.

round. We have several local bodies of water that freeze in winter and offer ice skating, ice fishing, cross-country skiing, ski-joring (traditionally they use dogs or horses to pull a skier, but we use a snowmobile), sledding, tubing, figure skating, and games such as ice hockey. We also snowshoe and cross-country ski around the countryside, and we love taking the snowmobiles out for a cruise. We camp in winter and summer in our homebuilt motor home, and we go backpacking. There's hunting, fishing, predator calling, and trapping that provide recreation as well as food and money. For summer activities, we like archery, shooting, photography, bicycling, canoeing, kayaking, and swimming.

We like making things. My wife and I both sew some of our own clothes. It's fun and it saves money. I wanted a wool coat but couldn't justify spending the money for a new one. We shopped around the thrift stores and purchased two wool coats for under $10 each. I used pieces off both coats to make the coat I wanted. For less than $15 and about five hours of work at my treadle sewing machine, I had a replica of a coat they wanted $200 for at the store. My wife has made lots of clothes for us and the kids. There's also knitting, embroidery, crocheting, and quilting.

Woodworking is a great hobby that also has income potential. In the past I've made furniture and have the tools to do that now if time permits. We know a guy who does wood carving to pass the time while he watches for fires from a remote mountaintop fire lookout. I'm hoping to make some wood-strip canoes in the future. I've put together muzzle-loading rifles from kits and built wooden archery bows from staves purchased online. I also make my own wood arrows using feathers from our turkeys and arrowheads from bone, stone, and steel.

If you don't already play a musical instrument, it'll be a good time to start. My wife can play about any musical instrument except a saxophone and has taught piano and guitar professionally. We like to sing and play with our family or with other neighbors and friends.

Board games can be fun for all ages. Light a couple of kerosene lamps and have everyone gather 'round the table for a game of chess, checkers, bingo, Scrabble, Monopoly, or any other game you have on hand. Cards are fun to play. We like playing poker using chips or spare change. No one gets to

keep more than they brought with them, so it's not about making money; it's just to have some fun. Games like Pitch and Hearts are easy to learn and fun to play in a group. When I was young, there used to be parties held in old country schoolhouses where locals met once a month to play cards. There were often donated door prizes for winning teams.

We used to meet with a group on a monthly basis for square dancing. My wife and I and our four kids still living at home back then always looked forward to those times. We even did some line dancing for a while.

Rural areas and small towns often have an active social calendar with parades and events for all major holidays. One of our favorites is the rendezvous held every spring. It's called a "living history" event in which participants dress in clothing like that used during the Western fur trade up to about 1840. You'll see women and girls in long flowing dresses and the guys (and some of the women and children) wearing buckskin clothing. They've often tanned and sewn the hides themselves. Muzzle-loading rifles, knives, and tomahawks are carried by everyone, and there are shooting and throwing matches held continuously during the weekend. Some of the time it's open to the public and some of the time it's for those in period clothing only. We love browsing along "trader's row," where people lay out their wares for public sale or barter. Cash is always accepted, but most merchants are open to barter as well. It's a lot of fun striking deals like it was done on the wild frontier.

There are clubs and organizations for every age and hobby. 4-H is an organization that teaches skills like animal care, gardening, cooking, public speaking, shooting, archery, and more. Once it was geared toward kids and families who resided on farms. Now you'll find a lot of urbanites taking part and learning valuable agricultural skills that used to be an integral part of rural living. If you've never had any homesteading or farming experience, it's a great place to learn skills you'll use every day on your homestead or survival retreat.

And don't forget Boy Scouts and, to a lesser extent, Girl Scouts. Even though these organizations have grown more cosmopolitan, they still place a major emphasis on outdoor skills. Summer camps for kids are a great place to learn outdoor skills and have a lot of fun too. Even if you're an adult, there's a place for you as a volunteer leader. They'll usually teach you the skills so that you can teach the campers. These are all fun places to be, and they have the added benefit of teaching you valuable skills for your personal use.

If you homeschool your children, find the local homeschool association. Ours put together field trips, sporting events, musicals and plays, science fairs, and picnics and dinners for the adults and children of our group.

Churches in rural areas are great places to meet and have fun. Most have programs and events for youth and adults. We always enjoyed New Year's Eve at our church. The church was open for members and their guests to meet and play games until the clock struck twelve. At midnight we'd usually sing a few songs and offer prayer for the coming year. Many never stayed that late, but it was still a fun evening no matter how long you were there. Everyone brought a snack food of some type so we had plenty to eat and lots of fun ushering in the new year. Churches also sponsor summer camps for kids and retreats for adults of all ages. Many have summer picnics, holiday celebrations, and other times to just get together and have some fun.

Craft sales and farmer's markets are usually held during the spring, summer, and fall. It gives you an opportunity to make a little money and talk to a lot of people. These are as much social events as they are commercial. In rural areas you get to know a lot of people, and it's fun to have them drop by your table and catch up on what's happening (or what isn't).

Socializing is a big part of rural life. I don't mean rural as in suburban mini farms; I'm talking about rural as in people who live close to the land, making their living from it.

No child that has any imagination whatsoever should ever be bored when living on a low-budget homestead. When I was young, we made tractors by nailing a tin can to a board and then nailing can lids to the sides for wheels. We made plows out of sticks tied together to pull behind our tractors. We made harrows by driving nails through a board and pulling the board (nail side down, of course) behind the tractor. We also made forts and tree houses. There were always piles of used/scrap lumber around. We had access to hammers and handsaws and were given permission to use any nails we salvaged from the used lumber. We made slingshots out of forked branches and powered by rubber cut from old inner tubes. We made bows and arrows out of branches cut from trees. We used baling wire for bow strings and tied on bird feathers for fletching. Tips were fire-hardened, and we went hunting for rabbits and squirrels. They wouldn't shoot an arrow over 30 feet, and I don't think we ever got anything, but it still provided hours of fun for practically nothing. It was a dream life for a young boy with some imagination.

We also fished, waded, and went swimming in nearby ponds, lakes, and rivers. There were ponds in every pasture and almost as many creeks. All had fish in them, and no one cared how many you caught as long as you didn't waste them. As I grew older, I hunted whenever the seasons were open.

Wean the kids off the video games and television. Get them reading and playing outdoors. Find some books on things kids used to do before the one-eyed-monster invaded our homes. Talk to senior citizens about the things they did as kids. Teach your children how to play with marbles and jacks and how to play games like hopscotch or jump rope. Make a swing out of rope and an old tire and hang it from a limb. Give them a little guidance and some raw materials and you'll be surprised at how much there is to keep them entertained.

16

Work Habits, Time Off, Hobbies, and Burnout

This life is a lot different than a nine-to-five job where you punch a time clock. There's no boss around to plan your workday or assign tasks. No one is going to dock your pay if you sleep in a couple of mornings or take an afternoon off to go fishing. In many ways, being your own boss and setting your own schedule is great. But it can also be a curse.

If the work doesn't get done, you'll pay for it! If you're growing your own food and you don't get the garden planted in time, you won't get any crops . . . and you'll run out of food. If you don't spend time weeding and watering your crops, they'll be stunted and production will suffer. If you put off cutting your firewood until you run out, you may find yourself cutting it in waist-deep snow. (I've seen that happen!) If you don't clean and maintain your chimney, you could wake up to a chimney fire. If you don't keep your fences maintained, you may lose your entire garden to raiding deer or your fruit trees to scavenging bears. If your milk cow gets out, it may be hit by a car and you'll be out one cow and possibly facing a lawsuit for the damaged vehicle. You have to be the kind of person who can schedule his or her time and work without supervision.

Of course, if the garden fails you can get a real job and buy groceries and milk, but if you're going to supply your needs through the grocery store, why are you homesteading? And that's assuming a best-case scenario. Suppose this is your survival retreat and the S has HTF and there are no more supermarkets? It wasn't that many years ago that

famines were common in the United States. Crop failures meant mass starvation. Go to the grocery store and see how much of the food comes from local sources. It won't be much. If modern transportation systems are the only thing that keeps food in the grocery stores, what happens if those trucks, trains, and planes can't run anymore?

Back when I was working at a "real" job and we heated with wood, we had a family crisis that kept me from getting my firewood cut on schedule. Winter hit early and hard that year and by the end of October, most secondary roads were closed by snow. I ran out of firewood about mid-January. No problem; I'll just buy some, right? Wrong! I learned very quickly that just because someone ran an ad that they were selling firewood didn't necessarily mean that they had any to sell . . . at any price! I called vendor after vendor with the same results. They'd be glad to sell me some firewood, but it would be a month before they had any. I finally found someone who actually had wood, but it was from a slash pile in "log lengths." I purchased three cords. Half of it was too green to burn. Most of it had gravel embedded in the surface from being dragged out of the woods with a skidder. I was constantly sharpening the chain on my saw because the rocks dulled it. But beggars can't be choosy! It got us through until I could get better wood delivered. I learned my lesson well, though, and have never again run short on firewood.

Before you panic and think that living the homestead life is nothing but endless drudgery and worry, let's look at how good things *can* be with a little planning and self-motivation.

Helen and Scott Nearing were household names among homesteader wannabes back in the '70s and '80s. (That's *1970s* for those new at this!) They divided their days into segments, with four hours allotted for "bread labor," four hours for community service, and four hours for professional or recreational activities. Now if you think about that a bit, they only scheduled four hours per day for activities that provided their daily necessities and produced income to purchase things like clothing and tools and pay taxes. They did this by living simply and establishing a routine that kept them focused on the things that were most important, and when they worked, they worked steadily and efficiently. (Maybe someday I can be that competent!)

ROUTINES AND SCHEDULES

I read a book on building log cabins where the authors looked back at how long it took to build their first cabin and stated that if they had laid one log per day from the very beginning, they'd have completed it in half the time. The problem was that they'd work like fools for a couple of days, then get tired, sore, and discouraged and do something else that was "fun." Then after a week (or a month or more!), they'd feel guilty, try again, and repeat the whole process. The lack of advancement kept them discouraged, which made it hard to get motivated to resume their work. If you're not careful, homesteading can be a lot like that.

Establish a routine and follow it. Working steady is better than working hard. What I mean is that you'll get more done by working four hours a day, every day, than working 16 hours one day, wearing yourself out, and doing nothing for the next week. Like the old saying goes, "work smarter, not harder." This is especially true if you're not used to physical labor.

Remember, though. that we're talking about efficient, productive work time. I've seen adults that grew up in the city taking half a day to dig a 3-foot-square by 18-inch-deep outhouse pit. They were out there four hours but spent most of that time resting on the shovel or stabbing ineffectually at buried rocks and roots.

It isn't always laziness either. Muscles that aren't used to hard work get tired quickly and effi-

ciency takes a plunge. Soft hands blister. Inexperience leads to a lot of wasted motion. Splitting wood is a prime example. Knowing where to hit, then hitting that exact spot is much more productive than swinging harder or using a bigger maul. Most people wear themselves out when splitting wood the first time. Their aim is bad to begin with and, because they don't know the best places to strike, each chunk of wood will take several more blows than an experienced wood splitter will need. Top that off with fatigue and the loss of fine muscle control that fatigue brings and not only will a person be less efficient, he'll also be more likely to injure himself. Then, if you aren't used to physical labor, you'll spend a week recuperating while the blisters on your hands heal.

If you aren't used to physical labor, it's going to take awhile to toughen up. Work for shorter segments of time on each project. Alternate tasks to use different muscles, and wear gloves to avoid blisters. A caution about gloves, though: don't

So, what constitutes "work" on the homestead? Cutting firewood is obviously work, yet I enjoy it immensely. I love the cool, crisp, fall mornings and being in the mountains and deep timber.

Writing is my major source of income but I usually limit it to four hours a day, because I tend to run out of creativity after that and I'd rather spend the time outside doing something physical.

become dependent on them. They're expensive and wear out quickly. The only time I wear gloves now is when working with firewood. (I don't like splinters or pine sap!) When using smooth-handled tools like shovels, I work barehanded. Your hands will toughen up over time.

Routines are also important for the mental aspect of getting the job done. We know one couple with a home business who go to a coffee shop every morning, have breakfast, then return home to begin their day. Their routine helps them "change gears" and shift into a work mindset. For me, it helps to get up, have my morning cocoa, eat breakfast, then begin work. Most of my life was spent at an eight-to-five-thirty job. The day always began the same; get up, get dressed, eat breakfast, go to work. I've followed this routine for years, and my brain just doesn't shift into "work" mode until after breakfast.

My wife and I had to make some compromises when I "retired" to become a full-time homestead husband. We're both morning people, meaning we'd rather go to bed around 10:00 P.M. and get up around 6:00 A.M. (We have children who resent looking at any clock before 12:00 noon!) However, our work routine is vastly different. I prefer to get up, get dressed, and eat, then get busy and keep working through the afternoon. I like to relax in the evening. She'd rather get up, get dressed, have our morning cocoa, and do "light" stuff like housework in the morning, read, or get on the computer. In the late morning she'll have brunch, then work outside in the afternoon and into the evening. I'm ready to knock off for the day about the time she's hitting her most productive time. It's taken some getting used to, but we're getting better at respecting the other's routine. There is no right or wrong when it comes to developing a work routine, as long as it gives you enough time to get what needs doing done.

So the first two things for getting the work done are to work steadily and efficiently. The third thing is to work smart.

Schedule your work so that the more labor-intensive tasks are done in the mornings or evenings when the temperature is lower. When I worked on the farm in my teen years, we did chores (feeding livestock and chickens, milking the cow, etc.) first thing in the morning. We then unloaded the hay from the wagons and stacked it in the barn. Stacking the hay was hot work because there was little air circulation in the barn. We spent the hottest part of the day cutting, raking, and baling because there was less physical labor involved—we just drove the tractors for these tasks. In late afternoon we loaded, hauled, and stacked more hay in the barn, then once again loaded and parked the wagons. The next day we did it all over again. Even now, when I cut firewood, I like to start early in the morning and get it over with before the sun gets too high.

While a daily routine helps, there are times you'll have to pour on the coal and get the overtime in. One thing every farmer knows is that "you gotta make hay while the sun shines." We've had rainy springs when we anxiously waited for the garden to dry enough so we could plant our crops. When conditions were finally right, we didn't stop adding compost, tilling, and planting until we were finished. The same thing often happens at harvest time. If we're going to be hit by an early frost, we'll get out there and cover what we can and harvest the rest.

One of the most important aspects of working smart is planning ahead. You need to know what needs to be done and when.

In the homestead life, some things are seasonal.

In the early stages of setting up our homestead, we all worked a lot of hours. Here, I'm digging postholes for our temporary woodshed while Becky (in the background) washes dishes on the wire spool we used for a work area.

The garden must be planted by a certain time or frost will kill the plants before they mature. (At least it works like that in our climate!) That means you'll have to plan ahead to have compost ready. You'll have to order your seeds early enough to allow time for processing and shipping your order. If you save your seeds, you'll have to do it during harvest season the fall before! In many places, spring brings rain. I've seen a lot of springs when we only had a one- or two-day window out of an entire month when the ground was dry enough to till and plant. If we missed that window, we were out of luck for the entire season!

Some things need to be done each year, but the time to do them is somewhat flexible.

In the summer, we try to get our winter's supply of firewood cut, in addition to completing building projects and keeping the garden watered, weeded, and mulched. The good thing about summer is that the weather is usually great. Sometimes, though, our project list gets kind of long and we find ourselves slipping into fall with a lot of things left on the agenda. Last spring, for example, we had a daughter and son-in-law move onto the property. We helped them plan and build their cabin, which took most of the summer to complete. On top of that, I fell off the roof and sprained my ankle while putting on the shingles. Thus in October we found ourselves needing to cut our annual firewood supply of 10 cords of wood. That's only about four trips if we use the truck and trailer (six with just the truck), but the work is labor intensive and with my sprained ankle it took us a lot longer to fill the truck. October was a rainy month, so we spent time watching the weather forecast and whenever we had a clear day, we dropped the other projects and cut firewood. Splitting isn't real time sensitive either (most years!), so we normally throw the cut firewood in piles to be split and stacked in the shed as we have time. Last year, however, there was some urgency to the task because we were late cutting it and the wood needed to be split and stacked before the snow came. We like to do things like this during the summer because the schedule is more flexible. It didn't work so well last year.

Fall is often a busy time for us. We'll be trying to complete any building projects we have left over, plus the garden will need harvesting and the food preserved. Foraging for huckleberries, wild (Oregon) grapes, mushrooms, rose hips, wild herbs, and

My wife and I both like to sew. I sew to save money; she sews to make money, selling her craft items over the Internet and at local farmer's markets. She also writes and has magazine articles and fiction stories published in various outlets.

Is an afternoon kayaking a river considered work or play? In this case it's pure fun!

an assortment of other goodies is usually best in late summer and early fall. If we have grain planted, it will need to be cut, threshed, cleaned, milled, and stored. Seeds need to be dried and saved for next year's garden.

Any animals raised for food will be butchered in the fall so that we won't have to feed them over the winter.

Bowhunting season for big game begins in September, so that means a couple of week's time in our hunting camp and, if successful, we'll be butchering and preserving anywhere from 100 to 300 lbs. of wild meat (depending upon how many tags we have to fill and what species we're successful at harvesting). If we still have things to get caught up on, we may skip the bow season and we'll hunt during the rifle season in November.

Trapping season for mink, muskrats, beaver, and otter begins in November, so I'll spend time getting traps ready, making cubbies, and scouting potential trap set locations, getting landowner permission (if I haven't already), and preparing fur stretchers and the other equipment for skinning, fleshing, and drying the fur. Depending upon my trapping area, that may mean getting the camper, boat and motor, and canoe prepped for some extended time in the woods.

Hunting season ends just before December, which is when the trapping season for land animals (bobcats, marten, fisher, wolverine, etc.) begins.

Late winter is our "recovery time." Often the snow is perfect for cross-country skiing, snowshoe-ing, and snowmobiling. The really cold or snowy days are spent in front of the stove, drinking hot cocoa and reading. We may put a movie on if there's one we want to see. The last two years we've taken a few weeks off to head south for warmer weather. This is our break between the time our fall tasks are finished and our spring work is yet to come.

Another aspect of planning ahead involves times when you need to run special equipment. For example, last summer I had to do some welding on my truck's side racks. I also needed to weld some steel handles to several shovels and do some welding on one of the trailers. I got the generator, welder, cutting torch, metal cutoff saw, steel, clamps, square, and tape measure all together. Then, when I had the truck, shovels, and trailer in place, I started the generator. The setup time to get the equipment and parts ready takes anywhere from 15 to 30 minutes (depending upon how much searching through the scrap metal I'll have to do). Cleaning everything up and putting it away takes about the same length of time, which means I use 30 to 60 minutes each time I have a welding project. By doing three at once, I save time because I only get the equipment out one time instead of three times as I would have if I'd done each job separately.

We also ran a cord to the cabin and, while the generator was running, my wife ground some grain in our electric grain mill and used the vacuum cleaner.

Keep a list of "inside jobs" for days that you can't work outside due to weather. These might be

This was taken in camp while a friend and I were hunting elk. Is hunting work or recreation? Yes!

great times to mill some grain into flour, do some sewing or inside home repairs, or maybe reload some ammo. There's always something that needs to be done, which leads us to the next section.

TIME OFF, HOBBIES, STRESS, AND BURNOUT!

For more years than I care to remember, I worked as a mechanic. In my junior and senior years in high school, I took three hours per day of auto mechanics at our local vocational technical school. I loved it! I thoroughly enjoyed working on cars. After three years in the Marine Corps, I continued to work as an auto mechanic.

Unfortunately, as time passed I grew tired of working on cars. The excitement was gone. Many of you may have had the same experience. Did you ever stop to think that the same thing can occur with homestead life?

It used to be that I couldn't wait for the week-end to arrive so that we could go skiing, backpacking, hunting, fishing, or just roaming the woods. Early morning sunrises at some pristine, high mountain lake brought joy to my heart. I lived anxiously waiting for early fall mornings to hit the woods with rifle or bow in hand while I searched for deer, elk, and bear. I dreamed of owning a snowmobile for snowy winter explorations and having my own fishing boat.

Well, we have two good snowmobiles, one fishing boat with motor, three canoes, and two kayaks. It's the middle of January and from my desk I can see the snowmobiles parked, fueled up, and ready to go. Just a half mile from our cabin is a full section (640 acres) of state land that abuts hundreds of thousands of acres of national forest. All I have to do is suit up, start my snowmobile, and take off riding. Instead, I'm looking at the thermometer that reads 6 degrees above zero and thinking it would be a great day to get another chapter of this book written!

Paintball games! This is my fifty-seventh birthday. There are over 20 people when we get together with our kids, their spouses, and the grandkids. In this case there were a few more because we also invited some friends to join us. Most have paintball markers, but we have extras to loan to those who don't. I purchased a charging station years ago, so we rent a 50-lb. bottle of CO_2 and have loads of fun.

Hunting is not as fun as it once was. "Then" it was for recreation; "now" it's for sustenance. Gardening is on the same level as hunting. I used to enjoy coming home from work to my garden, where I got immense satisfaction from tilling, planting, weeding, and harvesting the produce. We could go completely through the list of things that used to be recreational—things I did for fun and to restore my spirit—but are now part of the "job." There's an expectancy now, a pressure to succeed that wasn't there in my previous life. That can take the fun out of it . . . *if you let it!*

I've learned to keep the stress out of my hunting excursions. We always fill enough tags for our meat and there's no reason to believe this year will be different, so why get stressed over it? The same could be said of the garden. We've had years when one vegetable didn't do well, but in those years something else produced more than expected and it always balanced out. Foraging works the same way. The years that huckleberries produced poorly, the wild grapes were abundant. Don't let your fears keep you from enjoying today. Work steady, efficient, and smart and you'll do fine.

But take time off too.

All work and no play make Jack a dull boy. Remember I said that being your own boss and setting your own schedule can be both a blessing and a curse? It's easy to get overwhelmed or even lost in your work on the homestead. I can tell you right now—you will never have everything finished. There's always something that needs to be done, so get used to it. Learn to handle it or it will destroy you. You need to set aside time for recreation. Don't forget to have some fun and enjoy life. Otherwise you're going to become a burned-out wreck.

HANDLE STRESS, AVOID BURNOUT

It's important to realize that stress and burnout are not the same thing. Everyone experiences stress, but burnout is avoidable.

Stress is usually characterized by too much: too many demands, too much pressure, too many people wanting too much from you. With stress you still think you can cope if you can just get things under control again.

Burnout is characterized by too little: there's nothing left to give, you feel empty, burned out. There's no motivation *and no hope for change.*

Burnout is often the result of prolonged stress, so it's important to keep your stress level under control. These are some of the things you can do to deal with stress.

Manage Your Workload

This is tough to do on the homestead. Be realistic. I used to think the Nearing's three-part daily division was silly, but it's a great formula for managing stress and avoiding burnout. And it can work for us if we keep life as simple as they did. Most of the problems I've seen are caused by taking on too much! Remember what I said about the first-year garden? It's better to keep it small and manageable than to start with a big garden that will overwhelm you. That's the principle to follow on your homestead life as well. Don't overcommit!

Don't Take On Too Much Outside the Home

Learn how to say no. We firmly believe that taking part in volunteer activities is important, but you must balance those undertakings with family and work obligations. It's easy to give too much of yourself. Most people outside your family are much better at showing appreciation than family members. After all, when's the last time your children said thanks for doing their laundry or driving them to social activities? How many times has your husband thanked you for doing the dishes or dusting? Husbands, how often does your wife thank you for the time spent at work providing an income to put groceries on the table or a roof over her head? Yet volunteer a few hours for the PTA or other association and you'll be showered with recognition, praise, and thanks. It can be addicting! But if it's causing problems at home, is it really worth it? If you burn out, they'll just find someone else to do your work and cast you aside like a dirty sock. It will be up to your family to restore you to health. Learn to say no.

Put People In Their Appropriate Place

Lets face it: Does it really matter if the neighbor doesn't like you? You got along just fine for X years before you knew John or Jane Doe, and you'll probably do just fine without them in the future. Demanding people, gossips, and similar types that leave your stomach feeling queasy are not worth losing sleep over. They are leeches who feed themselves by destroying others. Don't let them feed off of you. If they want more than you're willing to give, curtail the time you spend with them. Avoid gossips. They're everywhere, but they're especially obvious in small towns and rural areas. If they'll speak maliciously about others to you, be assured that they'll also speak spitefully about you to others. The best ways to handle gossip is first, don't take part in it (that includes listening to it). Second, should you become their target, live your life in such a way to prove them wrong. And third, recognize that gossips are pitiful people with empty lives who can only feel good about themselves by putting others down. Set some boundaries and keep those kinds of people at a distance. Spend time with real friends and family who love and understand you. You'll enjoy life more.

Stay Healthy

Bad diet, lack of sleep, overwork, and no exercise affect not only your body but your mind and emotions as well. Preparing meals from scratch takes time, as does washing dishes by hand. It's surprisingly easy to fall into a junk food habit on the homestead. Homemade cookies may not have the preservatives of their store-bought counterparts, but they're still not health food. I like sugar and cream with my coffee. I like so much sugar and cream that we refer to it as my liquid candy bar. I limit myself to one per day.

Sleep on a remote homestead can be difficult at first because there's no background noise from things like traffic, forced-air furnaces, or air conditioners. You'll find the silence discomforting at first. Eventually the pendulum will swing the other way and you won't get much sleep when you're in town! The noise and fumes tend to overwhelm you.

Overwork can be a problem if you let it get out

This is my wife on one of our trips to Nevada. We take our U-Haul truck that we converted into a camper and spend a few weeks down south to escape the snow. It's mostly pleasure, but we take our computers and cameras and write a few articles while we're there, so in a way it's a "working vacation" . . . but then, that describes our life in general!

of control, yet in the winter you may need to make an effort to get some exercise. Bad weather can sometimes keep you caged indoors for weeks at a time. Be sure you take care of yourself.

Count Your Blessings

Be thankful for what you have. Remember why you entered this life in the first place! There's a tendency to forget the bad and remember only the good things of your past life. Keeping a brutally honest journal before you make your move will be invaluable after you begin your new life. The low-budget, make-do life has its ups and downs, just as every other kind of life. There'll be a lot of times you just wish you had enough money to go buy the things you need instead of scrounging through scrap piles to find building materials or finding an alternate way of accomplishing something. Doing laundry by hand and preparing meals from raw ingredients may sound romantic, but after awhile it can get to you . . . again, if you let it.

One time my wife spent a week in town with one of our children to help with their new baby. She went to town looking forward to eating frozen burritos, cardboard microwave pizzas, and all the other junk food we'd done without. The kids couldn't wait for her arrival because they were anticipating real meals prepared from scratch instead of the junk food they lived on! Everything in life is a compromise, and people tend to look longingly at what they don't have and don't appreciate the things they do have. Cultivate an attitude of gratitude.

Live in the "Now"

Don't fall prey to worrying about next year's crop, income, taxes, etc. If you spend your day worrying about the future, you've traded the happiness this day could have brought for anxiety about what may never happen. If you're constantly lamenting the past, you won't be able to enjoy the blessings or see the opportunities of today. It's okay to plan for the future; just don't let worry about it steal the pleasures of today. *Today is the most important day of your life.* Treat it like a special guest and give it your best.

Put Aside Unrealistic Expectations

Wild roses are beautiful to the eyes and fragrant to the nose, but the stems are loaded with thorns. One of our favorite quips when I was in the Marine Corps was a line from a song: "I didn't promise you a rose garden." Every lifestyle has its challenges. This one does too. You will have times of discouragement in any life. Happiness does not come from your surroundings; it comes from within.

Pursue a Hobby

Find new things to do. Learn how to play a musical instrument. Take some classes on photography or writing. Join a quilting club. Acquire a bow and some arrows and hit the range. Do something that's different and interesting.

Volunteer

Volunteering gets your mind off of you and your problems. By helping others, you get thanks from them, and it may help you put your problems into perspective. I'll never forget one time we helped the food bank distribute Christmas baskets. There was a guy there who rode his bicycle to the food bank (remember, this was in mid-December in northwestern Montana). He was living in a rental storage unit with no heat or water. But the most remarkable thing was that he was happy and thankful for what he had. Of course, there was also the well-dressed single woman who threw a fit because she got a chicken instead of a turkey. (Turkeys were reserved for those who had families.) It wasn't hard to tell why she was single.

Laugh and Make Others Laugh

It's hard to feel sad when you're laughing. It's even more difficult to feel sad when you're making others laugh. Laughter is, in many cases, the best medicine.

Try Some Stress Reduction Techniques

Relaxation, meditation, and exercise are all great for relieving stress. Don't get freaked out by meditation. It doesn't have to be a mystical experience. Meditation can be an "emptying" of mind as in some spiritual disciplines, or simply the deliberation of the mind on something that brings peace or relaxation. It might be a calming thought or concentration on a place, situation, or person that brings emotional tranquility.

Cultivate Contentment

This is slightly different than counting your blessings. Contentment is the one word manufacturers, designers, and advertisers fear more than all other words combined. The purpose of advertising is to create a feeling of dissatisfaction. They want you to believe that something is missing from your life unless you purchase their product or service. Everything is designed to create a feeling of desire. Don't fall for it! When I sit down with a catalogue, I quip to my wife that I'm taking a break to feed my discontent. It's a humorous way to put things in perspective. Also, review the section on needs vs. wants in chapter 2.

Take Control

Stress is a consequence of feeling out of control. There will always be some stress in our lives, because we cannot control everything around us. However, there are some things we have power over, so take control of those. There's an old saying that you can't keep the birds from flying over your head, but you can keep them from building a nest in your hair. It's the same way in life. Your life is not totally out of control. There are things you can do, so take charge of those things that are within your power to change.

BURNOUT

People under stress often recognize it, but burnout tends to sneak in under the radar. *A person who is burned out has nothing left to give.* Avoiding burnout is a matter of constant vigilance and regular maintenance. It's a serious, but often preventable condition. Be aware of the symptoms.

Symptoms of burnout include:

- Feeling lethargic, run down, or drained of emotional and physical energy.
- Dissatisfaction, or feeling negative toward your work, your life, or the people around you.
- Irritability with or lack of sympathy for the people around you.
- Feeling that you'll never be able to accomplish what's expected of you.
- Feeling isolated and/or withdrawing from responsibilities or those around you.
- Feeling hopeless; that you don't have time to think or plan for the future or find a way out.

In addition to the above symptoms, a person suffering from burnout may experience depression and physical symptoms such as lowered immunity, muscle aches, headaches, and a change in appetite and/or sleep.

Burnout occurs primarily because of a focus on what's important to others and completely neglecting your own needs and desires. I'm not advocating a hedonistic lifestyle but rather a balance between your needs and the needs of those around you. To combat burnout, focus on what's important to you. Cut back on whatever obligations you can and take some time to rest and reflect on your life and heal. If you can do so, take a vacation or sabbatical and spend it contemplating your life and what's most important to you. What are your hopes and dreams? Turn to your support network, because you need them to help you recover. In burnout, you often isolate yourself from friends and family because there's nothing left inside of you to give them. Let them carry some of the burdens you've been struggling with. Often, just sharing your heart is enough to begin your recovery.

A person who is burned out often needs help from others because he has nothing left to help himself. He's like a burned-out house. There's nothing of use left, only a charred foundation and ashes.

There's no more shame in asking for help to recover from burnout than there is in asking for help due to injuries from a vehicle accident.

• • • • •

Like I said at the beginning of this chapter, being your own boss and setting your own schedule is great. But it can also be a curse. Being aware of what to do—or not to do—at least lets you get started on the right foot.

17

The Neighbors: Getting Along with "Country Folk"

I heard the ruckus outside and knew what was going on. The neighbor's dog was on the porch again and fighting with my dog over her food. Grabbing a shotgun as I walked through the door, I stepped off the porch and fired a shot into the air. The neighbor's dog was already running for home but kicked it into overdrive at the sound of the shot. Two days later, the neighbors, who had been renting, packed up their dogs and belongings and moved away. It was one of the happiest days of our lives. For weeks we'd put up with their dogs roaming our property, chasing deer, stealing our dog's food, and fighting with our dog. Enough was enough!

Lest you think I'm just short-tempered, my wife and I had both asked politely well over a dozen times that they keep their dogs off our place. Each time they apologized and said they would. The final straw came when they told *us* to come up with a solution for their three-year-old daughter getting up early and letting the dogs out of the house without their knowledge. Our response was that that wasn't our problem. The dog was theirs, and it was their responsibility to keep it from being a nuisance. A week later the incident cited in the paragraph above occurred.

I wouldn't have shot the dog. It was doing what dogs do, but we *would* have taken it to the county animal shelter and let the neighbors bail the mutt out. If the problem continued, we'd have filed a complaint with the sheriff's department.

They had problems with other neighbors as well, and they, more than anyone else, inspired this chapter.

One thing anyone aspiring to move to the country should know is that there is no anonymity. This isn't the city, where it's easy to get lost in the crowd. Here, everyone knows whose check is good and whose husband isn't. That can be good . . . or bad!

This chapter is about the relational blessings and curses of rural living. With a little forewarning, you can circumvent some of the pitfalls that commonly turn neighbors and neighborhoods against you and, by following good advice, you can do things that will spring the doors of their hearts wide in acceptance.

Here are a few do's and don'ts to help you get along with your new neighbors.

RULE NUMBER ONE:
DON'T TELL US HOW THINGS
WERE DONE WHERE YOU CAME FROM

This is probably the quickest way to raise neighborhood hackles. First, if it was so great where you came from, why did you move here? We don't want to live like the people in the city or be a bunch of urban yuppies. If we did, we'd move there! We like not having dozens of zoning regulations. We like our laid-back life, independence, and freedom from busybodies sticking their noses into places they don't belong. Too many who move here want freedom to do as they please, yet want to tell their neighbors what they can or can't do. Let's look at a few examples . . .

Junk

Some people looking at a property up the road from ours asked the sellers if they thought the people with the junk vehicles would mind if they were asked to move them. The sellers replied that they'd probably mind it very much. The potential buyers gave a sigh and made a very wise decision. They purchased property somewhere else.

If you don't like seeing junk on the neighbor's property, then don't buy next to that parcel of land. If you do buy, build a privacy fence around your land so you can't see them. I can assure you that things are going to go downhill very fast if you try to coerce them into appeasing you. If you try to get county authorities involved, things will really get hostile.

Show some tolerance. If it's not a threat to your health and they aren't trespassing, it's not their problem, it's yours. Get over it! Live and let live.

Guns and Shooting

Want to be the local cops' joke of the day? Complain about people shooting guns. As long as they aren't endangering you or waking you up at night and are respecting your property rights, don't whine. Most likely, if the cops do show up, they'll join whoever is doing the shooting.

People in rural areas shoot guns. Sometimes they shoot them a lot. Give this some serious consideration before you move to the country. I can guarantee you're going to be mighty unpopular with the locals and law enforcement if you start complaining about people shooting guns.

You may see people carrying guns openly or concealed, in stores, offices, and vehicles. Many Western states allow concealed carry with a permit and open carry without one. Be happy about it. You don't hear much about gangbangers or drive-by shootings in rural areas. They don't like environments where the average citizen can and will shoot back.

Guns are a part of life in rural areas. If you can't handle that, stay away.

Wildlife and Open Range

Montana is an "open range" state. That means livestock is allowed to wander at will. That means you may awaken to the sound of cattle in your front yard. Don't call to complain to the local constabulary. It's perfectly legal for those cows to be there. (And, no, the rancher is not responsible for any damage they do to your landscaping!) If you don't want them there, run them off. If they keep coming back, put up a fence.

The same is true for wildlife. If you call the state

Shooting guns is a family affair in most rural areas.

CREATING THE LOW-BUDGET HOMESTEAD

Department of Fish, Wildlife and Parks to complain about beaver eating your trees, they *may* give you a nuisance animal control permit to trap them or have a trapper do it (who will charge you for it). However, don't expect them to do more than that. If ground squirrels, rabbits, pack rats, skunks, or other nongame or unprotected wildlife are causing problems, take care of it yourself. If a wolf, coyote, mountain lion, bobcat, or bear grabs your pocket pooch off your front porch, then call FWP. They might send someone out to investigate. Living in the country has its own set of blessings and trials. If you're in an area teeming with wildlife, learn the proper protocol for dealing with them.

"I know a better way . . ."

Please don't come in and tell us you know a better way to grow a garden, make a road, hunt, fish, or anything else. First, no one likes being talked down to, especially by newcomers. The way you did things in the city or flatlands (or wherever else you came from) might have some merits. If so, the best way to let the neighbors know is to show them rather than tell them. If you have some advice to offer, try posing some questions first. Instead of saying, "This is a better way to . . . ," try asking, "What happens if you do it like this?" At least that gives them the opportunity to tell you what might be wrong with your idea if it's bad, or it will open the door so that they'll listen to you and honestly evaluate what you tell them.

RULE NUMBER TWO: FOLLOW THE RULES OF THE ROAD

My father-in-law told a story about driving across Montana in his younger years. He was stuck behind a rancher driving a battered pickup truck who obviously had no place he needed to be anytime soon. Being young and impatient, he was about to pass the old codger when he saw him stick a handgun out the window. He quickly pulled back into his lane as the old guy proceeded to shoot at the fence posts as he drove past them. Being young but not entirely foolish, he decided that he had no place he needed to be anywhere soon either. And maybe it was a good day to just drive a little slower and take some time to smell the roses along the way. "After all," he said, "I'd rather be smelling roses than pushing up daisies any day of the week!"

Driving on rural roads involves certain realities and etiquette that the reader will need to know. Here are some of them.

Driving Tips

Want to get to know the neighbors quickly? Drive fast! Cause a few accidents, beat the potholes out a little deeper, and stir up clouds of dust. After all, it's fun to see chickens, dogs, squirrels, deer, rabbits, small children, and other living things run for their lives! Unless, of course, they're your children or critters. In that case, reckless drivers are dangerous and will be dealt with the same as any other threat.

And while we're on the subject of driving, make about 10 trips out every day. City folk are used to jumping in their vehicles and driving to the store for every little need or want. My wife worked at the local (seven miles away) convenience store/gas station and noticed that new people often made multiple trips daily to purchase a cup of coffee! Buy a coffee pot and use it. Many rural roads have gravel or dirt surfaces, and in the summer you'll stir up great clouds of dust. While no one may ever say anything to you about it, it is annoying.

Many rural roads are single lane. If someone pulls off to the side of the road to let you pass, go by them, then stop and wait to see if they can make it out again. If they can't, help them either by pulling them out with your vehicle or giving them a ride to someone who can. (You do carry a tow strap in your vehicle at all times, don't you?) In the winter, it's easy to get stuck in the berm left by the snowplow. If you leave someone stranded who was considerate enough to pull over to give you room, the word will get around. You'll probably find out that no one else will pull over for you after that, so you'll be the one driving to the side. If you get stuck, do you think they'll help get you back on the road?

Road Improvements

Years ago in a place far, far away . . . okay, that line isn't very original, but in another place I lived there was a couple who moved into a rural area and decided that the private road to their home needed improvements. So, they began going to other homes along the road trying to solicit money to improve the road. When they met resistance, they began to threaten that they would get the county to take the road over and everyone's taxes would go up. That's when things went downhill very quickly. For one thing, the county hadn't taken over a private road in years unless the tax base was rich enough that the county wouldn't lose money maintaining the road.

The county commissioners laughed at them. The locals shunned them, and when a title search was made, they found out that they had no legal access to the private road they'd tapped into. Their legal access was over an even worse road that was three times as long and crossed through national forest and timber company land! (Neither of which were open to improving the road.) They were the only residents using the road, and they didn't have the resources to fight a losing battle with those two titans. They moved back to California a couple of years later.

Moving to a rural area is a lot like getting married. Be sure it's what you want before you say "I do." Bad roads are a way of life.

Register Your Vehicles ASAP

Nothing labels you as an outsider faster than driving a vehicle with out-of-state license plates. And before you even put on the new plates, scrape off any bumper stickers advertising favorite causes from your former life, for reasons explained in rule six below.

RULE NUMBER THREE:
BE RESPONSIBLE

Much of what I've written so far comes from personal experience, so I asked some other people what they thought of newcomers in their neighborhood. Here are a couple of typical responses:

> *"Newcomers to my neck of the woods want to live a rural life. In a year or two, they own 30 horses on their 30 acres, have 3–15 dogs, and it is impossible to count their cats. The result is: 1) no grass on their place, 2) my livestock and other neighbors livestock isn't safe, 3) deer are chased constantly, and 4) quail and other birds disappear."*

> *"I think it's not really the rural life they want as much as an irresponsible one . . ."*

Responsibility is a major issue. Most rural people are considerate and helpful, but there's a difference between helping someone and becoming a nursemaid to obnoxious, self-centered imbeciles.

I've already mentioned the incident with the neighbor's dog. We suggested that they put up a fence and keep the dog there. They responded that they wanted to live in the country so that their dogs could run free. We didn't care if their dogs ran free as long as they didn't cause problems for us. We had one instance when one of our dogs caused problems with a neighbor. We offered to pay the vet bill for their dog (our dog got in a fight with theirs on their property), but they didn't think a vet would be needed. We immediately put our dog in the kennel, and that's where he stayed unless we had him out on a leash.

Don't let your kids be a nuisance. Teenagers racing up and down the road in dad's pickup are not a good thing. Kids driving motorcycles and four-wheelers across private property or screaming up and down the road are not a good thing. Small children showing up in your yard without invitation or adult supervision are not a good thing.

On a more serious note, we've seen people move to the country with older teens and adult children who had drug problems. They stole from others to support their addiction. Believe me, when things start disappearing soon after your arrival, it won't take a trained investigator to figure out where the problem is, especially when word gets around that your kid uses illegal drugs. (Remember, there is no anonymity. The word will get around.)

We all live in a community of sorts and have a responsibility to live in such a way that we do not negatively impact those around us. This includes taking care of yourselves.

We had one family who came to visit soon after they moved here. In the initial conversation, the wife looked over at a gas-powered water pump in the yard and mentioned that they had a friend who needed a generator and since we had two, it would be nice if we loaned them the one in the yard. She was informed that (a) that wasn't a generator, and (b) we didn't lend generators to other people unless we knew them to be responsible. We've had too many tools come back broken, or not at all. This same person went to a different neighbor's home and asked if she could have the carpet in their living room if they ever bought a new one.

One of our neighbors brought over an excavator to dig a hole for one of our projects. Always volunteer to pay for fuel and any other expenses when someone offers their services.

Don't move to the country with a commune or moocher mentality. No one owes you anything. Most people don't mind helping in cases of hardship, but you'll be expected to carry your own weight. Mechanical things wear out and need regular maintenance and eventual replacement. Every hour a generator (or tractor or rototiller or any other equipment) runs brings it an hour closer to needing replacement. Someone has to pay for it. If you borrow something, realize this and at least offer a few bucks to cover normal wear and maintenance.

You are not entitled to extra produce from neighborhood gardens. If they offer some it's okay to take it, but don't be greedy. We often give away extra plants we have (usually strawberries and raspberries), but we also sell them. The same is true of others who live out here. We buy or barter for things like milk since we don't want to be tied down by a milk cow or goat. We do not expect our friends to give us their excess. They bought the animal(s), built the fences, fed them, milked them, and cared for them. They don't owe us or anyone else the milk they produce.

If you borrow something, don't loan it to someone else, keep it until the owner comes looking for it, or worse yet, break it and give them back the pieces. It is your responsibility to return it in the same condition it was in when you took possession. If it breaks while you're using it, repair or replace it. If you can't afford to do that, then don't borrow it in the first place. When you're finished, return it promptly. If it uses fuel, fill the tank. Don't just give them the money for fuel and leave them with the inconvenience and expense of driving out for gasoline or diesel.

On a side but similar note: don't knock on a stranger's door and ask to ride their horses. We've had that happen! Horses are a big investment. They take a lot of training. They are living animals and far more sensitive to the person on their back than most people recognize. Novice or cruel riders can undo a lot of training, destroy their trust, and cause physical injuries to the horse. It isn't like borrowing a pickup. In most cases, there's a deep bond between a horse and its owner. Very few owners will just let you throw a saddle on their horse and take off riding.

I shouldn't need to mention this, but I will just in case you aren't familiar with country living. You'll often see things left and seemingly abandoned on vacant land. Don't assume it's free for the taking. If someone else owns the land, they also own what's on the land. They may be storing it for future use or may have forgot it existed. In any case, if you didn't buy it or someone didn't give it to you, it isn't yours. Leave it there.

Our neighbor butchered one of his buffalo and offered the hide to us. We were on our way to town and would be back within an hour, so we just said leave it by the road. (They're kind of messy when fresh, and we didn't want blood and hair in the car.) Now, there is only one full-time resident and two part-time residents living above us. The road dead ends about a half mile beyond our cabin. We have very little traffic, and theft has never been a problem. He left the hide beside the road, but it was gone when we came back.

I began asking around and looking over vehicle

tracks, and there was one vehicle that had come up our road in the "'tween time." It was a different neighbor from another fork of our road who was a recent arrival. He was contacted and surrendered the hide. His story was that he thought the hide was abandoned and picked it up for himself because he believed the coyotes would just drag it off.

It was a good story except for one thing: a couple of weeks later the owner of the buffalo was back. I mentioned what had happened. He described the man and the vehicle. It seems the guy had stopped and asked if he could have the hide and the owner said it was already spoken for. The thief drove on up the road and when he came back and saw no one around, he loaded it up and took it home. This same "neighbor" had opened up some abandoned roads across private property and complained about people shooting. His equipment was used to widen an existing easement without the landowner's consent. He eventually sold his place and left. One of the reasons was because the people were so cold and unfriendly. Imagine that! Good riddance.

Accept responsibility. You are not entitled to anything owned by anyone else. That includes tools, equipment, access to their land, garden produce, vehicles, or even good will. No one owes you anything. If they're kind enough to loan you anything, it's your responsibility to return it in good shape and in a timely manner. Your pets, livestock, and children are your responsibility as well. Keep them under control.

RULE NUMBER FOUR: BE AWARE OF LAND ISSUES

Out-of-state buyers often purchase land at what they think are bargain prices. They may be a bargain in other states, but here you probably paid too much. The sellers and real estate salesmen will love you, but the locals may harbor some resentment. Out-of-state buyers drive up land prices, which often means locals can't afford to buy land. Local wages don't reflect what you made in the city, which means that people who live and work here can't make the payments for artificially inflated land prices. It especially affects their children who are just entering adult life and looking for land of their own.

There's no personal slight intended, but in our area we've been inundated with Canadians, Califor-

Remember, some of your neighbors have fur, hooves, or paws. Don't let your dogs terrorize the local wildlife.

nians, and people from Washington state. Many of them came to the area with lots of money, which drove up land prices to the point that local people can't afford to buy land. Rural people in New England, the Southwest, and most every part of the country experience the same thing with wealthier newcomers from out of state.

Now if you really want to get a cold shoulder, buy land and subdivide it. (I've known several who thought they'd pay for their land that way.) That'll make the neighbors love you . . . not! Face it: they aren't living here for the money. They like rural life without heavy traffic and crime, and they enjoy wide open spaces. Now you want to establish a mini city just so you can retire rich. Of course, land speculation has its own risks. Artificially inflated prices sometimes come crashing down. Current residents often band together to fight proposed subdivisions in the legislature and courts and will either stop you cold or drive up your legal costs. I could tell you lots of stories of developers having to fight for permission to hook up to existing water or sewer lines (and often losing in court). Many places in the West are also enacting tougher laws for subdivisions, which cut seriously into profits and potential sales. Be careful or you might just wreck your finances and future.

RULE NUMBER FIVE:
BEWARE OF GOSSIP, GOSSIPS, AND FAMILY TIES

Watch for people with an agenda. They'll often be the first to greet you and offer friendship. What they may be looking for is an ally to join them in a local feud of some type. Don't be paranoid, though. Most rural residents are decent people. Just don't be joining any neighborhood committees or similar ventures until you've been around long enough to know what's going on behind the scenes.

On a similar vein, watch out for gossips. The best ones will say something like, "They're a great person except for . . ." Be aware that if someone is relating unflattering information about other people to you, they will do the same about you to other people. A very wise person once said, "What a person says about someone else tells me more about them than it does the other person."

Be careful of what you say as well. Ever hear the joke about the phone book in a small town that had 500 numbers but only four last names? It may not be that bad at your new residence, but be aware that many rural areas are filled with people who are related to one another. Anyone you talk to about anyone else is probably related to the people you are talking to. Never say anything you wouldn't want repeated anywhere.

RULE NUMBER SIX:
BE CAREFUL REGARDING
POLITICS AND RELIGION

Get to really know issues before you offer comments, criticism, or solutions. First, if you take a stand (either for or against) a person, religion, or political view, you may be opening a can of worms you'll never be able to close. Likewise, be cautious about volunteering for any political or religious campaigns, offices, projects, etc. Even though it might gain a quick circle of friends, it can also expand your list of enemies.

Second, quite often those with an agenda will be knocking on your door to line you up as a new recruit for their cause. In one small town in a neighboring state, there had been some hard feelings against a coach and a school official. The two were separate issues involving adultery and coaching decisions. Some of the townspeople began working against the people involved by bringing a lawsuit

and by electing different representatives on the school board. Another group began working to retain certain board members. The point of bringing this up is that both factions were trying to recruit newcomers to their cause. It brought some serious splits in town unity that actually resulted in some businesses closing, some people pulling their kids out of the public school, and changes in employment among school staff. There were hard feelings for years afterward.

What many people who've never lived in a rural or small town don't understand is that people may hold grudges for years. There were actually those who would cross the street if they saw people from the other faction coming in their direction. If you have a business, these things can result in bankruptcy. I could list dozens of examples I've seen over the years. Be very cautious about running for any public office or openly supporting those who are running until you've lived there long enough to know what needs fixing!

I am not saying you should never get involved in local issues. What I'm cautioning against is getting involved before you know what's going on behind the scenes. That takes a few years. If you're interested in community involvement, pick something that's not divisive. (See rule nine.)

In many ways, rural life is like living in a large, extended—sometimes dysfunctional!—family. It has its good points and some bad ones too! Tread carefully when it comes to politics and religion.

RULE NUMBER SEVEN:
LISTEN TO THE LOCALS (SOMETIMES!)

You're going to get lots of advice when you move into a rural area. Some of it will be good. Some will be worthless but benign. Some will cost you. Be careful who you listen to! But how do you know whose advice is good and whose isn't? Well, you can't for sure, but there are some things to look for when the suggestions come.

First, are they local residents? Conditions in some places vary considerably due to soil structure, weather patterns, and other criteria. It's not so evident on the plains, but in mountainous country the differences can be astounding. I know of one place where the amount of snow is three times as much as it is five miles to the west. The mountains have a pass there that acts as a gate to channel clouds through in winter. Because our weather moves from west to east, the mountains act as a dam, holding the clouds along their west slope and slowly routing them through the passes. All the time they're waiting, they're dumping snow. The point I'm trying to make is that advice from someone living 20 miles away may or may not be good. The advice from someone living nearby will probably be more accurate. If there's a discrepancy, listen to those who live closest to you.

Second, how long have they lived there? It takes a few years to get to know an area. Some things can't be answered no matter how long you live there. We've been at our current residence for eight years now and we still couldn't say what a "normal" winter is like. We've never seen two that were the same. What we *can* say is that they're long. We can advise people to have their firewood cut by the end of October unless they like cutting it in the snow (a very miserable experience). But then we've seen times when snow didn't make an appearance until mid-December! The main point is that those who have lived there the longest will probably have a better understanding of what works or doesn't work than recent arrivals.

Third, how close is their lifestyle to the one you'll be living? We live completely off-grid using solar panels for 99 percent of our electrical power. Others in the neighborhood depend on generators of various types. Some use both. A couple have hooked up to grid power. The advice each gives will vary according to their lifestyle. Do they have children? Do they homeschool or use public or private schools? Do they work from home or depend on outside employment? Listen to those who are living or have lived the way you plan to live. They know what works and what doesn't. If you keep ignoring their guidance, they'll quit giving it and instead will just sit back and watch you struggle.

RULE NUMBER EIGHT: GET USED TO THE SIGNS OF POVERTY

Most places a low-budget homesteader or survivalist are going to move to will probably have a high poverty rate. Face it: the people who want to make lots of money are going to be living somewhere else. That doesn't mean you must live in true poverty (true poverty is not having the essentials of food, shelter, water, and security . . . more about

that in the next chapter), but you will be surrounded by some of the effects of poverty.

Most noticeable will be the percentage of people needing dental work. There are support networks and government programs to help people with medical care, but when it comes to teeth, you're basically on your own. Get used to seeing people with discolored and/or missing teeth. It's a lot cheaper to have a tooth pulled than to have it fixed.

Vehicles are older and shabbier. The price of owning a new car is not just a higher purchase price. Taxes, licensing, and insurance rates are also elevated. It's this combination that keeps low-income people driving older vehicles. When people live on gravel roads, their vehicles will be dirty. In the spring they'll be muddy, in the summer they'll be dusty, and in the winter they'll be covered with slush and snow.

Casual dress is the norm. I don't mean people are dirty or their clothes are worn out (although the people coming in after a day of work may be wearing their work clothing, so those people don't count). What you'll find is that blue jeans are prevalent, slacks are rare. Carhartt jackets, jeans, and coveralls will be seen much more often than a suit and tie. In the winter, both men and women wear insulated boots. It's a much more practical way to dress. Trendy clothing just isn't deemed important.

The most important thing to remember is that externals (what we wear or drive or how we look) does not reflect who the person is on the inside. Forget all the slogans advertisers use like "the clothes make the man" and other nonsense. Some of the nicest, smartest, most honest and hardworking people I've known would scare small children just by the way they looked. Appearances are deceiving, especially in rural America.

We know a very petite, middle-aged woman who spent the first 20 years of her adult life working on a fishing boat in Alaska. An older woman we know has a slicked up, mid-50s Chevy pickup in her garage. In her younger years she used it to make a little money drag racing. (And she has the trophies to prove it!) Some of the most interesting people we know are Dumpster divers. One man repairs and sells what he finds in Dumpsters during the summer, picks and sells wild mushrooms in the spring, picks and sells huckleberries in late summer and early fall, cuts and sells Christmas trees in the fall and winter, and takes life easy from January through March. We have dozens of stories like this. Every one of these people would drop what they're doing to give you a hand when you need it. None of them would ever steal from you.

Despite what you may have learned in college, poverty does not make people thieves, lazy, or stupid. Never judge a person by the way they look, dress, speak, or spell. Get to know people.

RULE NUMBER NINE:
SUPPORT YOUR LOCAL COMMUNITY

This does not contradict rule six regarding politics and religion. There are dozens of organizations that could use your help. Habitat for Humanity, the Salvation Army, Big Brothers Big Sisters, Girl Scouts, Boy Scouts, and 4-H (just to name a few) are nationwide organizations that depend heavily on volunteers for the work that they do.

If you have a volunteer fire department, see if they could use some help. The same goes for search and rescue. They'll provide some valuable training for the homestead life as well.

We have several nonprofit thrift stores in a nearby town that usually need help. The proceeds from their profits go to support other charitable organizations in town. Schools often use outside fundraisers to support their programs and need people to help that way.

Churches usually rely on their own members for benevolent work, but if you have a skill they can use in areas such as vehicle repair, taxes, legal issues, construction projects, plumbing or electrical repairs, etc., they could probably put you to work helping others.

The main thing is to stay away from controversial issues, at least until you understand all the forces working behind the scenes.

Support your local community with your dollars as well. We try to buy local whenever it's possible or practical. Unfortunately, the two nearest towns are lacking in some services, but we do support those businesses offering products we need. If you don't, who will? Local merchants pay a heavy share of the taxes that support schools and other necessary services. If you lose that tax base, those services may be cut and your taxes raised as well. Additionally, getting to know merchants on a personal level helps you too. It doesn't happen everywhere, but we've had times when we forgot to bring money with us when we went to our local convenience store. It takes a half-hour to drive each way, so the manager told us to take the merchandise home and pay when we came out next time. Try that at Wal-Mart next time you shop there. These people are more than just names on a storefront; they are friends and neighbors. Support them when you can.

My wife helping at the local food bank. We've taken part in filling their holiday food baskets and transporting and splitting firewood for their woodstove in the past. Organizations like these are almost always needing volunteers.

We've also done some bell ringing for the Salvation Army at Christmastime. We have a lot of fun with the little kids who stop to talk to "Santa."

• • • • •

There's obviously more to getting along with your neighbors than what I've written here, and someone else might bring up issues that are completely different than those I've listed. Acceptance takes time and positive involvement in the lives of those around you. Work hard at being the kind of neighbor you'd want living next door and you'll probably do just fine.

18 Some Final Friendly Advice

All things come to an end eventually, and in this final chapter I'm taking the opportunity to review some important points already made and bring up a few new ones. So, as I look over the nearly finished manuscript, I want to conclude it with seven things you really need to consider before you make the break.

FIRST: BE REALISTIC

Don't expect to cure all of your ills by changing your location or lifestyle. If your son or daughter had a drug problem where you are, they'll most likely have a drug problem where you move. Drugs are everywhere, and if it's drugs they want, they'll find them. The same is true of alcohol abuse. The stress involved in changing your lifestyle might even make substance abuse worse rather than better.

Likewise with marriage or other relationship problems. Every lifestyle has its challenges. If you have no experience at growing and preserving your own food, animal husbandry, or the countless other aspects of the self-sufficient homestead life, you're going to add a lot of stress to your marriage and other relationships.

Unless you're single, don't think you can do it alone. Your family must be onboard, because it will affect all of you to some extent. If they're resistant to this new lifestyle, it's going to cause major problems.

If you work a full-time job (as I did the first couple of years) and think you'll still be able to do everything that needs doing on a fully functioning,

low-budget homestead, back off and take another look. You'll be burned out in a year or less. You're going to have to make some allowances. In those early years, my wife and children built a lot of the outbuildings and sheds while I was at work. The kids helped dig the hole for the root cellar. I did what they couldn't do to remodel the cabin on days off while my wife and the kids handled tasks like cleanup, chinking, and staining while I was at work. Reexamine your plans, and expect to take a little longer to reach your goals.

SECOND: MONEY IS IMPORTANT!

It may not be necessary to have lots of it, but having none is a bad idea. We had a cabin shell as a basis for our housing. We had windows and doors we'd bought used and scavenged at remodeling and dump sites. We still had to purchase flooring and roofing materials, plus paint and cement. Our outbuildings were put together from locally cut poles and scrounged metal roofing. All of the digging was done by hand, including making our driveway. Gravel was free at the local dump site, but we used our truck (and gasoline) to haul it home. We needed cash for our phone service. We acquired our first solar panel through barter but purchased the rest as we had the cash available. If we'd moved onto raw land without the cabin shell and hadn't been stockpiling building materials for a year prior to our move, we'd have needed a considerable amount of cash for building supplies.

We recently had a daughter and her husband move onto our property. They had to purchase all the building materials, plus some of the construction tools to build their modest cabin. Most of the larger items like the cement mixer (not a necessity but still nice to have), ladders, and levels were borrowed from us. We furnished the windows and door for their cabin. They purchased four solar panels, batteries, inverter, charge controller, and the wiring and bought a generator for backup. Even without the cost of the solar power systems, it cost a couple thousand dollars just to put a roof over their heads.

Don't forget about repairing or replacing things that break and wear out. If your chainsaw is going to quit, I can guarantee it will be when cutting firewood for the winter rather than when doing that cleanup job after a spring storm. The stock on my hunting rifle cracked when I checked the sights the week before the season began. A new stock set us back almost $100. I threw a rod in the engine of my pickup on the way to get hay for our horse. It was cheaper to just buy another truck. I have four chainsaws, and there've been times when all four have needed repairs at the same time. Never underestimate Murphy's Law—if it can go wrong, it will go wrong! Even things like shovels, rakes, mattocks, and hoes break at times, and they always do it when you need them most. Do your best to keep an emergency fund on hand for unforeseen expenses.

THIRD: KEEP "POVERTY" IN PERSPECTIVE

There are at least two types of poverty. True poverty is not having enough money or resources to provide such basic needs as food, water, clothing, and housing. Relative poverty is defined in a social context using different formulas. One way is to declare that everyone below a percentage of the median income is living in poverty. Another method is to add up what it would cost to acquire the basic necessities of life and use that amount. The issue here is that not everyone agrees what constitutes a necessity. Some items deemed essential include personal care items, furniture, transportation, and home and medical insurance. Some would even add in entertainment expenses such as cable television, newspapers, and tickets to movies or sporting events.

Obviously, any definition of poverty is lacking. A

This is a stack of steel purchased by a friend for construction of a tower very similar to ours to mount their solar panels on. It cost almost a thousand dollars. By scrounging materials ahead of time, we built ours for free.

This is their tower after completion.

CREATING THE LOW-BUDGET HOMESTEAD

subsistence farmer may grow all the food he needs, have a home that's paid for, and make his own clothing yet have a low income. It doesn't matter that his needs are met and his income is discretional. He isn't starving, homeless, or naked, yet he is still considered to be living in poverty. Furthermore, the person's lifestyle who falls $10 below an established poverty level is little different from one whose income is $10 above the same level, yet one is classified as living in poverty and one isn't.

While we may agree that any definition is lacking, we still need someone in officialdom to draw a line in the sand and define who is or isn't living in poverty. The U.S. Department of Health and Human Services published the following guideline for establishing poverty levels.

2012 POVERTY GUIDELINES FOR THE 48 CONTIGUOUS STATES AND THE DISTRICT OF COLUMBIA

Persons in family/ household	Poverty guideline
1	$11,170
2	$15,130
3	$19,090
4	$23,050
5	$27,010
6	$30,970
7	$34,930
8	$38,890

For families/households with more than 8 persons, add $3,960 for each additional person.

Source:
http://aspe.hhs.gov/poverty/12poverty.shtml

The goal of a low-budget, self-sufficient life is to produce almost everything needed on the homestead or retreat. Consequently, we require very little cash to meet our needs. (Which is a good thing, because making money is the most difficult aspect of this lifestyle!) Even though we live well, our income is considerably below the poverty line.

There will be organizations and people who apply pressure to get you signed up for everything the government has to offer. The vast majority of them have good intentions and just want to help

you out. You'll have to decide for yourselves if you want to participate in government programs. Just remember that the money isn't free. It was taken from those who work for a living, and in my opinion it should only go to those who sincerely need it.

Because we chose this way of life, we have not signed up for food stamps, Medicaid, WIC, or other government entitlements. We've been called foolish for not taking advantage of these programs. "After all," we're told, "someone is going to get that money. It might as well be you." The thing is, life is good on our meager income. We have no need or desire for government help.

FOURTH: HAVE A PLAN

I've touched on this before, but it bears repeating. When we moved here, we had some very distinct priorities which gave us a clear focus on what we needed to do and when. Your primary needs are always going to be food, water, and shelter. If you're starting on raw land, make these your first priority. When we moved here, we had a timeline where we had to have the necessities ready by the end of October. Our priorities were to remodel the cabin, set up the outhouse, build a root cellar, and cut our firewood. All of our efforts went to completing these four projects. We cooked and ate outside and showered outside by the rear corner of the cabin. Until the cabin was completed, the kids slept in backpacking tents inside the cabin shell. My wife and I had a bed with mosquito netting draped over it. The cabin walls still needed chinking and the mosquitoes came and left at will. It was truly a great day when the windows and doors were in and the cabin walls chinked.

Your situation may be different. You may have a livable home on the place. If so, you can concentrate your efforts elsewhere. Just be sure the basics are covered first; then move on to other projects. Our daughter and son-in-law bought a small motor home and lived in it while building their cabin.

The important thing is to have a well-thought-out plan before you arrive. Then stick with it.

Having a plan also lets you evaluate your progress. That's important for several reasons. When you're working on several projects at once, it can be difficult to feel as if you're making any headway. Discouragement sets in, and then it's even more difficult to motivate yourself. If you can look at your master plan, you'll see how much you've accomplished toward meeting your goals, and it will (hopefully!) inspire you to continue in your quest.

Being able to see the end will help keep you motivated. People often find new reserves of energy when they see the finish line, because they know their work is almost over and they can rest (at least for a little while!).

A plan keeps you on track and going in the right direction. There's so much that needs doing that it's easy to get distracted. You can end up spending so much time on side issues that the most critical things get neglected. It's like time management. There are always things that are important and urgent. "Urgent" means you're in a time crunch and must drop what you're doing and take care of the matter *now*. In well-managed situations, these will be things that happen unexpectedly, such as an equipment or vehicle breakdown. "Important" matters are those that must be done, but you have some flexibility as to when they must be done.

The third category covers those things that are neither urgent nor important at the time. If you spend too much time in this third category and neglect doing those things that are important, you'll soon find the important projects have become urgent projects. Now your pile of urgent tasks has grown until you spend all of your time in crises management. You'll be under constant high levels of stress and on the fast track to burning out. Always do the most important things on your plan first. Then when emergencies arise, you can handle them without getting behind or stressed out. If you get sidetracked, get back to your plan ASAP!

A plan helps you organize. If I can see that I'm going to need lumber for a specific project coming up next week, I can pick it up when I go to town for other things this week. By consolidating my trips, I save time and money. I haven't lost time by needing to make a special trip to town, which in our case saves about two hours. I've saved money on gasoline (about $10 per trip for us) and vehicle maintenance. Plus, I have two hours extra to devote to the project, which means I can knock off early or get an advanced start on the next project.

FIFTH: KEEP LIFE SIMPLE (KLS)

One problem we see is people continually upgrading stuff. What I mean is that they start small and simple, then keep adding to it. I call this the "it's only" disorder.

For example, they may begin washing clothes by hand but eventually upgrade to a wringer washer. "It's only" a small step up, but they've gone from a completely independent method (no need of electricity or outside resources) of washing clothes to a machine that requires electricity in order to operate. Again, it's only a small step up. They'll just run the generator a few hours when it's time to wash clothes. (If they've got a big enough inverter, it might run the washing machine on solar, but will they need more solar panels or batteries to handle the new load?)

The next step up is an automatic washer. Hey, they already have the generator going, so why not go with an automatic washer? It won't use any more power than the wringer washer does. It's only a small step up from the wringer washer, isn't it?

Of course, an automatic washer works best with a good well and pump system. So, you'll need a good pressurized water supply system and a generator (and fuel for the genny, or a larger inverter and/or more solar panels and batteries) to do the laundry now. But you see that's not the end of it. The new machinery is more complicated, meaning it uses more parts, and those parts will wear out faster than the hand-cranked wringer. Plus, you may need to hire someone to fix them when they break. Now you have more money going out to upkeep and repair, and since they don't last as long, you'll have to figure in replacement costs as well.

Now, there's nothing wrong with new stuff if you have the money to purchase, maintain, and replace those things, but it all adds up. If you keep doing this in every area of your life, you'll find yourself back in the same boat you came here to escape. You'll need a full-time job to pay for all the labor-saving stuff you purchased to make your life easier or more convenient. Now you have to work elsewhere to support your new lifestyle, but you purchased a home and acreage way out in the country and you can't find a decent local job, so you're commuting a hundred miles a day to your workplace. (Don't laugh. I've seen it happen!) What happened to your dream of self-sufficiency?

Think about this when you're eyeing that new truck or backhoe or rototiller or power log splitter or anything else that will make your life easier. Review chapter 3 of this book. Many times it's better to rent the equipment or hire the job done. That way the other person can enslave themselves to the task of purchasing, maintaining, and replacing the expensive stuff.

Animals or livestock can be almost as bad. We've had horses before and probably will again. They're so cheap right now that it's hard to resist getting a couple. We can rationalize that horses are good investments. They're a lot of fun to ride, they replace themselves, they can be quite affectionate, and they provide tons (literally!) of excellent garden fertilizer. They can be used for work, replacing vehicles that need gasoline, oil, etc., and they can help produce and harvest their own food.

What's the problem then? First off, even though they can help produce and harvest their own food, they don't do it alone. You're going to spend a lot of time laboring to keep them fed and watered. You'll need fences, corrals, and shelters, and it'll be your responsibility to protect them from predators. (I should tell you about the night a California couple sat in their house, shaking in fear with their pocket pooch, while a mountain lion killed two of their horses that were trapped in the barn. They didn't believe in owning firearms.) At some point they'll need trips to the vet. Even though they can replace themselves, a colt will cost as much to raise to maturity as the purchase price to buy an adult horse; plus you'll need to train the colt to make it useful. Unless you can make other arrangements, you'll be tied down caring for it all year long. They can hurt you a lot if you aren't careful (and lucky). I've seen some serious injuries caused by horses. Oh, one other thing: you can walk out of your door some morning and find them inexplicably dead in your corral. That can be a huge financial loss in some cases . . . and a big relief in others!

There is no free ride (pun intended!). Everything has a good side and a bad side. That includes animate and inanimate objects. Carefully consider the total cost of any "improvements" to your lifestyle.

SIXTH: EMBRACE THE HOMESTEAD WAREHOUSE

Every low-budget, homestead or survival retreat needs a parts storage area. Okay, it may look like a junk yard and it probably is, but the truth remains that unless you have lots of money and a city that has everything you need close by, you're going to do a lot of scrounging, and you'll need a place or places to store the stuff you accumulate. Additionally, if you're concerned about the S hitting TF, you aren't going to be able to go to your local hardware store forever, so you'll want a good supply of "stuff" stored on your property . . . just in case! If you're organized, you'll have your "parts department" sorted in categories. It'll look a little better that way, and it'll be easier to find what you need. You can even hide it in the back corner of your land and build a fence around it if you want.

This can also be your staging area where you store materials for future building projects. We have one area loaded with windows, doors, siding, and other building supplies. If we have a construction project on our mind, we take inventory to see what we still need to acquire. If we already have everything we need, we get started building it. If not, we make a list of what we're missing and begin actively searching for those items. This might mean trips to the dump, perusing yard sales or auctions, bartering, or even paying cash if all other options fail.

We also have a couple of old vehicles on the place. We use them for parts for our running vehicles, and we sell parts off of them. Old vehicles are a source of batteries, starters, alternators, fuses, lights, mirrors, radios, speakers, and other parts that frequently need replacement, along with miles of low-voltage wire. We've sold, traded, or given away used windows, bumpers, hitches, tires, rims, gas tanks, and other parts off our worn-out vehicles. Junk vehicles can also be used for weatherproof storage.

We have assorted piles of pipe and tubing, tires, heavy metal, sheet metal and metal siding, old bicycles, and other items we can use for homestead projects. Our solar panel tower was made with salvaged metal pipe and steel from bed frames. I constructed a similar one for a friend who paid almost $1,000 for the same amount of steel from a supplier.

The key to salvaging materials is to get what you can when you can get it. Do not wait until you need it to start looking.

I know that for many people, the sight of (or even thought of!) piles of junk makes them want to scream. If you're one of them, you might want to consider a different type of life. If you have enough money to buy what you need anytime you need it, you're not going to be living like this anyway. If you plan on the low-budget life, then the homestead

This is one of our piles of scrap lumber.

This section contains doors and windows.

Scrap iron is sorted into different piles. This is the "heavy metal" pile made up of angle iron, automotive springs, and steel pipe. I have other piles of rain gutters, light tubular steel, old 20-lb. propane bottles, and other miscellaneous scrap metal.

A 300-gallon water tank we keep filled during the summer in case of fire and a stack of old bridge planks that we'll be using to make raised beds in the garden.

One of our stacks of sheet-metal siding.

warehouse will be your reality. If you're reading this book because you're building a post SHTF life, then you're already planning for a time when parts, materials, and cash might be very hard to acquire. You too will see the value of stockpiling materials for future use.

SEVENTH: BE AS PREPARED AS YOU CAN BE BEFORE YOU MAKE YOUR MOVE

That means knowledge, tools, and materials. If you're doing this on a low budget, the more you learn and the more you purchase at yard sales, scrounge, or barter for and bring with you, the better off you'll be.

At least a year before your move, start scrounging for building materials (lumber, doors, windows, etc.). If you have to, rent a storage unit to put them in. If there's a Habitat for Humanity outlet nearby, shop there. They often have used doors, windows, cabinets, sinks, showers, and other materials for dirt-cheap prices. Know what those items go for new before you make any purchases. We've found most of their prices reasonable except for things like electrical outlets and switches, which we can get cheaper new at Home Depot. The more of this you have on hand before you make your move, the better off you'll be.

Put away extra food also. You'll be surprised at how much food it takes to live on for a year once you're actually doing it. If your homestead or retreat is remote, you aren't going to want to drive to town for the evening meal or to get an ingredient for whatever you're preparing for dinner. Try to have your pantry stuffed with anything and everything you'll need before you move. Purchase cookbooks that tell you how to use the basics for preparing meals. After you get settled in and organized, prepare all the fancy meals you want, but in the beginning stick to the easy stuff.

The same is true of tools. Be sure you have the tools on hand before you move. The tool list in chapter 13 is the minimum recommended for homestead life. It helps to have extras if you can afford them. We buy nails by the box (30 to 50 pounds) because they're a lot cheaper per pound that way and we want to have plenty on hand. Kitchen tools are the same. We have four pressure canners and have had them all in operation at the same time. We never have enough canning jars (we

have well over a thousand already). You don't need four canners to live the homestead life, but we got them cheap over the years, and having four sure makes large canning sessions go faster.

Begin working on your skills now! You can never know enough, but the more you know before you move, the easier it will be. You'll have a lot more opportunities to learn important skills while in town than you will after your move. Plus, the time to learn roofing skills is before, not after, the wind blows the shingles off your house.

Clothing is another item to have stocked up. Homestead life is hard on clothes. Shirts and pants tear or wear out and need to be patched or replaced. You'll want footwear for all seasons. We keep "mud boots" next to the door for wet, sloppy days. These are rubber, slip-on, knee-high boots we use for doing outdoor chores when it's sloppy outside. Have some good winter boots. We prefer rub-

The better you're prepared before your move, the smoother things will go. We came with a year's supply of food on hand, along with most of the tools and skills we'd need. Even if you can't buy a place now, you can start preparing in both supplies and skills.

ber-bottom boots with felt liners. The uppers can be either leather or nylon. They'll keep your feet warm and dry on cold, snowy days. I use leather boots with nine-inch tops when cutting firewood. Anything shorter will fill with sawdust and wood chips. Hats and sunglasses are another item people don't think about. A lot of your work will be outdoors. Your eyes and skin need shielding unless you enjoy the thought of entering your senior years with alligator skin and cataracts. Gloves have been mentioned elsewhere, but they're worth a reminder. They wear out quickly. We purchase ours in boxes of 12 dozen.

Don't underestimate the need for preparation. The full-time, self-sufficient homestead life demands a certain amount of skills to live. If you're preparing a low-budget, self-sufficient retreat, it's even more critical that you acquire the skills and knowledge you'll need to survive on your own. Face it: few people would have any respect for an EMT who didn't prepare himself before he ever set foot in an ambulance. Nor would you trust your money with a stockbroker who'd never studied the market. We expect a minimum level of skill or knowledge of every profession, from taxi drivers to brain surgeons. Why should homesteading be any different?

• • • • •

My grandfather (who was embarrassed by his lack of formal education, although he knew more than most high-school graduates know today) used to say he was too dumb to be anything except a farmer. If I had half of his knowledge, my life would have been much easier. He grew up in an age of transition. He began farming with horses and mules, and when he retired he was using tractors. My grandparents met 90 percent of their own needs and those of their four children from what they produced on the family farm. They had beef cattle and milk cows, chickens, and pigs; they grew corn, oats, wheat, milo, and soybeans; and they harvested their own hay. Their garden was nothing short of phenomenal. Their farms were diverse because in that era you needed to cover all your bases to stay afloat. They worked hard and

spent money wisely. Self-sufficiency wasn't something people sought back then; it was a way of life. It was like breathing. They didn't have to think about it. Most farm families of those days lived the same way.

Skip a couple of generations and look at how things have changed. Those small independent farms are nearly gone in favor of large farms using mechanized equipment and chemical fertilizers. Even the family farm is different. Most concentrate on one or two crops or products. Gardens are rare. They can make more money growing crops than they save by growing their own food. They may raise cattle for market or grow wheat or corn for market, but few do both. They, like most of us, are now specialists.

What my grandparents knew was more than just how to grow crops. They knew how to care for and use horses and mules. They knew what it took to raise cattle for milk, food, or market. They raised chickens and pigs for their own use and for sale. They butchered and preserved their own animals. I still remember days butchering chickens and the time they had pork curing in the milk house. They had hand-powered cream separators and corn-shelling equipment. My grandpa built outbuildings, sheds, and fences and cut firewood to heat their home. My grandmother sewed clothes, canned thousands of jars of food, and cooked everything from raw materials. Both of them could drive horses or tractors to work the fields. My grandmother told stories of plowing with a horse-drawn walking plow with a five-gallon bucket hanging on each handle. Each bucket held one of their twin girls who were too young to be left in the house alone.

They were knowledgeable, tough, and resilient. The reason I bring this up now is to caution anyone reading this book that there is a learning curve involved. Don't be overwhelmed, but do prepare! It's going to take years to become proficient at homesteading. This doesn't mean you shouldn't make your move unless you have or know everything you'll ever need. But being prepared will increase your chances of success. Start now to acquire the skills and materials you'll need for the low-budget, self-sufficient life you desire.

About the Author

Steven D. Gregersen is uniquely qualified to write about how to succeed on a low-budget, self-sufficient homestead. He learned such skills as crop and animal husbandry while working on the farms of various relatives; hunting and fishing from his father; camping and outdoor skills from the Boy Scouts; discipline, marksmanship, and first aid from the U.S. Marine Corps; auto mechanics from vocational school; and business administration as a small business owner. Through diligent study and hands-on experience, he has taught himself gardening, trapping, construction, solar power, food preservation, heating with wood, and a host of other skills essential to an off-grid, rural lifestyle. He, his wife, Susan, and four of their seven children established their 20-acre homestead in northwestern Montana in 2004. For an instructive, ongoing look at their daily life, visit his "Homesteading for Real" blog at www.dirttimeforum.com.